Transport and the Urban Environment

OTHER INTERNATIONAL ECONOMIC ASSOCIATION PUBLICATIONS

Transport and the Urban Environment

Proceedings of a Conference held by the
International Economic Association
at Lyngby, Denmark

EDITED BY
J. G. ROTHENBERG AND IAN G. HEGGIE

MACMILLAN

First published 1974 by
THE MACMILLAN PRESS LTD
London and Basingstoke
Associated companies in New York
Dublin Melbourne Johannesburg and Madras

Published in the U.S.A. and Canada
by Halsted Press, a division of
John Wiley & Sons, Inc., New York

SBN 333 15073 2

Printed in Great Britain by
R. AND R. CLARK LTD Edinburgh

Contents

PART III: EVALUATION AND CONSOLIDATION PANEL

List of Participants

Professor G. Albers, Institute of Town and Regional Planning, Technical University, Munich, F.G.R.

Mrs. Bodil Nyboe Andersen, Institute of Economics, University of Copenhagen, Denmark

Professor Tibor Bákacs, National Institute of Public Health, Budapest, Hungary

Mr. Jean-Philippe Barde, Environment Directorate, O.E.C.D., Paris, France

Professor W. Beckerman, Department of Economics, University College, London, U.K.

Professor Niels G. Bolwig, Institute of Economics, University of Aarhus, Denmark

*Professor E. von Böventer, Department of Economics, University of Munich, F.G.R.

Professor C. Cameron, Department of Social and Economic Research, University of Glasgow, U.K.

Mr. Ulf Christiansen, Danish Building Research Institute, Copenhagen, Denmark

Mr. Alan W. Evans, Centre for Environmental Studies, London, U.K.

Professor Luc Fauvel, Secretary General, I.E.A., Paris, France

Professor Finn R. Førsund, Institute of Economics, University of Oslo, Norway

Mr. C. D. Foster, London School of Economics, London, U.K.

*Mr. Edwin T. Haefele, Resources for the Future, Washington, D.C., U.S.A.

Professor Niles M. Hansen, Centre for Economic Development, University of Texas, Austin, U.S.A.

Mr. Ian G. Heggie, Nuffield College, Oxford, U.K.

Professor Sir John Hicks, All Soul's College, Oxford, U.K.

Lady Hicks, Linacre College, Oxford, U.K.

Mr. Chr. Hjorth-Andersen, Institute of Economics, University of Copenhagen, Denmark

Dr. Irving Hoch, Resources for the Future, Washington, D.C., U.S.A.

Dr. Erik Hoffmeyer, Governor, Danish National Bank, Copenhagen, Denmark

Mr. N. J. Kavanagh, Department of Industrial Economics and Business Studies, University of Birmingham, U.K.

Mr. A. V. Kneese, Resources for the Future, Washington, D.C., U.S.A.

Professor S -Ch. Kolm, CEPREMAP, Paris, France

Professor Lester B. Lave, G.S.I.A., Carnegie-Mellon University, Pittsburg, U.S.A.

Mrs. Judith R. Lave, G.S.I.A., Carnegie-Mellon University, Pittsburg, U.S.A.

*Professor H. Lévy-Lambert, Ingénieur en Chef des Mines, Société Générale, Paris, France

Professor Fritz Machlup, Department of Economics, Princeton and New York University, U.S.A.

Mr. Karl-Göran Meler, Department of Economics, University of Stockholm, Sweden

Professor Niels Mayer, Technical University of Denmark, Lyngby, Denmark

Professor Edwin S. Mills, Department of Economics, Princeton University, U.S.A.

Mr. Anders Müller, General Planning Directorate, Copenhagen, Denmark

*Professor Robert Mossé, University of Grenoble, France

* Presented a paper but did not attend the Conference.

Professor Frank E. Münnich, University of Dortmund, G.F.R.
Professor Knud Østergard, Technical University of Denmark, Lyngby, Denmark
Professor Remy Prud'homme, University of Lille I, Lille, and BETURE, Puteaux, France
Professor P. Nørregaard Rasmussen, Institute of Economics, University of Copenhagen, Denmark
Professor Jerome Rothenberg, Department of Economics, Massachusetts Institute of Technology, U.S.A.
Dr. Clifford S. Russell, Resources for the Future, Washington, D.C., U.S.A.
Professor Eugene P. Seskin, G.S.I.A., Carnegie-Mellon University, Pittsburg, U.S.A.
Mr. Alessandro Silj, The Ford Foundation, New York, U.S.A.
Mr. Irving Silver, Ministry of Urban Affairs, Ottawa, Canada
*Mr. Walter O. Spofford, Jr., Resources for the Future, Washington, D.C., U.S.A.
Professor Steinar Strøm, Institute of Economics, University of Oslo, Norway
Professor Dr. Rainer Thoss, Department of Economics, University of Munster, G.F.R.
Professor Henry Tulkens, Centre for Operations Research and Econometrics, Catholic University of Louvain, Heverlee, Belgium
Professor H. Uzawa, Faculty of Economics, University of Tokyo, Japan
Mr. Kjell Wiik, Department of Economics, University of Munster, G.F.R.

Secretariat and Editorial Staff

Miss Mary Crook
Mr. Ian G. Heggie
Mrs. Elizabeth Majid
Mr. Karsten Peterson

Programme Committee

Jerome Rothenberg, U.S.A. (*Chairman*)
Peter Bohm, Sweden
E. von Böventer, G.F.R.
Sir John Hicks, U.K.
Allen V. Kneese, U.S.A.
Shigeto Tsuru, Japan

Copyright Permissions

Introduction

J. Rothenberg

1 ONE CONFERENCE – TWO VOLUMES

This book is a record of somewhat more than one half of the proceedings of the International Economics Association-sponsored Conference on Urbanisation and Environment, held on 20–24 June 1972 near Copenhagen. The conference subject matter divided rather clearly into two parts, one concerned primarily with urban development and its impact on the environment, the other on more technical considerations about waste residuals, water quality management and pollution policy. There is carryover between the two parts. Indeed, it was the purpose of the conference to examine some of these carryovers explicitly. None the less, it was felt that a separation of the material into two volumes would facilitate their communication to relevant audiences, since each volume would thereby concentrate on material in a recognisable specialisation.

This does not at all mean that the separate volumes are intended for specialists alone. One of the chief motivating forces behind the conference was the realisation that the rapid and thoroughgoing tide of urbanisation might be carrying with it critical damage to the environment, damage that would not become understood until it was either too late or too costly to rectify. Widespread appreciation among the technical and lay people alike was called for. The books are therefore addressed to a broad audience of sensitive readers, not because they are 'popular' in viewing immediate human prospects with loud alarm, but because they may be quietly offering early insight into problems of great complexity which will have to be wisely dealt with soon, or failed at peril.

The present volume contains eight of the fifteen papers presented at the conference, the formal critique of each of these by designated discussants and the succeeding general discussion of each of these. In addition, there are two special statements included from non-economist participants of the conference – Mr. Bakács, a biologist, and Dr. G. Albers, a town planner. These express a view of some of the conference's chief issues from perspectives quite different from that of the economist, and set the latter in sharper relief as a result. Finally, there are included the full proceedings of the conference's last day, an Evaluation and Consolidation Panel in which important themes dealt with during the conference were summarised and drawn together by a designated panel, and then developed further in general discussion. These panel transactions deal with materials belonging to the subject matter of both volumes and are being included in both for that reason.

2 *URBANISATION AND ENVIRONMENT: AN OVERVIEW*

What is the relationship between urbanisation and environment? It is not one but many relationships, and depends on what one understands by 'urbanisation' and what one understands by 'environment'. For example, is 'urbanisation' to be taken as the process by which cities develop, or the relative emptying out of the countryside, or the larger process of industrialisation of which city building is an attendant element? Different contributors have borrowed from the different concepts. Similarly, is 'environment' to be taken as a reference to air and water pollution, does it refer to characteristics of social environments as well, like congestion or noise or crime or aesthetic obtrusiveness, or does it refer to the even broader notion of the whole relational setting – the network of linkages among inanimate and animate matter, subhuman and human – within which humans carry on their living activities? The conference has made allusion to all of these possible levels. It therefore pays to say something briefly about a number of them.

In its broadest sense urbanisation concerns a process whereby diminished human reliance on labour power in agriculture and striking gains in non-agricultural industrial pursuits led to a radical shift of population from rural to urban settings. This changed the environment for the urban migrant from a 'natural' to a created, culture environment – in Mr. Bakács' terms, we have yet to understand fully the biological consequences for man of such a changed environment. Not only was there a shift for many people from one existing environment to another by migration, but the process of industrialisation attendant upon this migration tended to change that pre-existing rural environment, and the process of city building, which was its counterpart, tended to change the pre-existing urban environment as well. So urbanisation can be a focus of various environmental concerns.

Although touching from time to time on various levels of inclusiveness the conference seemed to be willing to treat urbanisation as including industrialisation as well as city building, but it concentrated rather more on specific dimensions of the environmental relationship – the impact of industrial and city development on water quality, air quality, crowding and a few other social dimensions. In this introduction we shall do so too.

The link between industrialisation and urbanisation is direct. Industrialisation made advantageous a concentrating together of many non-agricultural producing and selling activities, and on a scale never previously encountered. These complexes could either be superimposed on existing urban concentrations or create new concentrations. In addition to shifting very large numbers of people from a 'natural' environment to a purely man-made one, and settling their descendants into the latter as well, the process changed both the rural and urban environments as it did so. The urban environment was changed because of the scale and density of the new urban concentrations and the nature of the new activities carried out there. Air pollution, water pollution and crowding, especially transport congestion, resulted. The rural environment was changed because some industrial activities were directly operated there; because waters polluted by urban activities carried their degraded quality into the countryside; because urban air pollution likewise was carried outside the urban area; and because the greatly augmented industrial needs for raw materials led to extensive and exhaustive exploitation of such resources in the countryside. The use of forestry products, metals and fossil fuels left especially significant marks on the landscape.

The very broad consequences of urbanisation, especially on the biological destiny of the human race, are treated eloquently by Bákacs, in 'A Biologist's View of the Consequences of Urban Change'. He is especially concerned with its eliciting a potentially disastrous population explosion, and with its subjecting city dwellers to an assault on their biological viability through stress, pollution, crowding, and insufficiency of basic recreative resources like open space and greenery. Economists do not often attend to impacts on well-being that are either unrecognised by their principals or are so long delayed in culmination as to be discounted as irrelevant. The perspective of the biologist is therefore a useful reminder that the economist's perspective is very special and may sometimes lead to neglecting the forest for the individual trees.

The other papers and discussions in this book address themselves mainly to the more detailed questions concerning the specific aspects of urban experience which give rise to adverse environmental effects, the determinants of the character of different urban areas from this point of view, and the public policy issues that arise in attempting to ameliorate the situation. These questions have not been answered exhaustively or definitively in the materials to follow, but they have been dealt with imaginatively and provocatively. The general discussion following each paper and formal critique has frequently served to widen the focus to some of the broader concerns suggested above. We shall now turn to the more detailed issues treated.

3 DETERMINANTS OF URBANISATION AND ENVIRONMENTAL IMPACTS

The urban impact on the environment would surely seem to depend on the size of the urban area, its density, its industrial composition. What determines the pattern of development among urban areas with respect to these variables? Research on this question has been carried out by examining the temporal record of individual urban areas, by using cross-section data on a number of urban areas, and by using time series information about a system of urban areas. Alternatively, the focus has generally been either the individual urban area relative to a largely undifferentiated 'rest of system', or a system of cities of different types. The difference is important. The first would explain the failure of a given city to grow larger in terms of national demand characteristics and resource and locational disadvantages relative to the rest of the system. The second would explain it in terms of the fact that *particular* other cities *were* growing at the time.

Two papers deal with aspects of this question, 'Central Place Theory and Regional Planning' by Münnich, and 'Migration and Urban Change' by Lave, Lave and Seskin. While it deals with other matters as well, the latter paper uses cross-sectional data to explain patterns of labour migration to metropolitan areas. Characteristics of the destination area are the chief explanatory variables for inter-regional migration. Where intra-metropolitan migration patterns are being explained, however, the much closer substitutability between central city and suburb leads to the use of variables which reflect differences between origin and destination.

The Münnich paper is an application of Central Place Theory. It begins with the presumption that commodities have markets of differing degrees of inclusiveness, that these form themselves into a mutually exclusive hierarchy of inclusiveness, and that this hierarchy represents a set of economic incentives to generate a set of specialised types of cities. Specialised type and size are closely associated in this theory, because of the hierarchy of market inclusiveness and assumptions about production and sales technology. Thus, explanation of the size and pattern of growth of any urban area is couched mainly in terms of its internal composition: that is, the specialised economic role it plays within the system of roles and other urban areas.

The Münnich paper examines an unbalanced relative growth pattern among urban areas of different type, and discusses public policy designed to ensure a pattern more in accord with the normative prescriptions of central place theory. This represents somewhat of an anomaly, since Central Place Theory is a predictive theory as much as a normative one. The conference discussion raised a number of factors which limit the predictive (and normative) power of this theory. They include scale economies in manufacturing and transportation, and the utility aspects of lifestyles in different types of urban area.

The second of these opens an important set of issues – the amenity character of urban places. While jobs attract workers, and thus strongly influence the size and growth of cities, the reverse direction of causation operates as well. Workers attract jobs. Prior existence of a potential work force with certain skills signifies a low real cost of assembling and using labour resources for many types of enterprise. Such labour supplies come into being not only as a result of past job creation decisions but also because of labour migration decisions that are influenced by the amenity characteristics of the area. The variety and cost of private goods available in the area are one component of this. So too are the quality, range and cost of government services in the area. In addition to these is another form of public good, but not one provided by government: environmental quality. This includes air and water quality, degree of crowding and crime incidence, among others.

The Lave, Lave and Seskin paper is directly relevant to this issue. They concentrate on the determinants of both inter- and intra-urban migration. In addition to a variety of well known influences in the earlier categories, components of urban environmental quality are demonstrated to have significant effects as well. The nature of these effects differ for the different components, for different types of migrants, and for inter- as opposed to intra-metropolitan migration.

Environmental quality can influence migration patterns and through them, overall urban development patterns. But what determines environmental quality? We argued above in general terms that at least some of these depend on the size, density and composition of the activities in the urban area. City size has been especially emphasised as an influence. Since size has been considered an important explanatory variable for other facets of urban experience, such an association with environmental quality would be significant for policy purposes. It would also, incidentally, indicate a two-way causation process between population movement and environmental quality: high quality attracts population, population attracts economic activities, economic activities degrade quality.

Empirical evidence concerning the relationship between urban size and environmental quality is clearly of great importance. It is a central issue of the conference. The paper by Hoch, 'Interurban Differences in the Quality of Life' directly attacks this problem. It attempts to give precise measurement to the impact of size on quality. Two methods are used. First, various components of the 'quality of life' – including a number of environmental variables – are related to city size by using cross-sectional data. A number of associations look promising. But 'quality of life', or 'environmental quality', are not single-dimensional notions. They comprise a multiplicity of factors, factors which do not vary uniformly with any known explanatory variable.

The problem is even more profound because ultimately 'quality of life', and even 'environmental quality', are subjective magnitudes, not objective ones. In so far as human tastes with respect to the different components of either differ substantially, no purely objective index will adequately represent the quality phenomenon. Quality must then be represented indirectly, through its effect on human valuation. Individuals, faced with the choice of exposure to different 'environments',* will presumably select the better and eschew the worse. So observations of households' locational choices carry information about differential environmental quality. But the information is not easy to decode, since real world observations do not record situations controlled to neat experimental requirements. Many attendant valuational components in the choosing situation vary among alternatives.

This last complexity is not an accident. It is a property of market systems. If one inherently scarce alternative is systematically more attractive than another, competition will raise the price of the former relative to the latter. Indeed, this price adjustment makes possible an indirect measurement of overall relative attractiveness among alternatives, since in principle the price differential between any pair of alternatives just equals the preferential differential for the marginal chooser between them. The market price differential is an approximation for the average preferential differential operative among market participants.

In using this principle to measure environmental quality, a critical question is which prices should be observed to record relevant differentials. Since locational-specific scarcity is a critical factor, land rent obviously suggests itself. But there are others as well. Hoch argues in his paper that the market system sensitively registers differential environmental quality through the effect that the resulting differential locational attractiveness has on market prices. But he claims that the labour market is the arena where these differentials

---

* I shall use 'environment' in this section to refer to the whole broad external setting of human welfare.

appear most strongly, arguing in effect that supply prices of labour reflect these differences. He uses wage level differences as his proxy measure of compensating differences for the effect of environmental quality. His observations on these suggest that environmental quality falls as urban size increases. A variety of explicit pollution and congestion processes are examined directly to bear this out.

This is a highly suggestive study. Much of the ensuing conference discussion of the paper, however, raised a variety of considerations which make inter-metropolitan wage level differences a potentially highly misleading indicator of environmental quality.

Admitting that urban size may have an influence on environmental quality, it is crucial that this influence is not invariant or inevitable. What mediates it is not only private market decisions concerning spatial concentrations and composition but also various types of public policy. Environmental degradation can be controlled, moderated, rectified: by sewage treatment, by heating and incineration regulations, by mass transit systems, and so on. Such mediation by public policy is not costless. It involves public administrative costs, but in addition, and much more importantly, engenders significant net resource costs in either the public or the private sector. They represent, for example, the cost of water treatment or mass transit facilities, or the higher private cost of low-sulphur fuel oil, or the private costs of effluent control or recycling, or the resource allocational cost of externally induced decreases in production of pollution-associated commodities relative to others. In addition to these, public policy toward city size itself may also incur costs in so far as city size is associated with various gains in terms of public and private good production and financing and consumption.

Thus, for any urban area of given 'private' characteristics – including size – the population can presumably change the quality of the environment to some extent by means of public policy, and hence incur the costs of doing so. These costs will vary for different target levels of environmental quality, and for each such level they will vary for each specified urban configuration. There are tradeoffs between a host of non-environmental urban opportunities and environmental quality. Size is one of the urban components for which there are resource tradeoffs. 'All other things equal', a larger city* is compatible with a given environmental quality only at a higher total of direct and indirect control costs. In general, there are tradeoffs among environmental quality, urban size, urban structure, and the flow of private and public non-environmental commodities.

We are familiar with production and consumption tradeoffs for private sector commodities. We view the market as a process by

* In other words, for proportional changes.

which these tradeoffs representing consumer tastes and production transformation costs are approximately optimally comprised. Can the broader problem be characterised similarly? The question is of great importance for both positive and normative theory. Normative theory purports to delineate the optimal pattern of urban settlement. For this it must have access to the gains and losses (in absolute and distributional terms) attendant on different detailed patterns, and this requires adjudicating among the various tradeoff options obtaining. Positive theory predicts observable urban development patterns by generating supposedly optimal choices for different types of participant and then predicting their interactive consequences through a market-type adjustment mechanism. These steps require much the same understanding of the tradeoffs, of the choices within each, and of the aggregative consequences of these choices.

Supplementing private sector market choices for this large allocation problem there are two kinds of relevant choice behaviour that have been formulated as rational maximisation processes. One is locational choice among jurisdictional areas. Individuals select among political jurisdictions on the basis of preferences concerning a variety of private and public good availabilities. The other is the political choices conducted within each jurisdiction to determine public expenditure, tax and regulatory policy. These choices are assumed to be arrived at by a form of representative aggregation of participant preferences. The three processes together lend a semblance of overall system optimising. But there are a number of obstacles to this end, involving the pervasive externalities associated with pollution and congestion, social intransitivities associated with political decision-making, interjurisdictional political externalities, and various imperfections in the public planning process. Böventer's paper, which is designed to present a theoretical introduction to the conference, discusses at length the normative and public policy issues relating to optimal development of urban areas, with environmental quality and its linked tradeoffs with urban size and structure included as components of the problem. Along with a number of imperfections in the overall decision processes and an agenda for needed research, Böventer presents a number of simple normative models to illuminate facets of the problem. The following discussion, especially a considerable contribution by Kolm, examines these formulations critically and extends the analytical grasp.

4 URBAN TRANSPORTATION

The first set of four papers deals with the individual urban area relative to the larger system of which it is a part. The second set of four deals with some of the internal relationships characteristic of urban areas. The central focus is on urban transportation, but as such, many other urban activities are implicitly treated because of the fundamental function of transportation to link activities and participants together.

This extensiveness is best seen in the paper by Mills, 'Sensitivity Analysis of Congestion and Structure in an Efficient Urban Area', and its ensuing discussion. Mills constructs a model of an 'efficient' urban area by specifying a set of urban activities, a given population to carry them out, and a set of production (but not consumption) tradeoffs by which they can be accomplished. Transportation is the activity that connects complementary activities. He centres on the tradeoffs between horizontal *versus* vertical settlement, and on the size of investments in transportation capacity *versus* traffic congestion. The 'efficient' city is generated by determining that allocation of activities which minimises the total cost of achieving them in a linear programming framework. Transportation is seen in this trenchant context to be intimately linked to the spatial structure of the urban area. Special features of the model, as well as its necessary level of simplification, prevent it from going further and showing how the nature of the transportation system helps determine even which activities will be connected together – as, for example, which workers will work in which locations, from which supplier a given firm will obtain its needed inputs, to which customers a given firm will sell – and at what levels.

Mills' particular purpose is to examine the effects of subjecting his model to a variety of exogenous changes in transportation variables. He obtained the seemingly very provocative result – contrary to the spirit of the last paragraph – that rather substantial changes in transportation costs had only minor influence on the spatial density pattern of settlement in the urban area. The discussion by the formal discussant and others demonstrated that certain special characteristics of the underlying model made the result less provocative, and also less generalisable to the real world than first appears.

The remaining three papers in the section, and Lady Hicks' formal discussion of the Mossé paper, which constitutes almost an independent paper, deal with much the same complex of issues: what constitutes the problems of urban transportation with regard to environmental quality, and what policy measures can be used to solve these problems? Of these, Foster's paper, 'Transport and the Urban Environment', is the most elaborate in setting out the problems and considering the various remedial measures that might be employed. Foster deals explicitly with the unique set of impacts that transportation has on the environment. Not only does this impact derive from its effect on induced density patterns of settlement and traffic congestion, but it consists in a long list of types of environmental degradation – like noise, accidents, aesthetic distastefulness, and so on. Foster critically considers at some length a wide range of policy approaches. Informational requirements, evaluation imperfections and other administrative constraints are emphasised as barriers to effective policy.

Some of the same issues in the specific areas of modal choice and highway management are treated at length in Mossé's paper, 'An Introduction to Urban Transportation Problems', Lady Hicks' formal critique of this, and Lévy-Lambert's 'Cost–Benefit Analysis and Urban Traffic Congestion'. Mossé's paper heavily emphasises the fault of the private automobile in generating the urban transportation problem. He attempts to decompose the problem by distinguishing among different categories of urban transport demand, with an eye toward manipulating these components at the hands of a central authority. The latter aspect reflects his concern that the present set of decentralised decision processes seriously fails to do justice to the technological coordination and financial problems associated with transportation. He examines at length the characteristics of an assortment of different modes to evaluate their contribution towards meeting the different forms of transport demand on the one hand, and their contribution towards generating congestion and pollution problems on the other. He would supplement the inadequate repertoire of present public modes with a a number of new modes, considering for illustration monorails, self-service taxis, and others.

Lady Hicks follows the question of modal choice more deeply. She relates the typical contemporary diffuse patterns of urban spatial structure with the need for flexible, personal transportation modes. While some more flexible public modes (not fixed-rail mass transit) may not be very ineffective, the private motor car will surely continue to have a dominant place, so Lady Hicks examines in detail various measures for improving the management of the existing road system. She finds prospect for considerable improvement in this direction.

Lévy-Lambert implicitly disagrees with this judgment. For him, the congestion aspect of the problem (but, in fact, more) requires a substitution of public transportation for the private motor car. He considers substantial parking charges for private automobiles as an instrument for accomplishing this. His paper is primarily devoted to displaying a cost–benefit analysis of such a parking charge scheme applied to Paris motorists. He develops an instructive analytical typology of benefit and cost impacts on different categories of transport use and users, and then applies this to the hypothetical Paris case by means of empirical data taken from a larger recent study of modal choice in France. His application points to a very substantial shift out of work-trip auto use into buses. This suggests a much higher degree of substitutability between public and private transportation than has been conceded for the U.S. Underlying it, however, is a supply availability of decent quality public conveyances, and probably a spatial urban form, that diverge significantly from assumed American conditions.

Finally, high uniform substitutability among modes implies that even substantial public policy intervention on any one mode is not likely to elicit large utility impacts on households, and may therefore have little long-run impact on household locational patterns. This is a circumstance under which Mills' finding would be duplicated in a very different institutional context.

5 TOWN PLANNING AND URBAN STRUCTURE: EVALUATION AND CONSOLIDATION PANEL

The final day of the conference was devoted to the presentation by Albers, 'A Town Planner's View of Urban Structure as an Object of Physical Planning', and the Evaluation and Consolidation Panel.

Albers' contribution was formulated during the course of the conference itself, as he became convinced, with the unfolding of the economist's specialised viewpoint, that the different viewpoint of the town planner should be displayed. His simple, brief exposition of the approach and analytical elements used in the discipline of town planning was highly illuminating, throwing into relief the special assumptions and interests of the economist, and therefore making the preceeding conference transactions somewhat easier to appreciate.

Albers begins with a brief historical sketch of the early history of theory and practice in town planning, continues with a discussion of the justification for and goals of planning, the analytical elements of the planning problem, and concludes with the character of a number of contemporary planning solutions for desired urban structure.

The historical justification for planning is of real importance to economists. The unfolding unplanned urban developments in Britain, France and Germany during the 19th century led to serious misgivings about absence of open space, ineffective development and use of municipal infrastructure facilities and often haphazard relative locations of activities that depended on smooth mutual spatial linkages. Planning attempted to rationalise the integration of fundamental elements of urban structure which decentralised private decision-making and an unengaged public sector together were apparently unable to do.

The problem raises important issues for economists. Students of urban processes have become aware that the substantial concentration of social, political and economic activities in space, with their distinctive, highly durable capital installations, which constitutes an urban area, involves many important externalities, market frictions and rigidities, significantly lagged responses, and non-market constraints on behaviour. Purely decentralised market interaction is not to be expected to lead to efficient allocational or desirable distributional outcomes. The task for the economist is to discern how decentralised market processes can be supplemented by centralised public sector processes to improve overall performance. Concern with environmental degradation has certainly made this need clear. Supplementation can, of course, take many forms, from altering market incentives to regulating private behaviour and to undertaking direct public responsibility for resource uses. The town planner's concerns and goals and methods can throw light on the economist's attempt to formulate effective criteria for the amount and kind of public intervention in urban land use and other markets.

The Evaluation and Consolidation Panel was set up at the conference to enable the participants to draw together and structure the accumulating experience of the meeting. The formal papers themselves interrelated, but even more the full and wide-ranging general discussions extended certain issues beyond that of the papers and even raised and developed issues that had been at most implicit in the papers. The format of the panel was for Ian Heggie, who had been in charge of taping and rapporteur activities, to begin with a retrospective summary of the conference. He also enunciated and described the set of ten topics which, because of recurring attention or intrinsic importance, were to be examined further by the other four members of the panel.

The topics discussed were as follows:

1. *Preferences* – the actuality and discoverability of the community's preferences respecting environmental and non-environmental commodities or ends.
2. *Objectives* – the criteria set for characterising desirable social situations, when environmental conditions are considered, and procedures for achieving them.
3. *Distribution* – the non-neutral distributional consequences of environmental degradation and of measures to remedy it.
4. *Micro and Macro Models* – advantages and disadvantages of micro *versus* macro models of environmental impact.

5. *Environmental Effects* – the relation between objectively observable ambient standards and economic gains and losses, including well-being impacts.

6. *Growth and Environmental Quality* – the effects of economic growth (including technological change) on environmental quality.

7 *Environmental Policies* – the characteristics and relative usefulness of a broad range of environmental public policies.

8. *The Role of the Economist in Influencing Public Policy* – how the economist can influence the political process to act, and act appropriately, on environmental issues.

9. *Causes and Consequences of Changes in Urban Structure* – to what extent environmental problems are the causes or consequences of changes in the urban structure.

10. *Agenda for Further Empirical Research* – problems, issues and topics in the general area where empirical research is especially necessary to resolve difficulties and make for intellectual and policy progress.

The first three of these were led by Tulkens, items 4–6 by Thoss, items 7–8 by Mäler, and items 9–10 by Mills. The introduction of each group of items was followed by general discussion. As evidenced by these pages, the discussion was vigorous and searching.

It will be noticed that a paraphrase of the general discussion following each paper and the panel presentations is included in this volume. This is not an afterthought. The format of the conference proceedings was designed to devote the bulk of the time to designated critique and general discussion, not to presentation of the papers themselves. Thus, the weight of the meeting lay in the discussions. As will be seen, these are not dutiful acquiescences, but controverting, probing, wide-ranging, informed and concerned deliberations. They sometimes raise important issues not included in the papers; they tie together issues from different papers; they comment, condemn and extend. They are an integral part of the record of the conference.

Finally, we must acknowledge the critical contributions which gave the conference its very existence, arranged for its superb accommodations, and ensured its orderly fuctioning: Prof. Fritz Machlup (President, I.E.A.), Prof. Luc Fauvel (Secretary-General, I.E.A.), Prof. P. Nørregaard Rasmussen (Vice-President, I.E.A.), and Miss Mary Crook (Secretariat, I.E.A.). The substance of the conference is heavily indebted to the work of the Programme Committee: Prof. Peter Bohm, Prof. Edwin von Böventer, Sir John Hicks, Mr. Allen V. Kneese and Prof. Shigeto Tsuru.

Part I

Urbanisation and Environment

1 Urbanisation and Environment: An Introduction to some Theoretical Issues

Edwin von Böventer

INTRODUCTION

The general relationship between levels of economic development, the degree of urbanisation and their effect on man's environment are well known. They are highly correlated and depend on the country's natural resources, its climatic conditions and its population density. However, general statements of this kind, or general quantitative analyses of these relationships, are of little practical value. Only slightly less trivial is the observation that a reduction in the speed of economic development, and of urbanisation, might reduce the rate at which the environment is being depleted.

Since economic development, urbanisation and the consumption of natural resources are likely to continue at a rapid rate, the problems of the environment relate to the *kind* of environment that societies should try to create. The problem is one of determining the *optimal environment* – optimal in terms of output structure, urban structure (and regional population densities) and the structure of environmental variables.

The structure of the production flows, and of consumption, in a national economy is determined by the relative supply of private and public goods and by the mechanisms that determine the overall, as well as the particular, shares of these two categories of output.

Secondly, a given degree of urbanisation – however defined – may be realised in a variety of ways. It is dependent upon the overall spatial structure of the economy, the city (metropolitan area) size structure, as well as the internal economic, social, political, administrative and architectural structure of the various urban areas. These variables are functions of past economic and social development and are crucial determinants of any future development.

It is also clear that the environment is a multi-dimensional variable and that each dimension requires data on the actual state, its past development, its spatial distribution and the main determinants of national and regional averages. What *kinds* of environment have developed at various places, and what kind of environment is desired? In this context the question is (i) how significant are national

averages, (ii) what national maxima or minima, and what ranges of
dispersion of average regional values, should be tolerated, and (iii)
what are the optimal values for each environmental variable for each
geographical area.

Clearly, all the feasible sets of values for the quality of the environment, for the degree of urbanisation or the spatial distribution of
activities, and for the level of economic development or per capita
consumption and investment, are interdependent and are interrelated in an extremely complex way. However, politicians and
planners need to know what the trade-offs are between the various
alternatives open to them. It is important to know which factors
make it difficult to ascertain, in quantitative terms, what these
trade-offs are. This leads on to a discussion of the relevant criteria
that are used in the decision process. In the following section I
leave aside the problems which arise out of conflicts between relatively few market participants, e.g. between groups and organisations
or between administrative agencies and groups of citizens, which
lead to strategic situations which in practice are solved through
negotiation (the rules being based on the power structure) through
the democratic processes, or by a combination of both.

QUANTIFYING THE ALTERNATIVES

When considering deviations from optimal combinations of development levels, urbanisation patterns and environmental effects, the
following factors are important (this excludes the lack of information
or any limitations imposed by different modes of property ownership).

(a) *Market imperfections*. These refer to discrepancies between
marginal costs and market prices.

(b) *Planning imperfections*. The deviations in optimal positions are
due to (i) deficiencies in the (internal) decision rules, i.e.
within both firms and public agencies, and (ii) deficiencies
in the assignment of jurisdictions (or responsibilities or authority) in the widest sense of the words. This refers to the horizontal and vertical structure of government (either public or
quasi-public) agencies and to their responsibilities, particularly
in relation to the spatial extension of communities, cities and
states. This raises the questions of the optimal degree of
centralisation or decentralisation of decision-making in
government, and the supply and price of public goods (some
of which spill over into neighbouring administrative units).

(c) *Imperfect planning horizons*. This refers to the imperfect consideration of distant effects that have their origin in the present. These latter imperfections may arise because of long periods of gestation and the inability of decision-makers to foresee correctly the effects of their decisions (this is partly due to the unknown relationships); the inability of society to appraise correctly the consequences of *known* effects before they are felt directly; and the appearance of external effects of all kinds.

These three factors are mostly interdependent. The creation of long-term capital goods, whether based on incorrect assumptions or assumptions subject to wide margins of error, have particularly important *external effects*. The location of a capital good is an important datum for the future decisions of households, firms or agencies which are affected by the service flows of the capital good. It thus makes a great difference whether such locational decisions are taken sequentially or whether they are taken simultaneously, i.e. within the confines of the same planning operation. Long-term investment decisions also affect the preference functions of society. They not only change the physical environment itself but also influence, via people's experiences, their knowledge and their tastes. The interdependence of acts and preferences is an important external effect and is not normally measured in cost-benefit analyses. This factor is nevertheless important since it acts as a possible obstacle to change. In the case of environmental degradation it may even be regretted that the adaptation of people's (superficial) tastes to basic needs is so slow – notwithstanding the soundness of conservative attitudes in other fields. However, these issues raise important problems of political choice as well as, more specifically, planning problems connected to the future of man's environment.

In summarising it is useful to distinguish between the following types of urban and environmental problems:

(a) The efficient organisation of the planning processes within the public sector and its relation to the supply of public services at various points in space.
(b) The assessment of real resource costs, in particular of the costs and benefits that are external to the decision unit, and the determination of 'correct' prices.

This presupposes that the effects on the environment are known; for this reason it is extremely important to have:

(c) An evaluation of the spatial effects of any economic activities on the state of the environment.

These three interrelated problems could be studied, if the necessary
data were available, by means of a static model, or within a comparative static framework. One would then have to state precisely what
it was that society was trying to maximise – what other objectives,
apart from a high level of G.N.P. were being sought and what short-
term and long-term weights we should attach to each objective. The
preference functions, and the relevant decision processes, must thus
be assumed and must be specified in fairly precise terms. In the real
world the important question is who chooses this objective function
and by what process are changes in the objective function affected.

In addition to these considerations one has to recognise the following three sets of interrelated problems:

(d) The need to adapt government planning machinery, including
the use of incentives and disincentives to regulate the private
sector, to take account of the above changes. In doing this,
however, one has to anticipate the kinds of external effects
that may arise, their spatial distribution, how they are likely
to change the future optimum outputs and locations, and what
kinds of additional planning methods the new situation
requires.

(e) The assessment of the future needs of society following various
economic changes; particularly from changes in technology
that are either likely to happen, or can be effected or induced,
by means of public action.

(f) The effects that all the changes mentioned under (d) might
have on the utility functions of people in different cities and in
different kinds of environment. The problem is one of ensuring
that the real needs of present and future generations do in
fact appear in the relevant utility functions. It is also a problem
of ensuring that the political processes also reflect these
changes and needs.

A detailed study of these problems will only be possible once the
three problems (a), (b), and (c) above have been tackled. Moreover,
it is no longer possible to distinguish between their various meanings.
Although preference functions can usually be treated as data, in the
analysis of future developments the utility functions themselves
become endogenous variables and are influenced by both the kind
and the rate of economic development.

THEORETICAL PROBLEMS

In planning for the future, and in trying to improve on past decisions,
one is handicapped by the imperfections (particularly by the lack of

knowledge of interrelationships) listed in the last section. In addition there is the theoretical problem of trying to reach an optimum by a series of adjustment processes which are not all under the control of a perfectly informed Planning Authority. Problems of imperfections, and those due to the decentralisation of the planning processes, invariably occur together. Their effects must thus be studied simultaneously. However, before questioning the significance of any deviations from an optimal position it is useful to inquire into the theoretical difficulties that are usually involved in this type of analysis. The central question is about the effects of decentralised planning: how does it affect economic efficiency and how do these consequences affect research and planning in the real world.

The basic assumption is thus that within a given legal and organisational framework (with specified initial conditions, technologies and preference functions) economic agents take decisions about the kind of environment they wish to live in and that they help create. A comprehensive theoretical model would need to specify the local markets for all goods, services, securities and money; the income and expenditure of all households, firms and government agencies; and, in the same way, the income and expenditure of all regions (or sub-regions) – including capital movement between each region (or sub-region) particularly for regional development purposes.

In this context, one would have to consider *for all* agents (e.g. households, firms, agencies) their *specific locations* (in terms of size, location and the qualitative characteristics of each residence as well as their locations within the agglomerations) and *all their activities*, including the kind of activity, its level as well as its spatial extension, its sources of supply, its final markets and its spatial interaction in general.

The specific questions that are relevant to urbanisation and environment are:

(a) For households:
   (i) the quality of their residential property, the quality and size of the dwelling unit, the distances to employment, shopping, cultural and recreational areas, and to government agencies;
   (ii) the incomes, taxes, and possible consumption of private and public goods (allowing for any variation in the quality of infrastructure services offered by the community);
   (iii) the amount of pollution the household has to put up with.
(b) For firms:
   (i) the levels of their production processes and any interaction they might have with other economic agents at other points in space;

(ii) the size of city and agglomeration, their locations within the cities (and relative to other cities), the range of public goods offered at each location and the prices paid for them, and the pollution that the firm's activities create.

(c) For all government agencies:
   (i) the organisational set-up in relation to the degree of centralisation, or decentralisation, of their activities and jurisdictions;
   (ii) the amount of public goods they supply;
   (iii) the sum total of all laws and regulations that must be treated as affecting, or restricting, the activities of all economic agents, particularly in regard to their environmental effects.

No single model can satisfy our needs. One cannot answer all the relevant questions at the same time; the system would get out of hand. It is likewise well known that general equilibrium models have to work with extremely rigid simplifying assumptions to meet both stability and existence conditions. These assumptions are so restrictive that the models lose most of their practical relevance. Within this introductory paper, however, only a few of the relevant issues will be raised. This will be done by utilising a number of very limited models which will focus on particular aspects of the overall problem. To do this the models will only be specified in sufficient detail for the specific problem being studied. Furthermore, in order to simplify still further, locations within cities (and relative to metropolitan subcentres) will not be considered. They would have to be treated rather like questions of optimal locations (or environments) within an entire economy and relative to other centres.

In considering the possible results of decentralised market solutions, one has to be aware of two areas where market based solutions are not feasible: (i) where the nature of the problem renders market choices impossible and (ii) where there are insufficient alternatives open to the economic agents. To discuss these issues, it is necessary to distinguish between national goods and services (private or public) and regional (or local) goods and services. In this context I shall consider three different situations: (a) there are large-scale economies related to the supply of public services within the public sector but, apart from this, no other agglomeration economies arise. The effects of (b) localisation economies and (c) urbanisation economies are analysed later.

Let me first turn to the many variables for which the economic agents can never be offered a choice. This applies to all public goods whose level of supply cannot be varied between regions. For this reason they are truly *national* public goods. This also applies to the establishment of national standards related to local supplies of public goods and to maximum acceptable pollution levels. For all national public goods, and national standards, the important problem is the determination of the relevant trade-off against private goods and the long-term consequences of each alternative for society. The real problem is how the public can be made aware of the long-term implications of their choices and how they can be persuaded to act accordingly. This is more than just an economic-political problem.

Free individual choice between a *number of alternatives* is likewise impossible in the case of *national* private goods which are only produced in one location. The producers have a wide choice of locations, but consumers are only offered one spatially determined variant of the product.

In the following section I shall concentrate on the theoretical questions of city sizes and agglomeration effects. I start with a model in which all the economic agents produce similar external effects (this will be explained below). I shall subsequently consider economic agents whose characteristics are significantly different. The main question in the next paragraphs is whether individual choices lead to economically efficient results.

Case I

As a first step let me consider the implications of the following simplistic example.

(i) Each location is distinguished by the public services – both levels and composition as well as the activities of waste disposal and any reduction in pollution – it offers which are paid for by the economic agents who choose each particular location.

(ii) The unit cost of each bundle of public services depends on the size of the community; there are, at least within a certain size range, economies of scale; these economies of scale apply to all the services normally supplied by a municipality.

(iii) There are no other agglomeration economies which accrue to the economic agents.

In this example there will be an optimal city size for *each type* of community (characterised by the level and composition of their public services). This is the size at which the unit costs of each bundle of public services are minimised. The number of cities of each type will depend on the number of economic agents who prefer each type of community. There is a formal analogy between the characteristics of this case and that of perfect competition. I shall return to this analogy later.

This simplistic model has two important characteristics:

(a) The average cost of supplying public services is minimised for each type of community (and average costs is equal to the marginal cost of increasing the size of the community); and

(b) all economic agents have a choice between different *types* of communities and (possibly) the different tax rates and/or income levels associated with each type of community. They will thus choose, on the basis of a set of indifference functions, the combination which suits them best. If the type of community is represented by a one-dimensional variable (indicating the level of public goods supplied), then the choices open to a particular economic agent with a particular set of indifference functions can be represented diagrammatically as shown in Fig. 1.1. A city of size L^* is optimal for this particular

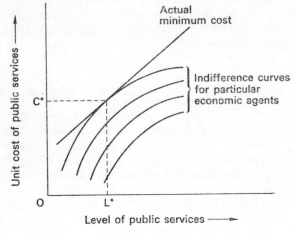

FIG. 1.1 The Choice of Optimum City Size: Case I

economic agent. However, even in this simplistic model, one further dimension (or set of dimensions) should be considered. They relate to the *type* of community: the range of regulations controlling permissible influences on the environment (pollution levels, etc.).

The important issues that arise even in this example are:

(a) What kinds of regulations should be introduced, and by what decision processes should they be introduced, in the common

situation in which individual economic agents and municipalities have to start with an existing community?
(b) How can the government encourage the development and use
of technologies that have fewer adverse effects on the environment? How are the marginal trade-offs to be determined and
what welfare criteria should be used?
(c) How can the preference functions (such as those shown in
Fig. 1.1) be influenced to take better account of the long-term
environmental effects of the above decisions?

Case II

As a slightly more complicated case, consider the following example.
This example utilises the same two assumptions, (i) and (ii), as Case I,
but assumption (iii) is different. In Case II we assume that there are
agglomeration economies in the private sector. These economies are
such that each economic agent is willing to pay a higher tax rate
for a city of a certain size than for any other city sizes. The agglomeration economies could arise (a) exclusively in the form of *localisation
economies*: only firms of the same type are affected by them, or (b)
there are *urbanisation economies* – as between firms of different types
– but these are exactly the same for all the firms affected by them. In
the latter case the crucial point is that all these firms enjoy the same
agglomeration economies although in other respects they might
be quite different. The two subcases (a) and (b) have one important
characteristic in common: there is a perfect symmetry between the
agglomeration economies received by each set of firms and those
emitted by them. One important feature is that all these firms have
the same indifference functions with regard to the type of municipality (say, Type L^* again) and to the maximum prices, or tax
rates, that they are willing to pay for public services. Each of the
firms considered also has the same effect on any agglomeration
economies that might arise; each of them makes the same contribution to the sum total of the agglomeration economies for each city.
The symmetry with regard to agglomeration economies makes this
example interesting and simplifies the analysis of its economic
efficiency. The unit cost curve of the public goods, as a function of
the size of municipality, is the same as Case I. But the corresponding
indifference curve (or isoprofit curve) of the economic agents is no
longer a straight line (in Case I the economic agents were indifferent
with regard to city size). In Case I they simply wanted to minimise
the cost of public goods – which implied that they maximised their
utilities or profits – since there were no agglomeration economies in
the private sector. The Case II situation is depicted in Fig. 1.2.
With a unit cost curve, and a set of indifference curves, like those

shown in the Figure (assuming that $I°$ is greater than $I*$ because the costs of the latter are higher throughout), the following results can be derived.

With a full knowledge of the alternatives (shown by the functions in Fig. 1.2) all these firms would prefer a city of size $N*$. At all other

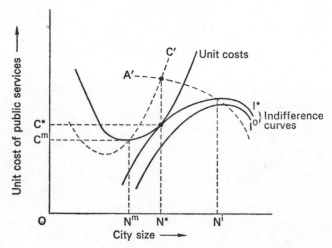

FIG. 1.2   The Choice of Optimum City Size: Case II

values of N, only indifference curves lower than $I*$ could be realised. One should also mention that the economic agents would simultaneously choose the optimal *size* and *types* of community as shown for Case I by Fig. 1.1. In Case II the cost function has to be reinterpreted: it is no longer the unit cost minima (C^m) that are relevant but the unit costs for each particular type of municipality (i.e. $C*$ instead of C^m for Type $L*$).

Is $N*$ really the optimal city size of Type $L*$ for these economic agents? Note that $N*$ is greater than N^m. This implies that the marginal cost of supplying this particular bundle ($L*$) of public services is greater than average costs. Thus each of these economic agents is paying less for the public services it uses than the (marginal) cost of supplying them. It should first of all be pointed out that, since all the economic agents are alike, there is no way of taking the difference away from them. It would always flow back to them unless there was a higher-order authority to take the money away from the city as a whole. However, this would not be economically efficient: the answer to the above question must thus be, yes. $N*$ is optimal. This is true for the following reason. On the one hand, beyond the city size N^m, each additional economic agent causes the average cost of public services to rise; on the other hand it also provides them with some benefit because it raises the level of their agglomeration economies by a greater amount. The net effect is thus positive. The attainable utility level, or profit level, for each of them rises up to N^*. Beyond N^* the net effect becomes negative. Thus N^* is a compromise which minimises the unit costs of public services and maximises the private sector agglomeration economies. If there were constant returns in the public sector, the optimum size would be N^i.

The same conclusion can be derived by considering the marginal functions. At N^*, the two marginal functions will necessarily have the same value if, for N^*, the two (average) curves are tangential to each other. The meaning of the marginal cost of public services (Line C' in Fig. 1.2) is obvious. The first derivative of the indifference curve (Line A') likewise shows the amount by which total agglomeration economies rise (in money terms) when an additional economic agent moves into this city. In conclusion it is clear that the same arguments apply *mutatis mutandis* if the indifference curves reach their maximum to the left of N^m. In this case, the optimal size of the cities will be smaller, and there will be more of them than shown in the above example.

Up to this point the application of a Tiebout-like model will only lead to an optimum solution if the number of different types of communities and regions is large enough. The communities only become attractive once a certain size has been reached and unit costs of public goods get significantly lower. For this reason, a central planning agency will have to ensure that the city growth process does indeed get started.

The scarcity of land presents a further problem. There are three possibilities:

(i) There is sufficient land available for new cities at (almost) negligible cost. In this case, sufficient competition between the economic agents in all cities would reduce hyper-profits to zero: this would be the profit maximum, or utility maximum, indicated by I^* in Fig. 1.2.

(ii) Land gets scarce as new cities come into existence and the owners of the land can extract rent. The situation will again be economically efficient although prices and income distribution will differ significantly, but hyper-profits will again be zero.

(iii) Land is scarce but is given free of charge to anyone who wants to take up economic activities in the community in question. In this case, there will be a discrepancy between average and marginal productivities (for each additional economic agent) and the situation will not be efficient. The communities will tend to be too large. The same result would obtain if in (ii) all rents were taxed away but were used by the municipal government for the benefit of all of its inhabitants. Thus in cases (i) and (ii) we have a pure case of a Pigovian external economy which is efficient and does not require any taxes or subsidies. If, in case (ii) rents were taxed away on equity grounds, the proceeds would have to be used by the national government.

Case III

The assumption that all economic agents have the same agglomeration economies is relaxed in this example. This assumption had the great advantage of symmetry: the external economies received and caused by each economic agent are the same. Now consider economic agents who are not alike in this respect. Since, in this case, everything depends on who first decided to locate in a particular community it is difficult to regulate the composition of the economic agents in a community. This leads to an assignment problem which is incomparably more difficult than the Beckmann-Koopmans stability problem in location theory. For these reasons, functions like those in Fig. 1.2 can only be determined if the composition of N can be specified for each value. Moreover, these functions now have different meanings; only the cost functions of public services remain the same.

The interpretation of the other two functions is more complicated. Assume that all the problems mentioned in the preceding paragraph have been solved and that the optimal size N^* for the composition L^* of public services has indeed been reached. Then it must be true for each economic agent that for N^* the highest possible level of indifference has been reached (I^*). For smooth functions, there would again be a point of tangency between the cost function and the indifference curve. The corresponding marginal functions will also intersect for N^*. Apart from this, however, the indifference function may be different for each of the economic agents that constitute N^*. And how do we now interpret the marginal function A'? A' shows what effect each additional economic agent, for a particular economic agent h, has on the agglomeration economies of each of the *other* economic agents. It is thus obvious that the marginal function A' can only be smooth if the other economic agents are ranked in a particular way. However, the important point is that the functions I^* and A' do not enable the activities of one agent b to be derived from a knowledge of the others (this represents a lack of symmetry). Now assuming that all economic agents know about the agglomeration economies, the derivability of h would be reflected in the corresponding function of all the other economic agents. If *on the whole* the existence of *h* were not derivable, then for *most* of the other economic agents the optimum city size N^* would *not* include the economic agent *h*. But this is of little use: in a system of completely decentralised decision making there is no way of keeping *h* out, as long as *h* is willing to pay the ruling price for public services (and for the land).

This is a situation that is often encountered in practice. Particular firms destroy the viability of certain neighbourhoods or sub-centres because they are able to sqeeze out others (by realising high profits and hence being prepared to pay high prices for that location), while making a small (or negative) contribution to the viability of the sub-centre. In this case two courses of action are possible: (i) try to obtain some of the information on the economic and social significance of the composition of a group of economic agents, e.g. effects on the environment, on the incomes and viability of the whole area; (ii) try to make use of this information for planning purposes by introducing zoning regulations which, at least to some extent, control the *composition* of the economic agents in certain areas.

It may seem surprising that no distinction has been made between producers and consumers (firms and households). For the above arguments such a distinction is not necessary because the various economic agents were different anyway and no details were given of what this difference comprised. It must be pointed out, however, that a nation of individuals deciding in isolation which type of community is best for them, and deciding it on the basis of a given set of utility functions, is quite unrealistic. The latter point has been mentioned before. In this context I should like to stress that the 'composition' of neighbourhood centres is certainly an important variable for all urban and environmental planning, and that, in analogy to (i) above, interactions between individuals within neighbourhoods are just as important in empirical studies as are agglomeration economies for firms. This leads into the realm of sociology. From the economic point of view, this is the other end of a series of approaches that start with conurbations and lead to the consideration of cities and sub-centres within larger spatial complexes. In any case, instead of considering individual economic units one might just as well consider groups of citizens or sociological groups.

PROBLEMS IN LESS ABSTRACT SETTINGS

The practical problem is not one of determining theoretical optima for situations in which everything can be planned *de novo*, but of changing the actual world as we find it and of leading developments in directions that are less detrimental to the environment than many past developments. Apart from the other points mentioned above, the following factors must therefore also be taken into account.

(1) Planning cannot start from scratch. All optima have to be considered in terms of a given socio-economic and institutional framework and the existing production and welfare functions of society (barring revolutionary changes in them). The optimisation process may, or must, thus try to change the world and the preferences of its inhabitants.

(2) There arise significant adaptation costs. This applies to all the changes proposed because the mobility of the system is limited. The mobility parameters are thus important in the determination of the optimum, or optimal, paths that are being sought. More information about them is necessary.

(3) For these reasons, subsidies and taxes (which are not needed in an ideal economic system) are justified on equity and/or efficiency grounds. Certain measures, which in a pure model and in the long run would have negligible distributional effects, do now influence income distribution and the competitiveness of certain sectors.

(4) Economic agents do not choose communities or municipalities in the way described in the last section. It is true that some people do move, but the important changes in the level, as well as in the composition of public services, and in their methods of finance, do have to be altered through the democratic process. This is particularly true for changes in jurisdictional and administrative boundaries, as well as in the degree of centralised planning.

(5) In justifying such changes, one has considerable difficulty in quantifying the interrelationships between the spill-over effects in one centre or region and other centres or regions. This is particularly true in relation to the functions that national and regional centres play as vehicles of economic and technological progress (and again, what is progress in this environmental context, and who decides on what definition is relevant?).

(6) Furthermore, some external and environmental effects first became visible in the biggest centres or agglomerations and thus helped to draw attention to these problems. Big agglomerations may thus be used to experiment with ways of fighting the deterioration of the environment. This does not hold, however, for effects that are not localised but which arise as a result of *all* economic activities regardless of whether they are spatially concentrated or scattered.

(7) One also has to consider the problems arising out of the need for international co-ope.ation, or international agreements, in those cases where goods are traded on a large scale and where production or consumption has significant environmental effects. All such effects, as well as the economic and institutional means of dealing with them, have distributional effects that cannot be ignored.

CONSEQUENCES FOR RESEARCH

As pointed out earlier, a comprehensive answer to most of the questions formulated in this paper could only be derived within a general equilibrium system – as is true of all comprehensive cost-benefit analyses. Since this is impossible, however, a systematic approach to the study of these questions must be based on a series of limited operational models which build upon one another (utilising the results of previous models) so that, in an iterative way, one moves towards an optimal position.

One important aspect, related to the relevant trade-off for decision-making, may nevertheless be formulated in a general way. Consider total welfare W as a function u of the vector of all outputs (final goods) and of the vector z of all the impacts the production processes have on the environment. If all inputs of labour and capital goods are given u will be a function of their output. To obtain the theoretical result that is relevant from our point of view, one may confine oneself, without loss of generality, to one commodity and one environmental effect and write (omitting any qualifications):

$$W = u\,(x,\,z) \quad \text{with } z = z\,(x).$$

Then $\qquad dW = \dfrac{\partial u}{\partial x}\,dx + \dfrac{\partial u}{\partial z}\,dz \qquad$ or $\qquad dW = \dfrac{\partial u}{\partial x}\,dx + \dfrac{\partial u}{\partial z}\dfrac{\partial z}{\partial x}\,dx,$

and for $dW = 0$,

$$\frac{dx}{dz} = \frac{\partial u}{\partial x}\bigg/\frac{\partial u}{\partial x} \qquad \text{or} \qquad \frac{\partial x}{\partial z} = \frac{\partial u}{\partial z}\bigg/\frac{\partial u}{\partial x}.$$

The result implies that, at the optimum point, the marginal utility of consumption and of putting up with environmental deprivation should be equal to the inverse values of the marginal rates of transformation or substitution of x and z. The latter relationship is determined by the available technologies. Generalising, this condition should hold for all commodities that are actually produced and that have an environmental effect z_{jk}.

One can consider a production frontier F for the whole economy

that links output quantities and their environmental effects. This is
shown in Fig. 1.3. If the level of production is raised, the (negative)
environmental effects become increasingly severe, while on the
consumers' side the propensity to accept *additional* environmental
effects becomes increasingly *smaller* as x rises. Thus by introducing

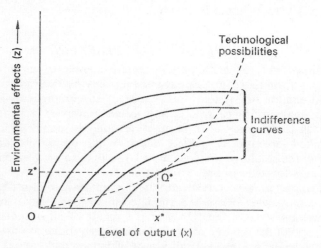

FIG. 1.3   Relationship between Output and Environmental Effects

a welfare function in the form of indifference curves for (x, z) combinations, one can derive the the optimum combinations of x and
z, as Point Q^* in Fig. 1.3, as a point of tangency to these smooth
functions.

The main practical questions in this context are:

– how can the government, and how should it, encourage technologies that *lower* the F function over the relevant range; or
– what kinds of limits on z should be imposed by law; and
– how can the government influence social indifference curves
  so that society becomes less ready to accept the negative environmental effects of production and consumption; so that
– on the whole *lower* equilibrium values for Z^* prevail, even
  though x is lower than is otherwise possible.

It should be mentioned that if factor prices are considered explicitly
in a slightly expanded model, then instead of simply relating the
marginal (disutility) of additional factor (labour) inputs (v) and the
marginal utility (U_x) of the additional output that can be produced
with the additional factor input (x_v) (i.e. $u_v = \mu \geq u_x x_v$) it should be

done so that the environmental effects are also taken into account.
One then has

$$u_v = \mu = u_x x_v - x_z z_x x_v = u_x v_x \left(1 - \frac{u_z}{u_x} z_x\right).$$

Here the marginal utilities are not considered for the marginal output
alone. The expression is corrected by introducing a factor that takes
both the marginal environmental effect z_x of producing x and the
marginal utilities of z and x into account, i.e. the marginal physical
product of v in x has to be greater than before.

Let me finally suggest a short list of some possible ideas for further
empirical studies of the kind mentioned at the start of this section.
It is clearly impossible to give an exhaustive list of ideas that might be
usefully explored in this context. The following list can only serve as
an example.

(a) *The determination of direct external effects* arising from the
activities of single plants or groups of plants. This follows directly
from the discussion in the above three paragraphs. This would start
with (i) a quantitative evaluation of the direct effects (z_x) followed by
(ii) the determination of market prices and (iii), as a third step, an
analysis to trace the effects by means of a simplified input-output
model or a simplified international trade model. In this way (iv)
market prices, corrected for external effects, could be derived for the
commodities in question, and then (v) the possible effects of these
adjusted market prices on demand could be evaluated through
demand studies. The question then is (vi) how does this process affect
optimal locations and incomes in each part of the country.

(b) *Optimal locations for plants* can be determined if certain
restrictions are placed on the total input of certain environmental
variables at each location. The environmental inputs can then be
auctioned. In this way (shadow) prices for the various outputs or
production processes, in terms of the environmental variables, could
be obtained. These values could then be used to answer the question
of whether or not the initial restrictions should be modified. It is
therefore important to realise that the numerical values for these
restrictions should be treated as variables.

(c) The *determination of city structures* by means of programming
models:

(i) For interacting sets of activities various scales, possibly also
varying compositions, could be considered by quantifying
the differences in costs and benefits to each activity (i.e.
industrial complexes, 'tertiary complexes', or groups of
people).

(ii) Optimal scales for the spatial agglomeration of these activities could be determined on the basis of the scale economies, and of the inter-agglomeration transportation costs, including the implied cost of commuting.

(iii) The aim is thus to derive an optimum system of sub-centres (and their locations) within agglomerations of various sizes.

(iv) This entails the study of the environmental effects of each system of sub-centres.

(v) In particular it implies the study of possible scale economies in those activities that protect the environment. Such a study clearly requires different simplifying assumptions from those listed under (a) and (b).

(d) One has to produce detailed (technical) studies of the technologies and costs of *pollution control and waste disposal*. Further studies of these kinds should be encouraged as a primary goal of any conference on environmental problems. It is difficult in this introductory paper, however, to offer any generalisations or a systematic presentation of possible approaches.

(e) *Transportation costs* can often be taken as given. This is not legitimate, however, in the context of studies on urbanisation and environment. An important aspect of these studies has for some time been the study of alternative systems of transportation in terms of their costs and benefits. The effects on the environment are again important in this context. These studies have to tie in with other studies that concentrate on the effect of transportation on optimal locations within metropolitan areas, as well as within the national economy and within inter-nations systems. An essential part of these studies is the estimation of short-run and long-run demand functions for public transportation: one has to know what kinds of incentives and taxes should be used for public and private transportation and what kinds of regulations are required for private passenger transport, if an optimum traffic system is to be developed.

(f) Apart from quantifying the *external effects* of economic activities, and of their effects on the environment, it is important to know how they can best be charged for or averted. It is well known that for industries with negative (positive) external effects output levels are higher (less) than is optimal from an overall point of view. The relevant questions are:

– In what cases should the use of production processes that create a lot of pollution be completely banned?

– In what cases should the output of pollution be limited, and how should these maxima (per unit of output or input) be determined?

- How should such maxima vary between different locations and different regions?
- How far should the industries be left to arrange their own pollution abatement?
- How can such regulations be implemented, what kind of administrative measures are needed, and how can the measures be best organised?

Discussion of the Paper by
Edwin von Böventer

Formal Discussant: Silver. von Böventer's paper attempts to synthesise our theoretical knowledge of the relationships between urbanisation, environment and economic development. It raises a number of problems and the author suggests a number of lines of research, of both positive and normative varieties, to broaden the scope of the investigation by building upon past research which, in this nascent field, has been somewhat disjointed.

It seems to me, however, that the author has not succeeded in analysing the most important questions common to urbanisation and environment, while the paradigm which he utilises to demonstrate their interaction is of questionable relevance. My remarks, accordingly, fall into two parts: first, I make some comments about his treatment of the problems which he does explicitly discuss; second, I comment upon areas which he deals with superficially but which deserve greater emphasis.

In his three models of increasing generality, the author demonstrates how difficult it is to achieve an efficient solution, even with a rather restricted model. While the demonstration is neat and succinct, the point which he makes seems to be largely irrelevant to the general discussion. Clearly, the derivation of an analytical solution to the problem of deciding the optimal size distribution and composition of a system of cities is very complex. What the author demonstrates is that the simple, diagrammatic treatment, which is useful for didactic purposes, rapidly becomes overburdened as we loosen or drop restrictions. But the same difficulty applies to a variety of situations in which spatial externalities do not play a role. One has only to introduce notions of variations in productivity and preference orderings, or non-zero costs of information, to generate the same level of complexity.

More important, the author's analysis seems to focus on the wrong problem. The growing concern with matters of urbanisation and environment arise from the feeling that real economic systems involve disparities between marginal costs and benefits which vary among groups of firms and individuals. In other words, the question is primarily one of distribution. The problem of efficiency arises in connection with public intervention which aims to bring about a redistribution of benefits and costs. The problem is not only one of distribution among income classes, but the distribution between existing firms and residents in an urban area, between urban areas and between current and future generations. These problems are of widespread concern in those countries which concern themselves with the urban environment. I had hoped that this opening paper would discuss these questions in more analytical terms.

The only planning problem discussed explicitly by the author, although others are mentioned, is the question of the optimal centralisation of decision-making. The problem of growth in a system of cities has been a traditional one in regional economics. Much of the literature on environment, on the other hand, has pertained to optimal systems of transfer and regulation, e.g. the taxation of pollution, congestion fees and zoning. A number of the papers submitted to this conference are concerned, at least in part, with these latter questions.

In his own analysis, and in his suggestions for the types of research which might be pursued in the area of urbanisation and environment, the author hints at some of the analytical tools which may be used to address these problems. Some more general comments are therefore in order. The first way of addressing environmental problems has been, at least analytically, through the application of welfare economics, since a large part of the subject has been concerned with externalities and distributional questions. This development seems natural. There has been much less work of the positive type in which the results of marginal adjustments have been interpreted as responses to environmental variables. The paper by Hoch (Chapter 3) is one of the better examples of this type. An important characteristic of environmental problems is that they are frequently concerned with questions of quality. Analytically we can think of goods which are composites of a number of characteristics. However, economic theory has not developed in a direction which enables us to evaluate the dimensions of the environment in order to compare different environmental situations. The work of Lancaster [1] is an instance of a recent attempt to develop economic theory in this direction. Besides being multi-dimensional another important characteristic of the environment is that, by and large, its features are not traded in markets. The study of public sector behaviour and output is therefore relevant. Here we can return to the author's diagrams and ask, first, how public goods can be measured so that we can make predictions about the locational choices of private sector agents between urban areas; and second, how the public sector is likely to behave under a variety of growth situations with regard to the four major types of distributional decision which I have mentioned. Casual observation suggests that small changes in the level of some public goods have large effects upon urban areas through migration within and among urban areas, e.g. crime prevention. The author's point that the real problems of urbanisation are related to changes in existing urban systems leads to the observation that very little exists in the way of a theory of urban growth. Instead we have several static models. Perhaps some of the elaborate analysis of modern growth theory could be adapted for this purpose.

My comments about appropriate directions for the advancement of research on urbanisation and environment rest upon a very broad interpretation of the scope of the environmental problems which affect urban areas. I feel that problems of air and water pollution, while most readily recognised as the substance of the study of environment, can be viewed as a manifestation of external effects generated by the spatial proximity of a variety of economic agents. Environmental economics and urban economics therefore overlap on a range of problems. The author also appears to recognise the breadth of the subject, though less so in his suggestions for research than in his theoretical treatment. For instance, the choice by the household of an optimal housing bundle (with associated decisions regarding commuting, labour force participation – or more generally allocation of the time budget – level of consumption of public services, etc.) when faced with a variety of residential environments, with associated tax rates and levels of accessibility, is a major concern of urban economics. Its investigation appears to complement much of the research in environmental economics. Similarly, on the production side, examining the influence of the external effects generated by individual firms, as the author suggests, requires a theory of industrial location – another major concern of urban and regional economics. More generally, any policy recommendation resulting from an analysis of the environmental effects generated by, and impinging upon, various economic agents in urban areas may, as a consequence of regulating levels of external effects, have substantial influence upon the structure of the urban economy.

It seems to me that several of the questions to which the author and I have alluded might provide fruitful opportunities for interdisciplinary research. The work on air and water pollution has already led to collaboration between economists and engineers. The concern with practical questions of regulation, when spillovers are important, suggests a potential for collaborating with political scientists. The paper by Russell, Spofford and Haefele [2] is an early attempt at such collaboration. A knowledge of legal systems could also be useful in proving environmental policies. Sociologists and social psychologists might greatly enhance our understanding of behavioural responses to various environmental situations.

In closing I should like to compliment the author upon a paper which raises a number of important points which will recur during the course of this conference and subsequently in the literature. That he was unable to treat them all systematically is testimony to the breadth and complexity of the subject-matter.

Rothenberg observed that one of the important issues raised by the author was that questions of the environment not only involve controlling activities constituted in their present location but of deciding on the optimum geographical distribution of these activities. This raised questions of long-term allocations involving choices between types and levels of activity, as well as between locations in cities of different size. This pointed to the kind of distributional issues involved in any general equilibrium framework.

He argued that we should distinguish between two types of distributional problem. The first was the overall progressivity or regressivity of the structure of public and private sector production and how this balance might be affected by environmental policies. The second related to appropriate and feasible policies towards environmental control: this raised a different type of environmental question. Within the structure of the externalities involved in environmental degradation there were different balances of distributional changes that different policies could render. Some policies involved uniformity of damage and thus involved no redistribution of relative income amongst the affected parties. Other problems showed a significant polarity of distributional effects. One group benefited substantially from the existence of the degradation while another group suffered losses. Any policy which sought to control the degradation would thus involve a substantial shift in relative real income.

Any attempt to frame appropriate public policies should thus go hand-in-hand with a fundamental understanding of the underlying distributional import of the problem as well as of the cure.

Mills said that public policies affecting income distribution were important and controversial. Research by William Baumol [3] and Marc Roberts [4] had strongly suggested that anti-pollution policies, paid for by polluters, would be regressive. Benefits from pollution abatement, on the other hand, were probably concentrated among high-income groups. Increased product costs for pollution abatement were almost certainly concentrated among low-income groups. The implication was that negative-income taxes or other redistribution policies would have to be somewhat stronger than otherwise. Attempts to abate pollution in ways that included specific distributional goals were therefore likely to be inefficient and ineffective.

Kneese disagreed with Mills' comment that we should down-grade the consideration of the distributional aspects of environmental problems. We were dealing with the question of public goods and, unless the lump-sum transfers that economists speak about were actually made, we were always up against distributional problems. They were inherent to the provision of public goods. To neglect them was to neglect an important aspect of the economics associated with the provision of public goods.

Hoch pointed out that any discussion of distributional effects should distinguish between (a) redistribution from rich to poor and (b) redistribution between different groups, without much reference to their incomes. With respect to (b) Foster's paper (Chapter 6), citing Mishan, seemed very germane: much, or all, depended on how society had assigned 'property' rights.

Evans thought that Fig. 1.2 depicted an unstable situation, in so far as the economic agents were taken to be profit maximising firms. Suppose the iso-profit Line I^* indicated a level of profit which was greater than zero so that excess profits were being earned by the firms located in the cities of size N^*. New firms would therefore be formed and would move into these cities increasing their size to, say, N^j. The unit cost of public services would then rise to C^j and the level of profits would be indicated by the iso-profit line passing through the point (N^j, C^j). This was shown in Fig. 1D.1.

Now firms would continue to be formed until profits fell to zero, this point being indicated in Fig. 1D.1 by the point at which the iso-profit line indicating zero profits cuts the unit costs curve to the right of the point (C^*, N^*). This point (N^e, C^e) was a stable equilibrium for firms since if additional firms moved into the city losses would be made leading to the exit of firms from the city: if the number of firms fell below N^e excess profits would be made and new firms would come into the city. The important point here was that whilst (N^e, C^e) was a stable equilibrium for firms it was not optimal.

It might be argued that, in long-run equilibrium, the level of profits indicated by I^* would for some reason be zero but in this case the point (N^*, C^*) would be a very unstable equilibrium. When $L^* = 0$ it was true that if any firms moved into the city losses would be made and city size would return to N^* as firms moved out of the city. If, however, the number of firms dropped below N^* then the losses would cause still more firms to move from the city and would lead to the city's eventual disappearance.

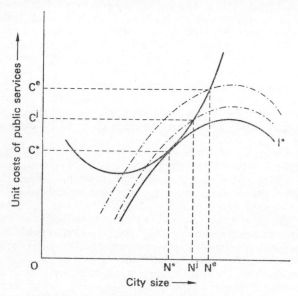

FIG. 1D.1   The Choice of Optimum City Size

A possible example of this contraction could be seen in Glasgow, Scotland, where high property taxes had apparently caused the liquidation of several firms in the central area and where every reduction in the number of firms had led to an increase in the tax burden. Obviously other factors were at work there but the example indicated that a model which allowed for instability might not be too unrealistic.

REFERENCES

[1] K. Lancaster, *Consumer Demand: A New Approach* (Columbia University Press, New York, 1971).
[2] J. G. Rothenberg and I. G. Heggie (eds.), *The Management of Water Quality and the Environment* (Macmillan, 1974), Chapter 7.
[3] W. Baumol and W. Oates, 'Environmental Protection and Income Distribution' (Unpublished manuscript).
[4] M. Roberts, 'Who Will Pay for Cleaner Power?' (Unpublished).

2 Central Place Theory and Regional Planning: West German Experience

Frank E. Münnich

This paper formulates the main hypotheses and preliminary findings of a research project which questions the intended use of Central Place Theory as a guideline for regional planning in the Federal Republic of Germany. It concludes that the expected development of all the main determinants of Central Place market hierarchies tend to destroy such a pattern rather than to maintain it.

2.1 *INTRODUCTION*

Few concepts in locational analysis have prompted so much research, and so many publications in the different sciences, as have Christaller's ideas on human settlements as hierarchies of Central Places. Geographers and economists alike have elaborated on almost every facet of Central Place Theory. The ensuing research has followed three main courses:

(1) Economists, who quickly realised the rather restricted basis of Christaller's work in economic theory, tried to add well-established economic theorems in order to bring Central Place Theory into line with the economic theory of location. Topics like agglomeration economies, balance of payments, price differentials, income differentials and so on were thereby included.

(2) Following Christaller's attempts, in Parts II and III of his original publication, many schemes were devised to test Central Place Theory empirically, e.g. using rank-size rule considerations and nearest-neighbour analyses.

(3) A reinterpretation of Central Place Theory was attempted because it was unable to explain many aspects of human settlements. This was nevertheless conditioned by a desire to preserve as much of Christaller's theory as possible because it was simpler and more operationally convenient than the usual theories of micro-economic equilibrium.

As a result Central Place Theory was only considered applicable to either thinly and evenly settled areas with a predominantly agricultural population [1] or to the tertiary sector of developed economies (mainly to retail trade and services [2]). This discussion, which extended from total refutation [3] to complete acceptance [4] of Christaller's original system, has not yet led to the formulation of any new, consistent and comprehensive concepts which either develop or reformulate Christaller's idea into a new theory which applies to the settlement patterns which exist, or are just evolving, in today's developed economies.

Besides this main stream of theoretical thought, which has remained predominantly academic, a quite different approach has slowly evolved in regional policy. Lösch, in the second edition of his *Economics of Location*, already points to the fact that, as early as 1941, Central Place ideas have been used as a guideline for relocation policy [5]. In 1956 Kroner stressed the importance of Central Place Theory for Regional Planning [6], but it took until 1965 before Central Place Theory was finally enacted as an integral part of regional planning policy. It is hard to trace this policy to specific events or people but there are at least three roots which, though interrelated, can be distinguished. The first was the increasing awareness of the huge regional differentials in income and wealth (and the supply of basic goods and luxuries) which developed between the highly industrialised areas of the Ruhr, Rhein-Main and Rhein-Neckar regions on the one hand and the mainly agrarian backward areas with poor soil, bad climate and low productivity (as well as the border areas of the German Democratic Republic) on the other. Besides specific programmes for education, road building, and so on, a general programme of subsidies for problem areas (so-called *Bundesausbaugebiete*) was created (it started in 1959) granting federal aid for industrialisation and the installation of infrastructure facilities. Parallelling this programme, with the same purposes and the same means, a programme was built up to support the development of Central Places (called *Bundesausbauorte*) without much theoretical basis. Both programmes have now grown into a fully-fledged system of subsidies for about 300 problem areas (comprising approximately three-fifths of the total area of Western Germany) and for about 100 cities and places which, with very few exceptions, are scattered throughout the problem areas.

A second incentive for regional planning policy is the economic and social crisis in agriculture. This crisis may be partly due to the free trade policy of the Federal Government (as well as to the increasing competition within the emerging European common market) but is mainly attributable to the structural changes associated with economic growth. The number of gainful workers in agriculture fell from 5·1 million in 1950 to 2·5 million in 1969 and is expected to drop to 1·7 million by 1980. This decline caused mass emigration from rural areas to the larger cities during the fifties and mainly during the sixties, to smaller and middle-sized cities. The Federal and Länder governments have attempted to balance the standard of living of the rural and industrial areas, to maintain the population of the plains and to only slowly alter the structure of agriculture. These objectives imply a policy of *Aktive Sanierung* whose implementation requires large-scale subsidies for (a) agricultural production and (b) the creation of new industrial employment in the 'problem areas' to help absorb the redundant agricultural labour force. Industrialisation, on the other hand, requires the provision of technical and social infrastructure on such a scale that any programme of industrialisation must focus on Central Places as possible industrial locations and cannot aim at a complete spatial dispersion of the new jobs to correspond with the dispersion of the agricultural population.

A third reason for concentrating federal assistance on a limited number of places has been related to the availability of funds and to their general effectiveness. Thus the direct goal of providing effective education, administrative and other public and private services to all parts of the population; combined with the technical requirements of an industrialisation policy necessary to stabilise the regional population distribution at large; and the increasing gap between requested and approved subsidies, led to the adoption of Central Places as the basic objective of regional policy. This approach had already become effective in the above-mentioned programme which started in 1959. Only in 1965 was the idea of a system of Central Places postulated as a general guideline for regional planning policy and enacted through the federal *Raumordnungsgesetz* (ROG) [7].

Unfortunately the law does not give a legal definition of Central Places, so that the operational meaning of the term remains obscure. Furthermore, due to the federal structure of Germany, the Länder develop their own definitions of Central Places which are not always compatible; for example, they differ in both number and in the meaning of different levels of centrality [8]. In several Länder research work is going on to implement the chosen definition by analysing the existing system of Central Places and its deficiencies. The Federal Government, on the other hand, in collaboration with the Länder, is about to develop a general federal programme for a regional planning policy (so-called *Raumordnungsprogramm*). This is supposed to be a comprehensive programme comprising all the relevant goals and objectives of regional planning policy in the immediate future. Within this programme, an attempt will be made for a unified approach to Central Place hierarchies, to ensure that federal subsidisation of regional development and Länder policy both follow the same well-established and well-accepted principles.

2.2 *THE CENTRAL PLACE CONCEPT IN SCIENCE AND POLITICS*

It is surprising that, in spite of the extensive criticism of Central Place Theory, it should still have been adopted as the basis of *Raumordnung*. There are only a few dissenting voices [9] and a few hints as to the possible differences in the notions used in science and in politics [10]. Within the professional world, on the other hand, there seems to be almost unanimous approval. In contrast to this majority opinion I want to show – if only in a preliminary way – that this policy is about to fix the German settlement structure to a pattern related to a stage of socio-economic development which has long since passed. To do so I start by considering the implications of using the Central Place concept as an objective.

Strictly speaking it is admissible to use the Central Place framework as a political objective only if it can be shown that:

(a) such a pattern is optimal for some (future) collective preference system subject to whatever constraints are expected to develop, and

(b) such a pattern is feasible, i.e. it can emerge from the uninhibited settlement decisions of migrating people or can be brought about by some direct or indirect kind of settlement and relocation measures.

As is well known, there is presently no way of predicting future preference systems. This problem is therefore usually approached by considering some partial goals, e.g. resource maintenance, sustaining an ecological equilibrium, regionally balanced economic growth and so on. Using Central Place Theory as a guideline usually means that only a few objectives are formulated, e.g. keeping or attaining a regional balance in the distribution of the population and in its living conditions. Such objectives are sometimes deduced from some principles of the German constitution on social adequacy and justice (*Sozialstaatlichkeit*). Despite some discussion, it seems that the principle of keeping agricultural areas settled is generally accepted. In the present situation this is clearly and intentionally directed against the market forces indicated above.

But whether or not we accept these objectives, the most important question is whether the proposed settlement pattern is feasible and, if so, what it will cost. In discussing this question we shall have to stress the role of market forces as the principal political means of influencing migration between towns as well as settlement patterns. There is little scope for direct administrative intervention in migration streams in favour of some preassigned destinations. In particular there is no means whereby migration streams can be directed back into rural areas. On the other hand, migration can be deterred from certain destinations in order to prevent areas from being settled or to prevent existing settlements being enlarged (e.g. in reserved spaces for recreational areas).

Indirect measures are likewise limited in number and are not very effective. Public investment (even if it is substantial) can usually only provide temporary employment (construction of roads, recreation areas, training fields, schools) or rather specialised employment in the provision of public utilities and administrative services (teachers, policemen, technicians, some handicrafts and civil servants). More important are the indirect effects on private investment for which public investment is often a necessary, but evidently not a sufficient, precondition. Investment in these types of infrastructure which yield the services necessary to keep qualified labour from migrating to places of higher centrality are particularly important in this respect. Investment by the private sector can only be induced indirectly by tax preferences, interest subsidies, credit guarantees, preferential status for entrepreneurs at public invitations to tender, and similar measures. The main problem with such a policy is to identify which places are to be subsidised. As indicated above, it is the explicit intention of regional policy to use existing Central Places, or Central Places which, according to theory, ought to be at some place, as nodes for economic development and industrialisation. The same principle holds for the provision of basic services to the farming population. In order to investigate the appropriateness of this political concept, as well as to provide a frame of reference for discussing the influence of market forces on settlement patterns, it is necessary to clarify the notion of Central Places. Because of the vagueness of the concept, the broad spectrum of ideas covered by the term, and the different meanings the word has for different writers from science and politics, we must adopt one exact notion. For the purpose of this paper, it is not necessary to give a complete reconsideration of Central Place Theory in formal terms. Instead, it will be sufficient to state some defining features of the concept, which also constitute the hard core of the notions usually used.

By Central Place structure we mean a nested hierarchical set of market areas irrespective of their specific shape. The hexogonal pattern, for example, is of no definitional importance since in practice many random factors, individual circumstances and singular events (special resources, a harbour, the topography) usually modify any regular patterns which might be expected on theoretical grounds. We can also dispense with the exact uniform distances for market areas of the same centrality. We retain as essential the notion of a hierarchy. By this I do not mean a graded step-wise or smooth rank-size relationship for settlements whose importance is measured by population or some measure of centrality. Such 'hierarchies' do not take into account the spatial outlay of the settlements and the functions they have for their surrounding areas. Instead we understand hierarchy as a nested ordering of market areas for different kinds of goods. That is, there are small market areas included in larger ones; there are places which, in differing degrees, sell goods to other places – the market areas of some goods being much larger and encircling many more places than those of other goods. The delivery structure between all settlements, viewed as a graph, is then a network of special structure: all arcs of this graph point in one direction only, away from the few sources which represent the most central cities and the initial extremities of all arcs going into one vertex representing market places which are adjacent to each other in real geographic space. This means that there may be settlements which purchase goods of higher centrality from several higher centres. In this case, however, these higher order centres must have adjacent market areas which meet exactly at these settlements. A good is called central if it is produced in place A but not in any area complementary to this place (the inhabitants of the complementary area buy it from place A). Centrality, therefore, is not established by the simple fact that differentiated production takes place; this higher production must be produced in a surplus amount and distributed to the whole population of the complementary area. It is this economically defined spatial hierarchy which establishes the spatial structure; not the size of the population or the differentiation of the product in any one place.

The question arises how this definition fits the intentions of the regional planning policy. As already indicated earlier the *Raumordnungsgesetz* (ROG) of 1965 is not very explicit on this point. Article 2 (I) 3 reads: 'Within distances which are tolerable to the dispersed population settlements . . . central places should be developed including the necessary educational, cultural and administrative institutions'.* No indication is given as to how 'central place' is to be interpreted in this context, and no indication is given as to which kind of Central Places this sentence refers. Article 8 on the other hand states that any definitions and delineations of areas mentioned in Article 2 must be developed jointly by the Länder and the Federation. So the statement of the *Ministerkonferenz für Raumordnung* of

* This and the following quotations are not literal translations.

8 February 1968 may be taken as the official interpretation of the text of the law [11]. It says, in short:

(1) The notion of Central Places under the law must be applied to Central Places of any order and their respective complementary regions in any part of the country.

(2) The definition of Central Places is as follows: There are areas in which settlements of different size and importance are economically and socially interrelated; they are called complementary regions. Within these regions certain settlements have developed a Central Place character in that they have institutions and a productive capacity able to supply their own population as well as that of the population of the complementary area.

(3) Four stages of central places are distinguished: upper, intermediate, lower centres and small centres or central hamlets. These four stages are mainly distinguished by their products. The two lower stages, which are often said to be indistinguishable in practice, provide for basic needs. The intermediate centres cater for more sophisticated needs and the upper centres supply the most sophisticated and specialised products. The types of products used for defining these centres are taken from the tertiary sector only with a strong emphasis on the top administrative services which, in the light of possible policy measures, is quite understandable.

(4) The statement gives minimum thresholds for the populations of the different types of centres and maximum time limits for the travel distances between them. The minimum population for the two lower types of centres, including their tributary areas, is 5,000 people; for the intermediate centre 20,000 people. The maximum time to be spent travelling by public transport is thirty minutes to the lower-stage centres and one hour to the intermediate centres. While the population figures are simply stated without any explanation the time limits are derived from some consideration of the frequency of trips and the tolerable time limit for these trips.

Without considering the proposed method of measuring centrality, and its normative implications, this statement clearly indicates that Central Places are defined in essentially the same way as outlined in the Introduction. There is further evidence supporting this assertion. A memorandum on Central Places [12] issued by the Federal Headquarters of the Associations of Towns and Municipalities clearly expresses the idea of nested market areas. The Federal Government itself in its first Report on Regional Planning [13] (ROB 66 in short) declared: 'Characteristic of the centrality of any settlement is that its market area extends beyond its local administrative area and comprises other settlements as well. . . . Central places can be classified by the quality of their central facilities and the range (diameter) of their market areas. . . . The productivity capacity of central places must be such that, besides the local population, the tributary area can be supplied.' In its second Report on Regional Planning [14] (1968) the Federal Government claims political importance for the statement of the *Ministerkonferenz für Raumordnung* cited above because 'it clarifies in a manner hitherto unknown in science or politics' that the main importance of Central Places rests upon the subsidiary function they perform for their hinterlands. Finally, the third Report on Regional Planning [15] (1970) discusses at some length measures taken in connection with Central Places and their efficiency. But this already indicates that the emphasis has shifted from definitions to policy.

Some qualifications must be added. First: despite the implication that *all* stages of the Central Place hierarchies in *all* parts of the country are implied by ROG, only the rural areas (which are distant from agglomerations) and the lower or lowest order centres have so far attracted attention. Little attention has been given to the Central Place hierarchies in, or near to, the large agglomerations and this has been without explicitly using the Central Place terminology. The discussion was confined to arguments based on the necessity of having a functional differentiation of centres and for the planned development of *Entlastungsorte* whose object was to give relief to the overcrowded agglomeration cores [16]. We can thus observe an imbalance of policy measures directed towards strengthening the Central Place structure of settlements in predominantly rural areas on the one hand and regional policy for industrial areas on the other hand.

Second: Central Places are defined in terms of several functions, all of which belong to the tertiary sector: the supply of basic goods (food, schooling, security, a minimum of administration) for lower order centres and a differentiated bundle of public and private services for the higher order centres. This is quite in line with many approaches in the academic field [17]. Even Christaller's original book may be partially interpreted in this way [18], despite the fact that Christaller's own expressed belief was evidently different [19]. The reasons for this restricted use of Central Place Theory are twofold. Central Place Theory evidently has some difficulty in explaining large agglomerations, and their structure of commodity flows, despite many attempts to detect a hierarchical Central Place structure within metropolitan areas [20]. The other reason is a recognition of the importance of those which influence settlement patterns in industries which are not dependent on special locations, e.g. mining. The restriction of Central Place Theory to service industries is somewhat unfortunate. There is little theoretical reason for this restriction and it does tend to destroy its rationale as an explanation of spatial structure if one restricts its use to a partial location theory for services.

The latter argument is obvious. But if Central Place Theory is no longer a theory of total spatial order, its use as a guideline for settlement policy implies that industrial location is either unimportant or that it can be managed according to needs derived from a service-dependent settlement structure [21]. Thus there is some internal inconsistency in the regional planning concept of the Federal and Länder Governments. However, it is not, in principle, necessary to restrict the applicability of Central Place Theory to the tertiary sector, the service sector, or, as we would prefer to say, the sector producing goods for immediate sale to consumers. The cost considerations which lead to market areas for consumer goods are equally applicable to intermediate goods. If raw materials are not distributed too unevenly over space, thresholds and ranges for industrial products and intermediate goods may exist, just as they do in the case of consumer goods and – entrepreneurs being even more aware of costs than consumers and being more rational – may lead to nested hierarchies. There is some empirical evidence to support this assertion – like the definite delivery areas for coal or cement and the price base pricing systems which exist in the markets for intermediate goods. However, there can be no doubt about the exceptional character of these examples. The question thus arises as to whether these hierarchies, and the ones for consumer goods, enhance or destroy each other. It has been demonstrated theoretically by Bos [22], that the explicit consideration of intermediate goods need not destroy the nested hierarchy of market areas. I will not elaborate on this problem, since definite conclusions can be reached from a Central Place concept which is restricted to the tertiary sector but is nevertheless interpreted as a theory of the complete settlement pattern. These conclusions will only be enhanced when the latter qualification is dropped.

Third: It might seem that the concept of Central Place Theory used in this paper stresses Christaller's ideas unduly, instead of those of Lösch or other, more modern, concepts. There are three reasons for this : the Central Place concept of the regional planning policy is much more in line with Christaller's model than with Lösch's where both differ. Indeed some indirect personal influence of Christaller on the formation of the regional policy is not improbable. Additionally, the features with which we shall mainly deal are the same for both models. Finally, it may be argued that Lösch's system gets near to being true by definition and has thus only restricted empirical meaning.

2.3 *RECENT RESEARCH ON THE DETERMINANTS OF CENTRAL PLACE*

The derivation of nested market areas depends crucially on graded ranges and thresholds [23]. Transportation cost – and therefore transportation technology – plays an important role in the determination of ranges. The usual assumption is that transportation cost is proportional to the volume of transport and to the distance travelled. But little attention is paid to the nature of this cost or to its relative importance as a proportion of total cost. As long as the social cost of transportation is not completely internalised, we would expect a steady decrease in the relative importance of transportation cost with increasing labour cost and progress in transportation technology. The declining importance of transportation costs is readily confirmed by considering the points of origin of many commodities (e.g. fresh flowers from South Africa, fresh food from California, butter from New Zealand). Approximately two thirds of all industry in Germany already has transportation costs of less than 5 per cent of total turnover, and this fraction is expected to increase to between 70 and 75 per cent by 1980 [24]. Transportation costs should therefore only enter locational decisions for a small and decreasing fraction of all industries. In Central Place terminology, the ranges of more and more commodities will increase. This development will clearly tend to destroy hierarchies if the ranges of sufficient goods become as large as the maximum distance between any highest order centre and any of its hinterland hamlets. This may be the case for many durable goods which are bought infrequently, like cars, refrigerators, furniture, and so on. The question of which enterprise should be considered as the 'producer' according to Central Place Theory will be taken up below.

There are many goods, however, especially convenience goods, for which this development will not take place, since they are sold from small sales outlets in the neighbourhood of household residences. In this case transportation costs take on a completely different form: they partly reflect the outlay for transportation facilities; they partly affect prices; and partly affect the time cost to consumers. The relative importance of these three components varies considerably; it is mainly dependent on the social status of the consumer, his income, where he lives, which method of transportation he and his family use, and on his taste. It is plausible to suppose, however, that these determinants will change over time so as to emphasise the time cost to the consumer. With increasing income, neither small price differentials between C.B.D.s or large shopping centres on the one hand, and suburban areas on the other, nor the fare for public transportation facilities, will really matter. Their relative importance, measured as a fraction of total consumption expenditure, will decrease rather than increase. Direct transportation costs decrease further because consumers tend to buy commodities in bundles and try to combine other trips with the home-to-work trip. Furthermore, people become more conscious of leisure time which they want to put to sensible uses. But the implications of increasing leisure, and the improvements in transportation technology, are counteracted by an increase in the spatial extension of the social environment (longer trips become more frequent partly because of suburbanisation, partly because of changed attitudes towards distance) and a decline in the performance of traffic systems (increasing congestion).

All this, of course, is only valid if transportation does not yield utility directly but is merely a means of acquiring goods. This condition may be fulfilled for convenience shopping in congested areas, but even then many trips are undertaken just for the pleasure of walking and window-shopping. In more rural areas it can also be observed that the purchase of Central goods is treated as a special excursion which gives satisfaction in its own right.

The growing importance of time will lead to changes in purchasing habits. In order to reduce the time spent on shopping, the frequency of shopping trips will diminish and the amounts purchased on any trip will increase, especially if adequate storage facilities like refrigerators, deep freezers and store rooms are available. This development will hold for convenience goods as well. It is therefore unclear how settlement patterns are likely to be affected by that part of transportation cost which the consumer has to bear directly in money or in time costs. Because of the increasing utility of spare time, and of convenience, small shopping opportunities within the neighbourhood will maintain their importance if only for unforeseen purchases. Increasing demand for potential, flexibility and additional service, however, necessitates a broad and differentiated supply. In addition to the really small neighbourhood outlets, fairly large shopping centres will thus also develop where they do not exist today. There is no doubt that settlements on the lower two stages of the Central Place hierarchy will not be able to sustain such facilities. We can therefore conclude that the development (in money cost) of transportation – included either in the product prices or as fares – will lead to larger market areas, while the impact of time costs on settlement patterns is ambiguous. People will patronise shopping facilities according to a step function of access time; some kind of a neighbourhood range will therefore remain intact.

There is another definition problem with transportation costs and its attribution to commodities and services. Such attribution can only be exact for goods which can be exactly defined and are transported separately over definite distances. But for food and hardware items, sold in chain stores and delivered by trucks operating scheduled services, such an attribution is almost impossible. The same is true of the money and time costs incurred by the consumer, because of the multi-purpose nature of many trips combined with joint purchases of different goods. Loosely related is a further definitional problem which also stems from the fact that producers sell, and consumers buy, not single commodities but bundles of commodities: are ranges therefore to be defined for single commodities or for sales outlets, for goods or for entrepreneurs? There may be situations in which the two definitions imply different delivery patterns. For example, different costs at different centres may lead to different f.o.b. prices and therefore to price relationships which differ between centres. In such a situation a consumer buying where it is cheapest should patronise several different centres whereas if he minimises total transportation costs he will patronise only one. But then market areas depend on the consumer's commodity bundles and not on price and freight costs alone.

The development of thresholds will also encourage larger production volumes because of the economies of scale which still remain in many production lines (at the moment we may disregard possible external diseconomies because they depend on the actual location and therefore only affect location decisions). Increasing returns to scale do not necessarily imply the strengthening of the top centres – thus stiffening the hierarchy – as is often assumed in the more sophisticated versions of Central Place Theory which rely on agglomeration economies. In considering the possible effect on nested market hierarchies we must distinguish between low density rural areas and high density urbanised agglomerations. In the former, where distances are generally large (in kilometres as well as in time), higher thresholds imply a larger threshold area. The producers who survive the ensuing competition, and the concentration process it involves, will be scattered over all levels of centrality or – more likely – will be spatially concentrated in higher order centres. This in turn causes a steady thinning out of the economic base of the lower order centres.

In densely populated areas the effects are quite different. Since densities are high, an increase in threshold (as measured in production units) implies only a small increase in market area measured in square kilometres. Since distances are small, differences in transportation costs are almost negligible and the consequent effects on location structure can be ignored. In both cases, however, the locational effect will be even smaller when the increase in thresholds takes place for goods with relatively high income elasticities when incomes are rising.

In this connection it is interesting to consider the long-term consequences of increasing density of population [25]. A rising density diminishes the area of the threshold (in square kilometres) but leaves ranges unchanged, so that excess profits must occur. In this case the final result depends heavily on freedom of market entry. If the density is already high, and the area is evenly settled with free (zero cost) market entry, competition from new entrants will wipe out excess profits and, in the absence of location economies, these new entrants will establish new production plants between those already there. This will clearly change the *k*-value of the market system at this level of hierarchy. If market entry is restricted, e.g. by high entry costs, and if the industry is highly competitive, e.g. a heterogeneous oligopoly, the rising density may induce innovative competition to exploit technical progress and the advantages of mass production. In this case the locational structure will remain essentially unaffected but the standard of living might rise considerably.

If the increase in population density takes place in a rather thinly populated area, with given Central Places of lowest order, and market entry is unrestricted, the new establishments will certainly be installed (if the thresholds permit) at Central Places. If the nested hierarchy has already been completed this may destroy the established pattern and foster the development of new centres which do not fit into the original Central Place pattern. Location economies might likewise attract the new plant to an already established centre of higher order which then gains importance and economic momentum. The outcome will depend, to some degree, on the economic importance of agriculture and on its productive technology. If agriculture is an important and prosperous branch of the economy, and the technology requires the even distribution of the agrarian labour force over the whole area (e.g. primitive transportation technology or low performance of traffic systems), then new production centres will tend to spread over the entire area. A decline in agriculture, on the other hand, will strengthen the evolution of centres.

In all cases, and especially in the ambiguous ones, the definite effect on settlement patterns depends on the existence of external economies and diseconomies of urbanisation and localisation. Localisation economies are of particular importance for shopping goods and highly specialised goods, not only because of the usual externalities in production and shopping habits, but also because of the general information given to consumers by a common location of producers of the same kind of product. While we are fairly confident about the ongoing importance of internal economies of scale, predictions about the development of both kinds of externalities are less certain. On the one hand, the attractiveness of large urban centres remains important for the white-collar labour force and gains importance for blue-collar workers (especially in relation to schooling facilities and employment opportunities), whilst localisation economies persist. On the other hand, however, increasing diseconomies of agglomeration may develop and may soon become important, e.g. congestion, waste disposal, the development of slums, dilapidating quality of the physical environment, physical and mental diseases caused by urbanisation, high population density or stress, air pollution, an increase in violent crimes, etc. They have clearly already had, and will increasingly have, a profound influence on the location of production plants as well as of households and thereby on settlement patterns. External agglomeration diseconomies are only one of the factors working against total agglomeration; another is the increasing demand for space. This topic will be returned to later. These forces are unlikely to destroy the attractiveness of metropolitan areas, but the evolving spatial pattern is likely to be different from that expected: it will be characterised by an upgrading of lower and (especially) intermediate centres in the outskirts of the large agglomerations and a decline in the nodes of agglomeration.

Another important determinant of the changing pattern of market areas is the changing organisation of trade [26]. Increasingly, chain stores and large department stores with nation-wide branches (including mail order houses) are displacing independent middle-size entrepreneurs. This clearly affects the Central Place hierarchy, in that it replaces several products of intermediate and low centrality by mere sales outlets whose production lines and business policy are centrally directed from some remote headquarters. It is actually impossible for these retail establishments to offer a different choice of products at each outlet. They sell the same range of goods advertised on nation-wide television, in illustrated magazines and on radio or billboards. This not only enables them to receive large quantity discounts, but also offers economies of scale. They furthermore show an aggressive market policy which spreads the supply of goods of high centrality to intermediate centres of, say, 20,000 to 50,000 people. This clearly shows the importance of independent merchants socially integrated into their communities for the survival of smaller centres.

But as urbanisation economies are ubiquitous in all agglomerations, the production centres and headquarters of such enterprises can be located anywhere within, or near to, agglomerations. For the distributing outlets, on the other hand, localisation economies may be important [27]. They therefore settle close to each other, so that the thresholds of the clusters of retail establishments increase considerably. Both tendencies form spatial delivery patterns for different goods and entrepreneurs which cut deeply into each other. The observable mutual penetration of market areas is different from the overlapping of market areas for goods of equal centrality which is characteristic of systems of nested market areas with $k = 3$ or $k = 4$. This feature of traditional Central Place Theory is due to the implicit assumption that settlements are points in space without any spatial extension of their own. If, for traditional Central Place Theory, we drop this assumption and consider the area of settlement explicitly, it immediately follows from the usual homogeneity assumption for markets, that the geographical area of each border settlement is divided into mutually exclusive market areas of higher order centres. The only heterogeneities of markets which are taken into account by classical Central Place Theory are those due to distance. But the observed kind of interpenetration of market areas implies the existence of additional heterogeneities due, for example, to consumer preferences [28]. Thus few oligopolistic enterprises, supplying the same large areas, have displaced the many small and medium-size merchants of Central Place Theory, who are assumed to locate their business as far away from their competitors as possible. When such heterogencities are taken into account, we can no longer define spatially separated market areas in which the applicability of Central Place Theory as a description of reality is preserved. The predominance of heterogeneous markets nevertheless need not render the normative use of Central Place Theory invalid, if it could be shown that overlapping market areas for heterogeneous goods was inferior (in terms of an existing welfare function) to distinct homogeneous market areas. Despite the plausibility of such a statement, however, we must recognise heterogeneous market areas as an important fact for all practical planning purposes.

Two other major determinants of future settlement patterns, which did not play an explicit role in Central Place Theory, must be considered. These are society's consumption of space and the role of certain social phenomena in the development of nested centres. Agricultural societies require a great deal of space and thus – provided transportation remains primitive [29] – causes the agrarian population to be fairly uniformly distributed. Many settlement patterns, in particular the pattern in Southern Germany and in the northern plains investigated by Christaller and Klöpper [30], did evolve during a historical period when such an economic structure and technology prevailed. Industrialisation, however, has moved the space needs of society towards lower land intensity in consumption as well as in production. This tendency is nevertheless changing as a result of an increasing demand for single homes and – much more important – by the increasing demand for land for recreational and economical purposes. It is space within the agglomerations, and around agglomerations, which is needed for the short-term (and short-distance) recreation of the urban masses. As many of the recreational facilities are highly land intensive, the decrease in daily working hours and weekly working days (as well as the increase in the duration of vacations) will result in a high demand for land near agglomerations which will have an important influence on the average densities around the population centres. If, for ecological purposes, further land must also be reserved inside the large metropolitan areas we shall need some kind of planned dispersion of population which will narrow the differences in the population distribution between the agglomerated centres and the long strips of land along their edges. This is clearly a development which has not gone unnoticed in ROG and ROBs; it is nevertheless given too little attention and cannot be satisfactorily dealt with as long as regional planning policy remains preoccupied with establishing and (vainly) trying to enforce Central Place systems on the plains.

The consequences of the increasing demand for space for ecological purposes in the rural areas cannot yet be foreseen. There are some people who argue that the steady flow of people into the larger towns will vacate the countryside, thus providing an opportunity for reafforestation and for a rehabilitation of the natural environment. Others argue that an orderly cultivation of natural environments and resources, and the preservation of open spaces and intensively used recreation areas, require such large labour forces that the cheapest way of cultivating these areas is by keeping some kind of extensive agriculture intact.

The social forces behind the development of settlement patterns are reasonably well known for consumers and the labour force. The importance of migration, and the consequent induced change in densities, though disregarded in traditional Central Place Theory, have been recognised by those responsible for the Central Place regional policy. The countermeasures, adopted by Federal and Länder Governments, to prevent the denudation of the plains have so far been ineffective, at least for the places of lowest centrality [31]. This is not at all surprising when one considers the significant influence of modern mass media and the parallel efforts in advertising which spread the idea of a uniform urbanised style of life over the whole country. We may even reverse the argument. The pull of attractive centres and large economies of agglomeration would have led, as they did in other countries, to an even more biased distribution of population (to larger and even more densely settled agglomerations) if no dispersing forces had been at work. These forces might have been due to geographical peculiarities like the distribution of coal mines in England and in former Germany. It may also have been affected by the political systems of the 19th century (feudalism restricting the outflow of tenants; extreme federalism in Germany) or, in earlier centuries, by the importance of transportation costs and agriculture. But I believe that the main forces have been social ones which still militate against labour force mobility. People have been adapted to, and are content with, a small social environment (which is often overlooked) in which they were fully integrated. The farmers, if they were independent, were proud of their independence and developed a feeling of kinship with the land. The attitudes of most agricultural people were directed towards preserving the old rules, adhering to traditions and opposing the new and the alien. Changing these attitudes, including the attitudes of those people still living in the countryside or in small towns, is a prerequisite for any further urbanisation. The continuing change in (conservative) rural attitudes – not only in those who migrate to the agglomerations but also in those who stay on the plains – has cleared the way for economic developments from the agglomerations to slowly filter into other parts of the country.

Less attention has been paid to the entrepreneur and to his attitudes and beliefs. We should like to propose that the existence of self-employed upper middle class entrepreneurs is essential for the existence of intermediate centres because, in spite of their title, these entrepreneurs confine their activities to their own social environment, i.e. the small town in which they live and the society which is based on these towns. They were independent craftsmen, royal merchants and industrial entrepreneurs who were both the opinion leaders and the honorary political leaders of their communities. They were responsible for evolution, if it occurred at all, but they also preserved their small communities from turmoil and revolution. And this was not only true of social and political revolutions, but also for economic revolutions. In economic terms, therefore, they were profit maximisers only in a very limited way; the risks they were willing to take were small and could not threaten their social existence. I need not emphasise that this is a broad and unspecified hypothesis which badly needs research by economists, historians and sociologists. On the other hand, we certainly must not disregard the importance of social factors, as is done by Central Place Theory.

2.4 *CONCLUSIONS FOR REGIONAL PLANNING POLICY*

We can sum up the indicated developments in the following way. The predominance of market imperfections, in addition to those due to distance, makes it possible that the market areas – for goods as well as for producers – penetrate each other profoundly. These imperfections, increasing returns to scale and increasing ranges and thresholds, together provoke a tendency to form nation-wide markets in all sectors of the economy. The centrality of intermediate centres consequently rises. The centrality of top centres, however, stagnates as the localisation of many service establishments, new production plants and headquarters is increasingly influenced by external diseconomies of agglomeration so that the attractiveness of the top-ranking centres slowly vanishes. New enterprises may even be deterred from old centres. This leads to the evolution of large areas of high and differentiated centrality whose parts have a distinct, but irregular, economic specialisation based (mainly) on socially determined spatial differentiation. Increasing income and leisure, more differentiated and sophisticated needs and the growing importance of time cost of consumer transportation require the organisation of high-ranking markets with high accessibility. Thus these market places must be within half to one hour's travel distance from their patronage. While low-ranking market places will be destroyed, 'friendly neighbourhood dealers' may survive because they are especially needed for emergency errands. While this development will cause relocation problems in and around densely settled areas, the thinly settled rural areas and smallest centres will not survive (or will require permanent and increasing subsidies to maintain their standard of living in relation to that of the metropolitan areas). On the whole, Central Place hierarchies will be completely destroyed and some kind of a binary distribution of population and economic activities will be substituted for them.

If this is true, two questions arise: Why do so many empirical studies of Central Place Theory still show, at least in the opinion of their authors, favourable results; and what are the consequences for regional planning policy in Germany? Let me deal with these two questions in turn. First: the good results are often deceiving pseudo-results for three reasons: (a) an alternative hypothesis has never been clearly stated; (b) the hypothesis tested is not in complete conformity with the theoretical formulation; and (c) the observed pattern is the result of past economic situations. I do not want to elaborate on the first two points but just make two observations. Most tests of Central Place theorems can only be interpreted as not contradicting the observed facts. This is nevertheless misleading, since no one appears willing to test the theorem in question *against any other theory* and its implications. Furthermore, many studies, especially those on rank-size rules, have tested the implications of Central Place Theory instead of the theory itself. This is clearly bad logic: if reality could be shown to be completely different from the implications of Central Place Theory, the latter would be false by logical induction. But if the facts are not significantly at odds with the implications of the theory, nothing can be said at all about the validity of the theory. The implications of a theory only constitute the necessary and not sufficient conditions for its postulates (axioms).

The third objection, reason (c), is much more important: if tests of Central Place Theory give reasonable results (and no technical objections can be raised against the testing procedure) the results nevertheless only prove past history and not the present or the future. Amazingly enough, few critics of Central Place Theory have observed that a stationary theory has been used to explain settlement patterns which have evolved over decades or centuries. As Klöpper [32] has shown, the settlement pattern of the northern plain in Germany has its roots in the 18th century. Certainly the importance, power and economic rationale of cities change, but these changes are long-term marginal changes which take place slowly and should be observable over time. In cases where sufficient supporting evidence for a Central Place hierarchy type of settlement can be obtained, a historical investigation should be included to show how the observed pattern relates to the economic forces which were operative during the period observed. The importance of history for settlements, and the fact that their development is influenced by strong recursive elements (and the expected probable development of the main determinants of the settlement structure), enable us to disregard the existing pattern when formulating goals for planning. The existing pattern is only relevant when dealing with constraints: it is the point of departure for future developments.

We have tried to show where this development would tend if market forces alone were operating. As indicated, this does not imply that this development is optimal, or even favourable, for society as a whole. However, in the absence of any optimising decision techniques, it is reasonable to accept this probable development as a broad guideline, to inquire into its adverse side effects and to adopt a policy which permits the former and prevents the latter. The proposed development for Germany should therefore not aim to cover the whole country with a complete net of hierarchically ordered Central Places at rigid distances. Instead, balanced agglomerations should be developed from the existing unbalanced ones and intermediate towns which are presently solitary urbanised settlements within predominantly rural areas should be strengthened. All other areas should be kept as open reserved spaces (with restricted uses) after their natural environment has been restored.

REFERENCES

[1] E. Neef, 'Das Problem der zentralen Orte', *Petermanns Geographische Mitteilungen*, 94 (1950), p. 12.
[2] E. v. Böventer, 'Towards a United Theory of Spatial Economic Structure', *Papers and Proceedings of the Regional Science Association*, 10 (1962), pp. 184–5.
[3] B. Dietrichs, 'Die Theorie der zentralen Orte, Aussage und Anwendung heute', *Raumforschung und Raumordnung*, 24 (1966).
[4] R. Klöpper, 'Zentrale Orte und ihre Bereiche', *Handwörterbuch der Raumordnung und Raumforschung*, 2. Auflage (Hannover, 1970), col. 3858. Klöpper argues that the location of industrial production follows the centrality pattern established in predominantly agricultural areas.
[5] A. Lösch, *The Economics of Location*. Quoted from Wiley Science Edition of 1967, p. 133; G. Kroner, 'Die zentralen Orte in Wissenschaft und Raumordnungspolitik', *Informationen des Instituts für Raumordnung*, 14 (1964), p. 436, note 2.
[6] G. Kroner, 'Die zentralen Orte in Wissenschaft und Raumordnungspolitik', *Informationen des Instituts für Raumordnung*, 14 (1964), p. 436. See also note 1 on p. 436.
[7] *Raumordnungsgesetz*, Bundesgesetzblatt (1965), Pt I, pp. 306–10.
[8] G. Kroner, 'Die Bestimmung zentraler Orte durch die Bundesländer', *Informationen des Instituts für Raumordnung*, 20 (1970).
[9] e.g., B. Dietrichs, 'Die Theorie der zentralen Orte, Aussage und Anwendung heute', *Raumforschung und Raumordnung*, 24 (1966).
[10] G. Kroner, 'Die zentralen Orte in Wissenschaft und Raumordnungspolitik', *Informationen des Instituts für Raumordnung*, 14 (1964), pp. 421–2 and pp. 436–56.
[11] *Raumordnungsbericht* 1968 (ROB, 1968). Bundestagsdrucksache V/3958, p. 149.
[12] Bundesvereinigung der kommunalen Spitzenverbände, 1966, quoted in H. Brügelmann, E. W. Cholewa, H. J. v. d. Heide, *Kommentar zum Raumordnungsgesetz* (Stuttgart, 1970), pp. 18–20.
[13] *Raumordnungsbericht* (1966), quoted in H. Brügelmann, E. W. Cholewa, H. J. v. d. Heide, *op. cit.*, pp. 20–21. No literal translation.
[14] *Raumordnungsbericht* (1968). Bundestagsdrucksache V/3958, p. 85.
[15] *Raumordnungsbericht* (1970). Bundestagsdrucksache VI/1340, pp. 36–9.
[16] *Raumordnungsbericht* (1968). Bundestagsdrucksache V/3958, pp. 151–2.
[17] E. Neef, 'Das Problem der zentralen Orte', *Petermanns Geographische Mitteilungen*, 94 (1950), p. 11; E. v. Böventer, *Die Struktur der Landschaft*. In: 'Optimales Wachstum und optimale Standortverteilung'. Schriften des Vereins für Socialpolitik, N.F., Vol. 27 (Berlin, 1962), p. 111; V. v. Malchus, *Theoretische Aspekte zur Untersuchung von Verflechtungsbereichen zentraler Orte*. In: 'Versorgungsnahbereiche als Kleinzentren im ländlichen Raum' (Hannover, 1969), p. 43.
[18] W. Christaller, *Die zentralen Orte in Süddeutschland* (Jena, 1933), pp. 139–40.
[19] W. Christaller, *op. cit.*, p. 259.

[20] H. Carol, 'The hierarchy of central functions within the city'. *Annals of the Association of American Geographers* 70 (1960); D. Bökemann, *Das innerstädtische Zentralitätsgefüge*. Karlsruher Studien zur Regionalwissenschaft, Heft 1 (Karlsruhe, 1967).

[21] W. Christaller, *op. cit.*, p. 259; R. Klöpper, 'Zentrale Orte und ihre Bereiche', *Handwörterbuch der Raumordnung und Raumforschung*, 2. Auflage (Hannover, 1970), col. 3859. Another theory-oriented approach is followed by von Böventer.

[22] H. C. Bos, *Spatial Dispersion of Economic Activity* (Rotterdam, 1965).

[23] B. J. L. Berry, H. G. Barnum and R. J. Tennant, 'Retail Location and Consumer Behavior', *Papers and Proceedings of the Regional Science Association*, 9 (1962), especially p. 105.

[24] *Raumordnungsbericht* (1968). Bundestagsdrucksache V/3958, p. 36.

[25] Cf., e.g., E. v. Böventer, *Die Struktur der Landschaft*, in 'Optimales Wachstum und optimale Standortverteilung'. Schriften des Vereins für Socialpolitik, N.F., Vol. 27 (Berlin, 1962), pp. 93–4.

[26] Different lines of research on the same topic have been followed e.g. by: B. J. L. Berry, 'Ribbon Developments in the Urban Business Pattern', *Annals of the Association of American Geographers*, 49 (1959); B. J. L. Berry, H. G. Barnum and R. J. Tennant, 'Retail Location and Consumer Behavior', *Papers and Proceedings of the Regional Science Association*, 9 (1962); B. J. L. Berry, *Geography of Market Centers and Retail Distribution*. (Englewood Cliffs, 1967); R. K. Schiller, 'Location Trends of Specialist Services', *Regional Studies*, 5 (1971).

[27] For cases where localisation economies are evidently unimportant see: R. K. Schiller, 'Location Trends of Specialist Services', *Regional Studies*, 5 (1971).

[28] M. Beckmann, 'Market Share, Distance and Potential', *Regional and Urban Economics*, 1 (1971).

[29] E. v. Böventer, *Die Struktur der Landschaft*. In: 'Optimales Wachstum und optimale Standortverteilung'. Schriften des Vereins für Socialpolitik, N.F., Vol. 27 (Berlin, 1962), p. 101.

[30] R. Klöpper, *Entstehung, Lage und Verteilung der zentralen Siedlungen in Niedersachsen* (Remagen, 1952).

[31] *Raumordnungsbericht* (1970). Bundestagsdrucksache VI/1340, pp. 36–7.

[32] R. Klöpper, *op. cit.*

Discussion of the Paper by
Frank E. Münnich

Formal Discussant: Cameron. Münnich has raised a familiar problem in regional economic planning. If the employment and consumption opportunities in high-income industrialised metropolitan areas are markedly greater than for residents of low-income, labour shedding agricultural areas, how does central and local government attempt to 'balance the standard of living of the rural and industrial areas, to maintain the population of the flat land, and to only slowly alter the structure of agriculture'?

Given the political difficulties of directing migration streams, and the limited methods of controlling or inducing private investment decisions so that they occur in locations specified by government, the West German authorities have adopted a policy of focusing their public investment and planning efforts throughout a hierarchy of 300 central places. The rationale for this polarised approach is not unusual in a context where public investment is obviously limited. Thus polarised provision of both public and private services and, hopefully, of industry is expected to generate greater internal and external economies than any other alternative spatial arrangement. What is novel in the West German approach is that the hierarchy of Central Places is graded in terms of upper, intermediate, lower and small centres. All of these, except perhaps the upper centres, are very small with a population of 20,000 in the intermediate centre and its surrounding district and only 5,000 in the smallest centres.

The author's contention is that with a reduction in the importance of transport costs, the growing oligopolistic nature of service activity, the economies of localisation in service siting and the benefits to the consumer of buying at a clustered location, the economic rationale for the smallest centres is now non-existent. Moreover, the diseconomies of scale in the largest centres are liable to push activities out of such centres. All forces are therefore working to promote the rapid development of inter-mediate centres. It follows that any policy which tries to focus public effort upon sustaining these very small centres is liable to fail.

May I say in passing that this prediction seems to be borne out by the studies by Borchert [1] in the *Upper Midwest Economic Study* which showed that between 1930 and 1960 the very small trade centres tended to grow markedly less quickly than the medium and large centres. However, Borchert's work did not show that the largest centres were losing out as the author predicts, although it is conceivable that such a trend may have appeared since 1960.

The difficulty with the author's paper, however, is that it too readily assumes that what market processes generate is likely to be socially optimal. There are problems here. One is that it is the politician who is increasingly concerned with achieving certain goals in terms of settlement patterns, so that the economist's job becomes one of evaluating the costs (and perhaps the benefits) of alternative patterns. Even if the politician is not actively specifying particular settlement patterns there is fairly overwhelming evidence from many developed countries that the population flow out of low-productivity agricultural areas is not sufficiently elastic to match the reduction in the supply of job opportunities caused by capital substitution. The result is persistent underutilisation and/or unemployment of labour, with no automatic equilibrating mechanism balancing demands and supplies of labour in every location. Thus whether the economist likes it or not he is forced into evaluating alternative objectives and policy means with regard to alternative migration streams, alternative streams of private and public investment and ultimately alternative urban patterns for population and economic activity. Furthermore, such calculations ought to be made not only in terms of the costs to the individuals, corporations and public bodies affected by spatial policies, but also to the governmental sector as a whole and ultimately in terms of national opportunity costs.

I wish to raise some questions within this broad context bearing in mind that broadly we are likely to have three different kinds of urban centres within the agricultural areas. First we have very small centres performing limited government, medical and retailing functions for a scattered agricultural population. Then we have larger centres which have developed a more complex base and which market their products, whether sources or manufacturers, over a wide area. These centres do not depend upon the rural hinterlands for all of their demand. The other type of centre is the large metropolitan area with a highly complex base and a significance in national terms.

Now if we assume that there is no alternative but to accept continued labour movement out of agriculture, the question is whether to seek to channel these migration flows and whether and how to provide new employment opportunities within the rural areas. There are no general prescriptions here which hold for every country but the question must be judged in the light of the destination preferences of the migrants. This whole question of migrants (destination) preference has hardly been touched upon by researchers, though Hansen has been doing some work in the area. There is, however, some evidence to suggest that some migrants have a strong preference for migration to centres close to their origin partly because this allows them to maintain social ties, partly because the new working urban environment is familiar and partly because job information is precise. If this is indeed so, the question may then become one of how should the state choose, and thereafter enhance, employment opportunities within 'preferred' urban centres within the regions.

This evaluation must take into account any marginal absorption costs falling upon the governmental sector, longer-run public service costs, particularly in education and health, any net costs for private individuals already residing within the centre, and the long-run earnings and employment prospects for the migrants. We only improperly understand the factors contributing to expanding employment opportunities, urban centre by urban centre, but if we see comparative advantage developing from some combination of

(a) vigorous local entrepreneurship,
(b) strong backward and forward linkages from key sectors producing goods in income elastic demand,

(c) good input/access to major national and, or, international markets,
(d) attractiveness to mobile capital,

then there is some evidence to suggest that, on average, such a combination
is unlikely to occur in the small, or indeed, even the intermediate centres
specified by the West German government. It would therefore appear
unwise to facilitate migration streams which favoured very small centres
with limited prospects for a long-run growth in employment.

Thus whilst the author has rightly drawn our attention to the market
factors likely to affect the spatial distribution of local retailing and whole-
sale services, we must also add another dimension relating to long-run
employment opportunities in non-consumption sectors. In this context,
however, Central Place Theory is largely irrelevant.

Second Discussant: Hansen. My criticism of Münnich's paper is directed
less towards the author than towards the apparent decision of the Federal
Republic of Germany to base its regional planning policy almost exclusively on Central Place Theory. In particular, it is disturbing to note that
'it is the explicit intention of regional policy to use existing Central Places,
or Central Places which according to theory ought to be at some place, as
nodes for economic development and industrialisation'.

Central Place Theory is essentially based on the notion of a hierarchy
of market areas and it is not really able to come to grips with the dynamics
of the urbanisation-industrialisation process. It has rather dealt primarily
with trade and service functions and has been essentially static. It is curious
to find an almost total absence of references to that body of regional
economics that has attempted to formulate a dynamic theory of industrial
location. Especially noteworthy in this regard is the work of Wilbur
Thompson [2] and the recent literature on growth centres [3, 4].

Finally, it may be noted that effective regional planning in the future
will have to transcend customary distinctions between core and hinterland
areas. In the United States, and probably in most other industrialised
nations, the life styles of most people are increasingly 'urban' in many
respects, though it also is true that city dwellers increasingly manifest a
desire for the amenities of the countryside. What is emerging is a new scale
of life and work that transcends the customary bifurcations between rural
and urban, metropolitan and non-metropolitan. This process will be
accentuated in the future by the advent of a whole new spectrum of
communications permitting significantly less dense population settlement.
Present cities and transportation networks reflect such factors as the need
to be near energy sources or to move people and objects. In the future more
emphasis will be given to moving information, and in principle it will be
possible to work, shop, receive intellectual and cultural achievements, and
'visit' relatives, friends and business associates from one's own home.

Thus the city is no longer so much a physical entity as a pattern of
localisations and connecting flows of people, information, money, commodities and services. A number of concepts have been suggested to
encompass this expanding scale of urban activity, but the most satisfactory
perhaps is that of an 'urban field', which represents a fusion of metropolitan

areas, and non-metropolitan peripheral areas, into areas with a minimum population of 300,000 persons extending outwards for approximately 100 miles, that is a driving distance of about two hours. In the past, metropolitan growth has tended to draw off productive population and investment capital from hinterland areas, but in the future centrifugal forces should reverse this pattern.

Of course, for the immediate future it must be recognised that not all rural areas will benefit from industrial decentralisation and from increased mobility and the high income elasticity of demand for leisure-oriented activities. In the declining, relatively stagnant areas, it is often difficult to maintain essential services, especially if the population is widely dispersed. In such cases Central Place Theory may be of value in identifying appropriate service centres.

Prud'homme remarked that the author described, analysed, evaluated and criticised government policy for German cities. He did not explain, however, whether the policy was simply *stated* or whether it was actually *implemented*? His paper only referred to statements, not to facts; to laws, not to figures, and we all know that stated policies are not always implemented. French regional planning provides us with several examples. For instance, the 'equilibrium metropolises' policy, which implies that eight large cities would get more than their usual share of central government revenue does not appear to have been implemented. Indeed, these stated policies are often not meant to be implemented. It does not follow, however, that they are useless or futile. They perform an important function, of a political rather than of an economic nature, and they might perform it quite well. What was useless, or futile, was to take them at their face value.

Kolm raised the question of the definition of objectives. The paper mentioned 'decline in rural areas'. Why did some people object to this decline? Economists always thought that objectives could be reduced to the pair distribution-efficiency; but this point of view was often unhelpful, if not untrue. Specifically, in the context of rural and village life, there was a very important objective which did not fit well into this framework. It existed in Europe (it did not seem to exist in the U.S.) and was extremely important to statesmen, politicians and enlightened citizens in general. It was related to the fact that man-made rural and village environments – old stones and landscapes – were the soul of West European civilisation. To conserve them was to protect our cultural heritage. And the capital they represented was non-reproducible (a Walt Disney medieval town was not a reproduction of the real thing). Although they were strongly felt, these preferences were nevertheless badly revealed because arguments about cultural heritage did not find much favour in growth orientated circles. Politicians thus often disguised this objective as a standard question of distribution or efficiency.

This objective was neither to keep living 'museums' nor to maintain outdated rural life. It was to preserve a rural and urban environment made by History. This objective was just beginning to be explicitly recognised for rural areas, and this enabled appropriate conservation measures to be adopted. For example, in France, peasants in mountainous areas will receive subsidies related to their role as 'nature' keepers. A similar idea for Germany was exposed in the author's paper.

It was better to pay directly for this objective than to obscure it by calling it something else. The usual way of paying for it was by subsidising the prices of agricultural products: this was a very bad method. We should also note that, if we wanted to prevent the depopulation of the countryside, we must provide adequate public services to the people living there. All the services necessary to maintain human life in these areas represented a demand for tertiary activities and this was the case for which Central Place Theory was most appropriate.

Rothenberg questioned how the environment was defined. Was it a life style, a life pattern, or a life space. We were talking about preserving, adding to, or changing the life style and life spaces of a substantial portion of the population. This was really a question of preferences: who wanted what and what for whom? And who deserved the right to say who should get what and at whose cost?

Russell raised a question quite opposite to the one mentioned by Rothenberg. He suggested that we should be looking for places at which to make cuts, rather than trying to see how much of the universe we could bring into the problem. It was only by making cuts – i.e. by separating problems which were only weakly connected (or by using market prices from reasonably well-functioning markets) – that we could define systems for which practically useful models might be constructed and applied. Universal models remained abstract and, while abstract models had their utility and aesthetic appeal, it was only infrequently that they assisted the people who were responsible for solving real problems. He suggested that pollution (or residuals management) was such a separable area.

Mills doubted whether a country like the U.S. should have a policy toward city sizes. But in any case, charges for pollution or congestion were an improper and ineffective way to affect the city size distribution. Hoch [5] and Tolley [6] had shown that the direction in which such charges affect city size was not predictable on theoretical grounds. His guess was that such charges would have substantial effects on urban structure, but little on urban size.

Lave on the other hand suggested that internalising externalities, i.e. by setting social marginal cost equal to price, would have a great effect on city size. It would certainly change the production structure.

Hoch, referring to his own paper (Chapter 3), felt that proper charges (pricing) for residuals and congestion were likely to make cities larger.

Beckerman, replying to the arguments about taxes on cars (for congestion) and the optimum size of cities, said that we should bear in mind that automobile usage was already subject to many taxes of one form or another, particularly in Europe where petrol (gasoline) taxes were extremely high, and where there were also often high indirect taxes on the purchase price of the cars themselves. Hence, if motoring in cities was subject only to the *optimum* tax, it might well be that the total effect would be to increase motoring rather than to reduce it, since it was highly likely that the present level of taxes on motoring were higher than the optimum if we only allowed for the divergence between the private and social costs of motoring. Of course, a congestion tax would be more efficient as a means of bridging the gap between private and social costs, and the substitution effects of the present package of taxes to which automobiles were subjected in Europe would not be the same as a congestion tax. Nevertheless, the total negative effect on motoring in Europe due to the various taxes was probably sufficiently large for it to be impossible to assume that their replacement by an optimal congestion tax would necessarily reduce motoring in cities and hence affect city size.

REFERENCES

[1] J. M. Henderson, *et al.*, *Upper Midwest Economic Study* (University of Minnesota, Minneapolis, 1961).
[2] W. Thompson, 'The National System of Cities as an Object of Public Policy', *Urban Studies*, Vol. IX, No. 1, pp. 99–116.
[3] A. Kulinski, (ed.), *Growth Poles and Growth Centers in Regional Planning* (Mouton, Paris and the Hague, 1972).
[4] N. M. Hansen (ed.), *Growth Centers in Regional Economic Development*, (The Free Press, New York, 1972).
[5] I. Hoch, Income and City Size, *Urban Studies* (October 1972).
[6] G. Tolley, 'The Welfare Economics of City Size', *Amer. Econ. Rev.* (forthcoming).

3 Inter-urban Differences in the Quality of Life*

Irving Hoch

This paper carries forward a line of inquiry formulated in two previous papers [1, 2] by developing and testing a number of interrelated
hypotheses about urban scale, a term employed to embrace both
urban population size and density. It is hypothesised that with
increases in urban scale there is a *net* decline in the quality of life,
including economic, environmental and social aspects. There are
likely to be some positive effects with scale, but such seem more
than balanced by other, negative, effects. However, equilibrating
mechanisms are at work, and the net quality decline tends to be
balanced by increases in money wages for performance of the same
work. This is not to argue that what exists is optimal: there is the
possibility of improvement through a number of institutional changes,
particularly through better pricing. However, awareness of the
trade-off of quality for income should be useful in appraisal of
proposed policies that probably go too far, through focus on the
cost side and neglect of the offsetting benefits of urban scale.

These notions are given more substance through a theoretical
statement in the following section. The remainder of the paper is
devoted to empirical tests of hypotheses, and documentation of
propositions, carried out in two major sections. The first focuses on
economic magnitudes and makes interurban comparisons of money
wages, money wages adjusted to achieve homogeneous populations,
and cost of living indexes. These measures, in turn, permit estimation
of quality decline over time, and by scale, net of cost-of-living, or
market, components.

The second major section focused on presumed non-market
phenomena which, by hypothesis, are the source of compensatory
payments for the quality declines beyond those of increased cost-of-
living. These include effects within both the physical and the social
environment.

Within the physical environment, there is good evidence that air
pollution increases with both urban size and density; with some

* Judith Drake served as research assistant for the work on this paper and
Elizabeth Pavlosky typed the original manuscript. Useful comments on the
initial draft were made by H. Tulkens, G. Cameron, E. Mills, R. Prud'homme
and J. Rothenberg.

variation, this conclusion holds for particulates, sulphur dioxide and nitrogen dioxide. (Parenthetically, there is some evidence of at least small declines in average levels for each of those pollutants in recent years.) Solid waste disposal costs increase at a rate greater than do wages, noise is much greater and flooding more likely as urban scale increases. There are climate effects which on net are probably negative. Only in the case of water waste management are there economies of scale, and even here imposition of stream standards appears to cause increasing costs per capita with urban size.

Topics treated under the heading of the social environment include traffic congestion, crime and health and welfare effects. In all cases there is some evidence of declining quality with scale. In the case of crime, this appears despite the introduction of a number of additional explanatory variables, whose neglect might have caused some confounding of the scale effect.

Though the paper focuses on establishing empirical magnitudes and relationships, it is hoped that policy applications are manifest.

3.1 THEORETICAL ARGUMENT

The central thesis of this paper is embodied in Fig. 3.1, which exhibits a model of the aggregate labour market for 'typical' urban

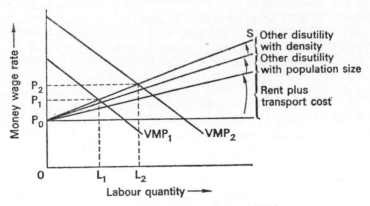

FIG. 3.1   Model of Urban Labour Market

areas. In the simplest interpretation of the model, aggregate output is treated as a single product, that is, each city has its own production function for 'urban output'. Demand for labour is then viewed as identical to value of marginal product (V.M.P.). Assume VMP_1 holds for an initial time period, and VMP_2 for a later time period. Alternatively, the two V.M.P. curves can refer to different locales.

In any event, VMP_2 involves a situation of greater productivity of labour than does VMP_1, e.g. because of technical advance over time, or because City 2 has a more productive natural resource base than does City 1. The supply of labour is treated as equivalent to a perfectly elastic long-run supply at a real wage rate of P_o. This can be amplified by arguing that (1) P_o can be secured in non-urban employment and that (2) preferences are such that P_o is accepted as the long-run norm or standard of living; deviations from P_o for the economy as a whole cause expansions or contractions in the birth rate until P_o is again attained. (The assumption can be made more realistic by attaching a time subscript to P_o and arguing that the standard of living shifts upward over time.) Although P_o is the real wage rate received by labour, the supply of labour in any typical urban locale is the curve S, which augments P_o by a money payment compensating for declines in quality of life that occur with increasing urban scale. (S will shift up or down in specific locales depending on amenities specific to each place, e.g. local climate.) Such declines in quality or disutilities can be classified into (1) rent plus transport cost, (2) other disutilities occurring with increased population size, on net, and (3) other disutilities occurring with increased density, on net. Alternatively, one can classify the disutilities into (1) market costs, estimated by a conventional cost-of-living index and (2) non-market costs, including the value of time spent in urban transport, primarily in the journey to work. Non-market costs can be further catalogued into those of population size and those of density. (Population density is seen as a function of population size and other factors; however, because those other factors vary between urban areas, and because density varies within urban areas, it seems useful to separate density from size, subsuming both under the heading of urban scale.) The first classification of disutilities is seen as more useful in the present, theoretical discussion; while the second is more useful in estimation, given the form of available data.

In Fig. 3.1, equilibrium occurs at L_1, P_1 and L_2, P_2, respectively. Assuming that population is a scalar of labour, Urban Area 2 is larger than Urban Area 1: as of a point in time, any urban area has its own 'optimum' size, identified here as the equilibrium level. With increasing urban size, the money wage rate increases, although the real wage rate is constant.

The discussion may be expanded to derive some additional implications for both prediction and policy.

For stark simplicity, assume an urban production function with only one product and two 'major' factors of production: labour and urban land. (This might be made more realistic by specifying that buildings are a form of land, e.g. if people lived and worked in caves.)

Within the urban area, the distribution of population can be described well by the function:

$$D = Ae^{-bk}, b > 0 \tag{1}$$

where D is density, or population per unit of land, k is distance from the urban centre, and A and b are parameters [3]. The centre is the focus of urban activity, accounting for the form of the density function.

It seems reasonable to argue that land rent is well correlated with population density: with an increase in the number of people within a given area, there will be a bidding up of the land value of that area. Therefore, assume that land rent facing households can be described by a function of the same form as the density equation; further assume that there is an exact trade-off of transport cost for rent, so that rent plus transport cost is a constant at any distance from the centre. Finally, assume that there is a decline in the quality of life as a function of population size and that the disamenity involved is constant at any point in urban space; wherever one locates within the urban area, he is subject to the same level of disamenity, e.g. a form of air pollution that is a function only of population size and not of density. (The matter of disamenity related to density is deferred for the moment.)

Fig. 3.2 presents this case in diagram form. For a given population size, rent R, transport cost T and cost of disamenity C are shown as

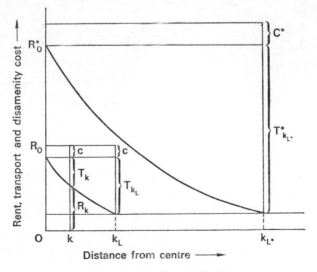

Fig. 3.2 The Rental Market

functions of log of distance from the centre k. At any point, k, $R_k + T_k + C$ is a constant. At the centre, transport cost is zero, and at the urban-rural boundary k_L rent equals its opportunity cost in non-urban use. An increase in population causes an increase in all components of cost, represented as R^*, T^*, C^*, and hence, a corresponding increase in equilibrium wage rate. One can view the labour market and the rental market as involving two equations in a system. Thus, a shift up in V.M.P. as in Fig. 3.1, raises wages, attracts more people, raises rent, transport cost and population disamenity, limiting the increase in labour to a point where the wage increase just covers these increased costs. (Intuitively, it can also be seen from Fig. 3.2 that density increases with population.)

Fig. 3.3 establishes the correspondence between the rental and labour market in more detail, exhibiting distributive shares. Equilibrium occurs at $P_1 L_1$. The real wage rate is P_0, and $P_0 L_1$ are total

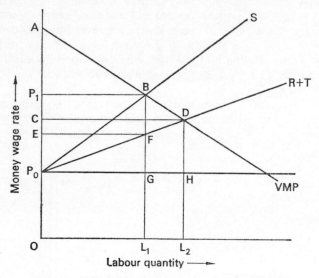

FIG. 3.3   Distributive Shares on the Labour Market

real wages. At L_1, the total amount paid for rent plus transport equals the rectangle $P_0 EFG$, which also corresponds to k_L times $(R_k + T_k)$ in Fig. 3.2; the total value placed on the disamenity by households equals $EP_1 BF$. The triangle $P_1 AB$ is the residual product after labour is paid its V.M.P. It may be interpreted in several ways. It can be viewed as profit, distributed to residual claimants. In real world applications, such claimants can be identified with the land used in urban production (e.g. factory sites), or with the urban landowners (the local squirearchy) plus, to some extent, local government officialdom and those enjoying its patronage. Depending on the definition of output, P_1AB may or may not include payment by households for urban land used in consumption. If the value of that land use is included as part of the aggregate output of Fig. 3.3, obviously there has been double-counting. But such double-counting will also occur if the total spent on land and transport in Fig. 3.2 is treated as a separate form of output to be added to that of Fig. 3.3; or more generally, in national income accounting, there is double-counting when both wages and urban rents are included in aggregate income. Put another way: utility or real income does not equal money income. If we have included consumer rent in P_1AB, real income in the system is P_1AB plus P_0L_1. The rectangle P_0P_1BG is 'intermediate output' used to produce, but not part of, total utility.

In Fig. 3.3, if the population disamenity did not exist, long-run real income would increase for households by the rectangle L_1GHL_2, and for urban land by the area CP_1BD, assuming consumer rent is included as a residual claimant in Fig. 3.3. It is worth stressing that the disamenity has impact on money income, as well as on rent; studies of the impact of pollution on land values appear to have neglected this consideration. Further, holding population constant, the disamenity cost per unit of labour is BF at L_1; but removal of the disamenity will cause an increase in consumer rent plus transport per unit from FG to DH, and not from FG to BG.

The effect of density can be hypothesised to differ from that of population size both because it may involve other types of disamenity and because it will vary within the urban area. In particular, say we have a shift in V.M.P., as in Fig. 3.1, leading to a growth in population, in turn causing a bidding up of land values. However, assume now that disamenity associated with density inhibits the increase in land value as a function of density, with greatest inhibition occurring at the centre, and least at the urban-rural border. The consequences will include changes in the parameters of the rent function, and corresponding population density function. In Equation 1, A should increase less than proportionately with population increases, and b should decline in absolute value. These expectations were confirmed when cross-section estimates of A and b were regressed on urban size, using estimates of A and b made by Muth for 1950 [3], and corresponding estimates of A and b for 1960 developed by Barr [2].

With a density disamenity component in the supply of labour, there is the further complication that the form of the rent plus transport function $(R+T)$ has presumably been affected, i.e. if the density disamenity were removed, there would likely be some shift in the $R+T$ function. This suggests that some additional information can be had by moving from geometric model building to an explicit system of equations. But perhaps as a first approximation, the $R+T$ function (as a component of labour supply) might be assumed stable.

Some policy implications emerge from this discussion. First, there has been much advocacy of limiting urban size because of presumed imposition of negative externalities on old residents by new migrants

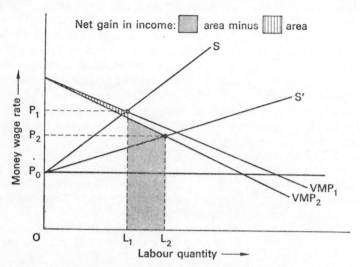

FIG. 3.4   Presumed Consequences of Better Pricing

to the city. In its least sophisticated form, the argument neglects the possible existence of compensatory payments equal to P_1-P_0 in Figs. 3.1 and 3.3. In a more sophisticated variant, the argument seems equivalent to drawing a marginal curve to the supply curve, S, and arguing that this marginal's intersection with VMP yields a socially optimum solution. But this seems a monopsonistic solution and, consequently, one involving a reduction in real output, relative to a situation of unrestricted entry.

However, this is not to argue that we are in the best of all possible worlds. In particular, some (if not all) of the urban scale disamenities are liable to involve zero pricing for valuable resources: absence of effluent charges, absence of congestion tolls, etc. Proper pricing is likely to yield increases in real income for the system, with the limiting case that of the sort of shift occurring in Fig. 3.3 – from S to $R+T$, and from L_1 to L_2.

Fig. 3.4 portrays what seems a more realistic situation: proper pricing reduces some of the disamenity, with S shifting to S'; but such a policy also costs something, posited here to be a relatively small decline in V.M.P., from VMP_1 to VMP_2. The consequence is that real income *and* city size increase.

This discussion has involved a great many simplifications and assumptions, including rational, informed and homogeneous households; only one product; and long run equilibrium. However, some analysis relaxing these assumptions suggests the basic conclusions may hold for a wide range of more involved and realistic cases [1, 2].

3.2 ECONOMIC MAGNITUDES

This section develops empirical comparisons of money income and cost of living by urban size and density. A number of regression equations are presented, being the resultant of a good deal of experimentation with alternative equation forms and variables. In specific cases, the equation form selected gave the best fit among the alternatives tried. Urban scale is measured by Standard Metropolitan Statistical Area (S.M.S.A.) population and central city density, for these variables generally performed better than alternatives such as urbanised area population and density. The log of S.M.S.A. population is used throughout, being a better measure than S.M.S.A. population, *per se*. Central city density refers to the average over the total city area.

3.2.1 MONEY INCOME

Good evidence is available on the relation between average money income and urban size, employing Department of Commerce data on per capita income over time for each of 231 S.M.S.A.s. Classifying by population size groupings and by a North-South regional breakdown, income per capita was obtained for each category. The income measure was then divided, in turn, by U.S. income per capita and by income per capita for the set of all S.M.S.A. counties. (A separate classification was developed for each year, so that, with population growth, an individual S.M.S.A. could move from one class to another over time.) The relatives obtained are presented as Table 3.1, which also exhibits non-S.M.S.A. relative to U.S. per capita income.

In all years, income increases with population size within a given region, there being a marked North-South differential. Over time, there is some reduction in S.M.S.A. values relative to the U.S. average, explicable as a consequence of rural to urban migration; and, of course, there is a corresponding increase in non-S.M.S.A. relative to U.S. per capita income. These shifts appear to have tapered

TABLE 3.1

AVERAGE INCOME FOR S.M.S.A. POPULATION CLASSES RELATIV
TO U.S. AVERAGE AND S.M.S.A. AVERAGE INCOME

Population Class Region and Pop. in 000	1950	1959	1962	1965	1966	1967	1968	196
			Average Income Relative to U.S. Average Income					
North								
1. 0–<250	1·060	1·018	1·018	0·995	0·983	0·977	0·964	0·96
2. 250–<500	1·068	1·036	1·011	1·011	1·010	1·006	0·989	0·98
3. 500–<1,000	1·183	1·106	1·099	1·070	1·065	1·059	1·049	1·05
4. 1,000–<2,500	1·235	1·183	1·164	1·127	1·125	1·125	1·119	1·11
5. 2,500–<9,000	1·258	1·257	1·250	1·242	1·235	1·229	1·224	1·23
6. ≥9,000 (N.Y.C.)	1·400	1·369	1·395	1·364	1·347	1·369	1·370	1·37
South								
1. 0–<250	0·852	0·819	0·808	0·820	0·829	0·835	0·846	0·84
2. 250–<500	0·934	0·889	0·867	0·887	0·878	0·879	0·882	0·88
3. 500–<1,000	1·026	0·939	0·898	0·912	0·931	0·934	0·944	0·955
4. 1,000–<2,500	—	1·108	1·032	1·023	1·016	1·026	1·027	1·020
			Average Income Relative to Average Income for All S.M.S.A. Counti					
North								
1. 0–<250	0·914	0·903	0·912	0·899	0·891	0·887	0·874	0·874
2. 250–<500	0·921	0·919	0·906	0·913	0·916	0·912	0·896	0·898
3. 500–<1,000	1·019	0·981	0·984	0·967	0·966	0·961	0·951	0·957
4. 1,000–<2,500	1·065	1·049	1·043	1·018	1·020	1·021	1·015	1·012
5. 2,500–<9,000	1·084	1·114	1·120	1·120	1·112	1·115	1·110	1·119
6. ≥9,000 (N.Y.C.)	1·207	1·214	1·250	1·233	1·222	1·242	1·242	1·247
South								
1. 0–<250	0·735	0·726	0·724	0·741	0·752	0·758	0·767	0·769
2. 250–<500	0·805	0·788	0·777	0·801	0·796	0·798	0·799	0·803
3. 500–<1,000	0·884	0·833	0·805	0·823	0·844	0·847	0·856	0·869
4. 1,000–<2,500	—	0·983	0·925	0·924	0·922	0·931	0·931	0·928
			Non-S.M.S.A. Relative to U.S. Average Income					
	0·725	0·739	0·756	0·770	0·778	0·775	0·773	0·778

(Derived from data appearing in *Survey of Current Business*, May 1971, Tables 1 and 2, 20–31. Population classification is made for each year, using estimates implicit in the source; thus, there were 82 northern S.M.S.A.s in Class 1 in 1950, and 61 in 1969. The source classified Baltimore, Md., Washington, D.C., and Wilmington, Del. as in the Mid-East U.S., in turn treated in this Table as a subcategory of the North. All averages refer to per capita incomes.) N.Y.C. indicates New York City.

off around 1965, with little change thereafter. Per capita incomes relative to the S.M.S.A. average show much less of a shift than occurs relative to the U.S. average; however, some small relative declines appear to have occurred for the lowest population size groups in the North. (It could be hypothesised that the increasing gap between small and large places might reflect greater decline in environmental quality in the latter group.) On the whole, however, there is general stability of pattern over time, perhaps most marked from 1965 to 1969.

This inference is reinforced by regression results employing the sample of 231 S.M.S.A.s for each year. The log of per capita income, deflated by the consumer price index on a 1957–59 base, was regressed on the log of S.M.S.A. population and regional dummy variables, employing a breakdown into four major regions, with the West effect set equal to zero. Results appear as Table 3.2.

TABLE 3.2

RESULTS FOR REGRESSION OF DEFLATED S.M.S.A. AVERAGE INCOME ON POPULATION AND REGION

Statistic and variable[a]	1950	1959	1962	1965	1966	1967	1968	1969
constant	1362	1497	1611	1665	1711	1778	1836	1821
population elasticity	0·0662*	0·0721*	0·0671*	0·0700*	0·0704*	0·0688*	0·0687*	0·0719*
ε: standard error of estimate	0·0116	0·0086	0·0088	0·0085	0·0085	0·0084	0·0080	0·0078
E: North-East	0·942	0·958	0·972	1·003	1·015	1·027	1·030	1·041
C: North Central	1·019	1·012	1·010	1·073*	1·077*	1·075*	1·069*	1·076*
South	0·808*	0·821*	0·813*	0·876*	0·894*	0·905*	0·924*	0·933*
²: adjusted R^2	0·3748	0·5040	0·4976	0·4687	0·4447	0·4211	0·4103	0·4280

[a] Results from regression equation: $\log A = c + ne + nc + s + \alpha \log P$; antilog form of fitted equation is: $A = C(NE)(NC)(S)P^\alpha$, where A = average income for individual S.M.S.A. deflated by consumer price index; P = S.M.S.A. population in thousands; ne, nc, s = regional dummy variables, with West set equal to zero; $NE = 10^{ne}$, etc.; if $NE \neq 1$, the other dummy antilogs = 1. C = antilog c. Base for Consumer Price Index: 1957–9 = 1·00.

* Indicates significant at 0·05 level in fitted equation (log form).

(Derived from data on 231 S.M.A.S.s appearing in *Survey of Current Business*, May 1971, Tables 1 and 2, 20–31.)

The elasticity of income with respect to population is quite stable over time; the standard error in each case leads to acceptance of the hypothesis the elasticity equals the overall average of 0·0694. Thus a one per cent increase in population brings with it an 0·07 of one per cent increase in per capita income. In contrast to absence of apparent trend in the elasticity, there are pronounced regional shifts. Thus, both the North-East and the South show a steady increase in per capita income, relative to the West, while the North Central region exhibits a sharp increase in 1965, but stability both before and after. The regional shifts seem consistent with major U.S. migration flows, and are suggestive of equilibrating processes at work. From the evidence, it appears plausible that disequilibrium, and consequent equilibrating changes, have occurred primarily at the regional level, for the city size relationship has been quite stable over the last 20 years.

3.2.2 MONEY INCOME FOR HOMOGENEOUS POPULATIONS

The data of Tables 3.1 and 3.2 can (and do) cover non-homogeneous populations, limiting the kind of inferences that can be drawn. Thus, it might be hypothesised that increasing income with S.M.S.A. size reflects only increases in average labour quality (skill, education, etc.). Contrary to this hypothesis, however, two sets of estimates, made about a decade apart, yield similar patterns of increasing income with size, for homogeneous populations. The first set appears as Table 3.3, and summarises results obtained by Victor Fuchs using a sample of around 50,000 observations from the 1960 Census. Fuchs obtained an expected hourly wage for given region and urban size grouping, based on average U.S. wage rates for 168 cells set up in a race, age, sex and education cross-classification, which were then weighted by the population frequency occurring for each cell in the given region and size class. The ratios of actual to expected wage rates were then calculated; for the standardised populations involved, wage rates increased with urban size, as shown in Table 3.3.

The second set of estimates were based on Bureau of Labor Statistics (B.L.S.) area wage surveys for 1968–69. Hourly wage rates for four male and three female occupations were obtained from this source; these were deflated by the Consumer Price Index on a

TABLE 3.3

MONEY INCOME DIFFERENTIAL FOR HOMOGENEOUS
POPULATIONS BY CITY SIZE AND REGION, 1959 (FUCHS
ESTIMATES)

Locale, Population in 000	*Actual/Expected Wage Rate by Region*			
	North-East	*North-Central*	*South*	*West*
Urban Place				
<10	0·92	0·85	0·76	0·89
10–<100	0·95	0·93	0·83	0·95
S.M.S.A.				
<250	0·96	1·03	0·89	1·01
250–<500	0·96	1·03	0·94	1·00
500–<1,000	0·99	1·11	0·96	1·05
1,000 +	1·10	1·16	1·06	1·14

(From: V. R. Fuchs, *Differentials in Hourly Earnings by Region and City Size, 1959*, National Bureau of Economic Research, Occasional Paper 101, New York, 1967, Table 8, Ratio of Actual to Expected Hourly Earnings, p. 16.)

1957–59 base to allow easy comparison with the Fuchs results. The occupational definitions are precise and narrow, so that the population involved should be relatively homogeneous. Deflated wage rates were regressed on log of S.M.S.A. population, log of central city density and regional dummy variables. Results appear as Table 3.4, with both the S.M.S.A. size and density effects positive, but with S.M.S.A. size exhibiting much greater statistical significance.

A comparison with the Fuchs estimates of Table 3.3 was carried out using wage indexes by S.M.S.A. size for three of the male plus two of the female occupations of Table 3.4. Each index was subtracted from the corresponding Fuchs index and the hypothesis of zero population mean was tested for the difference variable. There were 80 observations by way of five occupations, four S.M.S.A. groupings and four regions. Differences between the indexes were very small for all regions save the South, owing to low 1968–69 wage rates for males in the South, perhaps reflecting a high concentration of black workers in the janitor and labourer categories. The t test statistic for the difference variable was 1·1, so the zero mean hypothesis was not rejected. This indicates no significant change in the income differential over a decade, and squares with the results for money wages, involving non-homogeneous populations. This in turn suggests relatively stable levels of labour quality by S.M.S.A. size, over time.

3.2.3 COST OF LIVING INDEXES

Wage rate differences for homogeneous populations should contain cost of living differences as a component. The B.L.S. has estimated cost of living indexes for 39 metropolitan areas and for four non-metropolitan areas covering the four major regions of the country. There are indexes for families of four and for retired couples, with each family type further classified into low-, middle- and upper-income groups. Excluding Honolulu, which had a very high cost of living, presumably reflecting ocean transport costs, the remaining 42 observations were used in a set of regression equations employing log S.M.S.A. population, central city density and region as explanatory variables. Regional effects were significant only for the South relative to all other regions, with little difference occurring between North-East, North Central and Western regional effects; the latter regions were therefore combined into a Northern region, with effect set at zero. In all cases, the regression of cost of living on S.M.S.A. population and Southern regional dummy variable yielded coefficients significant at the 0·05 level. The introduction of central city density improved the R^2 in some cases, though t ratios declined. Results for this set of cases appear as Table 3.5. (Some additional

TABLE 3.4

REGRESSION RESULTS FOR HOURLY WAGES, 85 S.M.S.A.s 1968–69, ON 1957–59 BASE

Explanatory Variable	Female Occupations				Male Occupations		
	Keypunch Operators, Class B	Steno-graphers, General	Switchboard Operator-Receptionists	Typists, Class B	Mechanics, Automotive	Labourers, Material Handling	Janitors, Porters and Cleaners
Constant	1·29	1·41	1·20	1·27	2·42	1·97	1·61
Region[a]: NE	−0·07	−0·07	−0·02	−0·00	−0·36*	−0·35*	−0·08
NC	−0·05	−0·08	−0·04	−0·03	−0·18*	−0·07	0·16*
S	−0·17*	−0·14*	−0·12*	−0·12*	−0·51*	−0·66*	−0·34*
Log S.M.S.A. population[b]	0·20*	0·22*	0·21*	0·15*	0·27*	0·13*	0·08
Log cc density[b]	0·04	0·02	0·10	0·02	0·10**	0·22	0·12
R^2	0·47	0·45	0·65	0·45	0·69	0·73	0·58

[a] Western Region set equal to zero.

[b] Both S.M.S.A. population and central city density in units of 1,000. Population estimated as of 1969; density was 1960 value.

* Significant at 0·05 level; ** significant at 0·10 level.

(Data on wages from Bureau of Labor Statistics, *Area Wage Survey, Specific Metropolitan Area*, 1968–69, Bulletin 1625–1 to 1625–90, Washington, 1970. Wages deflated by Consumer Price Index, 1957–59 = 1·00.)

exploration indicated that Percentage Growth in S.M.S.A. Population, 1960–70, was a good explanatory variable, with coefficient always positive and often significant. This might be explained by rent increases due to lags in housing construction relative to population increases. However, not much was gained in explained variance, with the statistical significance of S.M.S.A. population often dropping sharply. Table 3.5 is retained as most useful for our purposes here.)

TABLE 3.5

COST OF LIVING INDEXES RELATED TO POPULATION SIZE, DENSITY AND REGION

Variable and Statistic	Indexes for Family of Four, 1967			Indexes for Retired Couple, 1967		
	Low Income	Middle Income	High Income	Low Income	Middle Income	High Income
Average Income Level	$5,900	$9,100	$13,000	$2,700	$3,900	$6,000
Regression Results						
Constant	96·29	95·78	91·91	99·20	93·99	87·17
Southern Region	− 7·30*	− 7·55*	− 5·88*	− 7·87*	− 7·10*	− 7·13*
log 1967 S.M.S.A. population (in 000)	1·57	0·76	1·66	0·96	2·15**	4·46*
1967 central city density (in 000)	0·13	0·44*	0·53*	0·17	0·35*	0·37**
(adjusted R^2)	0·484	0·674	0·637	0·458	0·602	0·631

* Significant at 0·05 level; ** Significant at 0·10 level.
(Based on: Cost of Living Indexes for family of four from J. C. Brackett, New B.L.S. budgets provide yardsticks for measuring family living costs, *Monthly Labor Rev.*, April 1969, p. 3–16; cost of living indexes for retired couple from M. H. Hawes, 'Measuring retired couples' living costs in urban areas', *Monthly Labor Rev.*, November 1969, pp. 3–16. S.M.S.A. population and central city density interpolated for 1967 from 1970 and 1960 values in U.S. Census Bureau, Census of Population: 1970, *Number of Inhabitants, Final Report*, PC(1)-A1, U.S. Summary; and *County and City Data Book*, 1967.)

Using the Table 3.5 equations for the family of four, estimated indexes are presented by S.M.S.A. size and region in Table 3.6; city density was set at its class average for each population class, in turn. It is noteworthy that the increase in cost of living is a function of income class, with a much more pronounced effect as income rises. Thus, relative to the smallest population size class, New York City's cost of living is estimated as 6 per cent higher for low-income families, and 17 per cent higher for high-income families. (If anything, the effect is more pronounced for the retired couples' indexes.) Some possible explanations are:

(1) With progressive income tax rates, higher-income people need a greater increment of income to achieve a given increase in disposable income.

TABLE 3.6

ESTIMATED COST OF LIVING INDEXES BY URBAN
SIZE AND REGION

Index (U.S. average = 100)

S.M.S.A. *population* *class (in 000)*	*Low* *Income*	*Middle* *Income*	*High* *Income*	*Estimated* *Weighted* *Average*
North				
0–<250	99·79	98·51	96·37	98·28
250–<500	100·83	99·69	98·15	99·62
500–<1,000	101·53	100·68	99·57	100·53
1,000–<2,500	102·19	101·21	100·48	101·27
2,500–<9,000	103·72	104·28	104·48	104·20
9,000+	106·14	110·49	112·19	110·10
South				
0–<250	92·49	90·96	90·50	91·58
250–500	93·53	92·14	92·28	92·86
500–<1,000	94·23	93·13	93·69	93·79
1,000–<2,500	94·90	93·66	94·61	94·52

(Based on: Low, Middle and High Income Indexes calculated from Family of Four Index regression equations of Table 3.5.

Weights for average index based on U.S. income distribution adjusted for individual population classes to reflect divergence of per capita income from U.S. per capita income, using Table 1. U.S. income distribution for 1967 from U.S. Census Bureau, *Current Population Reports*, Series P-60, No. 75, 14 Dec. 1970, Table 8.)

(2) There may be a relatively greater stock of older, cheaper housing in large areas.

(3) Rent control in New York City is likely to be of greatest benefit to low-income groups.

(4) Upper-income groups probably make up a larger percentage of the population in large cities, and some locally produced goods may have a high-income elasticity and hence higher prices in large areas.*

A weighted average index was developed by applying estimates of the U.S. income distribution for 1967, adjusted for individual population classes to reflect divergence from the U.S. average. The basic data source employed was a U.S. income distribution appearing in U.S. Census Bureau, Current Population Reports, Series P-60, p. 75, 14 December 1970, Table 8. The end points of the income classes were scaled up by the ratio of S.M.S.A. to U.S. income, for each S.M.S.A. class. Then the population in each of the original income classes was estimated by interpolation, to yield weights for each of the three cost-of-living indexes. It turned out that the weighted index was quite stable, i.e. fairly large changes in the

* This point was suggested by Professor A. Nove, University of Glasgow.

income distribution would yield only small changes in the weighted index.

3.2.4 INFERENCES ON 'QUALITY OF LIFE'

Inferences on 'Quality of Life' by urban size, and over time, can be derived from the results developed to this point. These seem of some interest in themselves, and may point the way to some useful applications.

Key estimates are brought together in Table 3.7, whose first three columns exhibit indexes of per capita money income, money wages for homogeneous populations, and the cost of living as a function of urban scale and region, with the U.S. average equal to 1·00 for all indexes. (The estimates for homogeneous populations were obtained as follows. Relative wages by size classes were derived from Table 3.4 by assigning appropriate values to the independent variables. These relatives were then averaged with the corresponding relative wage estimates of Table 3.3, for given classes. Results were then extrapolated to the remaining population classes.)

The difference between the S.M.S.A. index of average income and the wage index for homogeneous populations can be interpreted as involving a labour quality factor. More precisely, the difference will represent that factor plus any differential effects due to payments made to urban land and capital. There are likely to be such factor mix effects with urban size because urban land rent per capita is likely to increase with size, and because there is likely to be greater capital per worker with increasing urban size: higher money wage rates with size should cause some substitution of capital for labour. An estimate of the totality of these effects, intuited here to be primarily that of labour quality, can be obtained by dividing the average income index by the money wage index for homogeneous populations. Results appear in column 4 of Table 3.7.

By treating the homogeneous population wage index as the best estimate of total compensatory payments with scale, estimates of payments for net declines in quality of life are obtained by dividing through by the cost of living index. The resultant appears in column 5 of Table 3.7. It can be interpreted as containing extra-market effects not accounted for by the cost of living, e.g. the value of journey-to-work and other travel time, including congestion costs; decline in environmental quality; evaluated risk of loss through crime and accident, etc. The effects need not all be negative. Certainly, there are some benefits of urban scale, including greater variety and choice in both consumption and production. With larger markets, greater specialisation can occur, making economic the production of many

TABLE 3.7

SUMMARY AND INTERPRETATION OF URBAN SCALE EFFECTS, 1967

Magnitudes Relative to U.S. Average

S.M.S.A. population class and region Population in 000	Per capita money income (1)	Money wages for homogeneous population (2)	Cost-of-living index (3)	Inferred index of labour quality and factor mix = (1)/(2) (4)	Inferred compensatory payment for net quality decline = (2)/(3) (5)
North					
0–<250	0·977	0·975	0·983	1·002	0·992
250–<500	1·006	1·021	0·996	0·985	1·025
500–<1,000	1·059	1·051	1·005	1·008	1·046
1,000–<2,500	1·125	1·099	1·013	1·024	1·085
2,500–<9,000	1·229	1·165	1·042	1·055	1·118
9,000+	1·369	1·205	1·102	1·136	1·094
South					
0–<250	0·835	0·860	0·916	0·971	0·939
250–<500	0·879	0·910	0·929	0·966	0·980
500–<1,000	0·934	0·940	0·938	0·994	1·002
1,000–<2,500	1·026	1·000	0·945	1·026	1·058

(From: Column 1, actual 1967 values from Table 3.1; column 2 estimated from data in Tables 3.3 and 3.4; column 3 from estimates presented in Table 3.6.)

commodities that cannot occur in smaller places, e.g. opera, ballet, major league sports. However, it is hypothesised here that *net* effects are negative, and this is borne out by Table 3.7.

In general, the results of Table 3.7 square well with intuition, though results for New York City (the 9 million + case) may raise some questions: one might guess that the labour quality-factor mix index is somewhat high, and inferred payment for non-market quality effect is somewhat low. For S.M.S.A.s below a million in population, the labour quality-factor mix index is approximately the U.S. average in the North, and somewhat below the average in the South. The index then rises progressively with income, turning out about the same in both North and South for the one to 2·5 million size class. The divergence of the South from the North in wages seems primarily a matter of the cost-of-living index (perhaps reflecting lower winter costs) with some small additional effect stemming from labour quality-factor mix. The inferred payment for non-market quality effect rises progressively with S.M.S.A. size, except for a slight decline when New York City is reached, an anomaly – perhaps – noted earlier.

Treating the index of money wages for homogeneous populations as a quality of life index in effect accepts people's perceptions and revealed preferences as a proper measure of the quality of life. Under this approach, the index can be employed to deflate aggregate consumer income, given the distribution of income by S.M.S.A. size, and trends in deflated income noted; in particular, some estimate of the magnitude of conventionally unmeasured declines in quality can be made. This was carried out here for the three years 1950, 1959 and 1969 under the assumption that the homogeneous population wage index was the same for all three periods. (Recall that evidence supporting this was established only for the last two periods.) Aggregate personal income by S.M.S.A. class was obtained and deflated by the Consumer Price Index, 1957–59 base, to account for changes in the general price level. Then the estimated quality of life index was used to deflate aggregate income for each corresponding S.M.S.A. class. Source data and the sums of deflated personal income for each year are shown in Table 3.8.

For 1950, the 'quality' deflated total approximately equals the conventional measure of income; treating the 1950 ratio of the two measures as base, there is a quality decline of about 1·0 per cent in 1959, and of about 1·2 per cent in 1969, i.e. it is estimated that personal income (in constant dollars) overstates 1969 'real income' or utility, relative to 1950, by 1·2 per cent. The magnitude of the decline is about six billion dollars in 1957–59 prices, or about 8·5 billion dollars in March 1972 prices. The decline due to a shift of population

TABLE 3.8

PERSONAL INCOME DEFLATED BY PRESUMED 'QUALITY OF LIFE' INDEX

Population size, class and region, population in 000	Personal Income Deflated by Consumer Price Index (1957–59 = 1·00), in Millions of Dollars			Assume 'Quality Life' Ind by
	1950	1959	1969	Populatic Size
North				
Non-S.M.S.A.	45,889·0	56,626·6	84,554·4	0·900
S.M.S.A.				
0–<250	20,070·4	21,731·0	25,639·0	0·975
250–<500	18,768·5	22,004·0	33,975·7	1·021
500–<1,000	24,401·0	38,187·2	49,902·1	1·051
1,000–<2,500	36,321·0	54,107·4	89,516·1	1·099
2,500–<9,000	43,455·8	70,348·8	116,025·8	1·165
9,000+	23,948·7	30,990·0	45,469·9	1·205
(Total North: Y_N)	(212,854·4)	(294,004·0)	(445,083·0)	
South				
Non-S.M.S.A.	26,556·1	34,073·8	55,145·7	0·800
S.M.S.A.				
0–<250	12,033·4	12,197·1	15,859·0	0·860
250–<500	7,365·1	11,956·7	17,475·3	0·910
500–<1,000	11,115·8	17,107·4	21,952·2	0·940
1,000–<2,500	—	5,856·2	24,096·3	1·000
(Total South: Y_S)	(57,070·4)	(81,191·2)	(134,528·5)	
Grand Total: Y	269,924·8	375,195·2	579,611·5	
Totals after Deflation by Quality of Life Index				
Total North: D_N	203,396·7	278,436·0	419,782·9	
Total South: D_S	67,106·2	93,969·8	154,026·1	
Grand Total: D	270,502·9	372,405·8	573,809·0	
Ratios				
D/Y	1·002	0·993	0·990	
D/Y relative to 1950	1·000	0·991	0·988	
D_N/Y_N	0·956	0·947	0·943	
D_N/Y_N relative to 1950	1·000	0·991	0·987	
D_S/Y_S	1·176	1·157	1·145	
D_S/Y_S relative to 1950	1·000	0·984	0·973	

(From: Undeflated Personal Income data by S.M.S.A. from *Survey of Current Business* May 1971, Tables 1 and 2, 20–31. Table 3.8 excludes Alaska and Hawaii. Quality of Life Inde set equal to column 2, Table 3.7. Deflation carried out by dividing through by Index.)

and income from smaller to larger places is balanced somewhat by a relative shift from North to South, since the Southern deflators yield increases in real income. However, within regions, the decline is more pronounced for the South, i.e. there has been a greater shift to larger places in the South than in the North.

Those anticipating more striking losses through environmental degradation may be mollified by the qualifications that (1) there is no accounting for environmental degradation common to all places; (2) these are net effects, where benefits of scale, as well as costs, should enter; (3) these estimates do not purport to measure gains that might emerge from better institutional arrangements and/or an environmental clean-up (here, see Fig. 3.3); and (4) consumers' perceptions and preferences may well be changing, assuming consumer sovereignty is accepted in the first place.

The estimates developed here may be subject to the critique that there may be an identification problem, since observed intersection points of labour supply and demand may not lie on the long-term supply curve. In particular, if *VMP* shifts up and short-run supply has not fully adjusted, the observed intersection for price and quantity will lie above the long-run supply curve. (Here, see Fig. 3.1, with the interpretation that labour quantity lies between L_1 and L_2.) The argument deserves detailed investigation, perhaps using distributed lags, but some initial counters can be noted. First, population growth in recent years has been greatest for middle sized S.M.S.A.s [2]; any bias due to incomplete supply adjustment will tend to occur in the middle of the population size range, rather than at the extremes, tending to limit the impact of such bias on estimates. Further, there is marked stability of size relationships in Table 3.2, and in the results for Table 3.3 relative to Table 3.4. Such results fit the interpretation that disequilibria are neither large nor long-lived, i.e. observed points are likely to be close to the long-run supply function, rationalising the use of single-equation estimates.

3.3 *NON-MARKET PHENOMENA*

In the previous section, quality of life effects, net of conventional cost-of-living differences, were presented in terms of a scalar estimate for each urban size class. The present section attempts to go behind the scalar to a vector of sources of quality effects, usually involving non-market phenomena. Sources are classified as falling within the physical or the social environment; in all cases, there is some evidence of quality decline with increasing urban scale, in line with the scalar results shown in Table 3.7, above. Admittedly, the present vector is incomplete and could be extended; however, it covers most of the usually noted categories of non-market phenomena. Again, there are problems of measuring and comparing utilities, met here by the rationale that effects hold for the typical or average urban resident. In the present study, there has been little attempt to impute dollar values to the quality changes; such imputation seems a promising subject for future inquiry, perhaps paralleling the work of Lave and Seskin on air pollution damage [4].

3.3.1 THE PHYSICAL ENVIRONMENT

3.3.1.1 *Air Pollution*

Statistically significant results are obtained when air pollution levels are related to measures of urban scale. Table 3.9 summarises results for regressions of particulates on log of S.M.S.A. population, using 1965–66 data covering 76 urban sreas. Nitrates and sulphates here are specific kinds of particulates. In all cases, the coefficient of log of S.M.S.A. population is positive and significant.

TABLE 3.9

REGRESSION RESULTS FOR THE RELATION OF MEAN PARTICULATE LEVELS, 1965–66, TO LOG OF S.M.S.A. POPULATION

Dependent Variable (Geometric Mean)	Constant	Coefficient of Log S.M.S.A. pop. (in 000)	t Value	R^2
Particulates (all)	30·61	25·06	3·58*	0·15
Nitrates	− 0·42	1·07	3·49*	0·14
Sulphates	− 1·19	4·02	3·75*	0·16

* Significant at 0·05 level.
Geometric mean in units of micrograms per cubic metre.
(Based on: Air pollution data from Public Health Service, National Air Pollution Control Administration, *Air Quality from the National Air Surveillance Network – 1966 edition*, Durham, N.C., 1968. The 76 cities employed had observations for all three pollutants. S.M.S.A. population for 1966 estimated as 0·4 (1966 population) + ·6 (1970 population). 1960 population from *1960 Census of Population*. 1970 population from U.S. Bureau of Census, Advance Population Reports.

Because there was concern that nitrates and sulphates were not good proxies for gaseous pollutants, available data for sulphur dioxide and nitrogen dioxide were regressed on S.M.S.A. population for two time periods, listed as 1967 and 1970 in Table 3.10. (Because there were many gaps in the coverage, the '1967' sample consisted of observations in either 1967 or 1968, with the 1967 observation used if data were available for both years; the '1970' sample consists

TABLE 3.10

REGRESSION RESULTS FOR THE RELATION OF NITROGEN DIOXIDE AND SULPHUR DIOXIDE TO LOG OF S.M.S.A. POPULATION

Dependent Variable (Mean level in $\mu g/m^3$)	Constant Term	Coefficient of Log S.M.S.A. Pop. (in 000)	t Value	$\bar{R}^2$
SO$_2$, 1970	– 13·33	14·09	2·90*	0·07
SO$_2$, 1967	– 28·64	25·43	2·89*	0·07
NO$_2$, 1970	41·55	32·77	2·91*	0·07
NO$_2$, 1967	69·56	39·44	3·39*	0·11

* Significant at 0·05 level. $\bar{R}^2$ = adjusted R^2.

(Based on: Air pollution data obtained from Thomas B. McMullen, Division of Atmospheric Surveillance, Environmental Protection Agency, Research Triangle Park, N.C., 1971. S.M.S.A. population from U.S. Bureau of the Census, *U.S. Census of Population: 1970, Number of Inhabitants PC (1)-A1.*)

of observations in either 1969 or 1970, with the 1970 observation used if data were available for both years. The 80 urban areas employed had observations in both the '1967' and '1970' sample.) In Table 3.10, log of S.M.S.A. population is again statistically significant for all cases, though adjusted R^2 is relatively low.

When central city density was introduced into the particulate relation, its coefficient was not statistically significant. However, central city density was statistically significant for both sulphur dioxide (SO_2) and nitrogen dioxide (NO_2), as shown in Table 3.11.

TABLE 3.11

REGRESSION RESULTS FOR NITROGEN AND SULPHUR DIOXIDE WITH INTRODUCTION OF DENSITY

Pollutant, Variable and Statistic	1967	1970
NO$_2$ (in micrograms per cu. metre)		
Constant	56·36	56·94
Log S.M.S.A. population, in 000	26·32*	17·27
W (log S.M.S.A. population)	8·15	12·74*
Central city density, in 000	4·50*	3·90*
$\bar{R}^2$ (adjusted R^2)	0·24	0·17
SO$_2$ (in micrograms per cu. metre)		
Constant	5·18	8·74
City density, in 000	7·02*	3·40*
W (city density)	– 5·70*	– 3·30*
$\bar{R}^2$ (adjusted R^2)	0·51	0·41

* Indicates significant at 0·05 level.
W: Western regional dummy variable, equals 1 for urban area in West, 0 for all other regions.

(Based on: Same as Table 3.10; central city density from *U.S. Census of Population: 1970.*)

In the case of sulphur dioxide, the introduction of central city density and a regional slope shifter for the West caused log S.M.S.A. population to become statistically insignificant, with very low t ratio, though its coefficient remained positive. Hence, it was dropped from the equation. In the case of nitrogen dioxide, statistical significance occurred either for log S.M.S.A. population or a Western regional shifter of that variable, after central city density was introduced. The Western regional effect was negative for sulphur dioxide and positive for nitrogen dioxide, in line with expectations, given type of fuel consumption (for SO_2) and automobile usage (for NO_2) by region.

It is of interest that the 1970 results, relative to those for 1967, suggest some decline in pollution level over time. This conjecture is given substance through statistical test. Using the data spanning the four years 1967–70, the ratio P_t/P_{t-1} was formed, where P refers to specific pollutant, and t to year. (When a gap occurred in the series, the ratio was estimated. Thus, if P_{t+2} was available, but P_{t+1} was not, P_{t+2}/P_t was treated as equal to $(P_{t+1}/P_t)^2$, with the square root entered as the observation in this case.) Geometric mean values for the ratio were 0·820 for sulphur dioxide and 0·936 for nitrogen dioxide, i.e. the average annual decline was about 18 per cent for the former and about 6 per cent for the latter pollutant, over 1967–70. The log of the ratio was used in forming the test statistic, and in each case the hypothesis of zero population mean was rejected.

Use of the ratio, rather than the log ratio, would introduce an upward bias. Thus, sample values of 5 and one-fifth have a geometric mean of 1, and an arithmetic mean of 2·6. Testing was carried out using $\bar{x}/(s/n)$ where $\bar{x}$ was the sample mean for the log of the ratio, s was sample standard deviation and n was sample size. Values obtained were as follows:

	$\bar{x}$	s	n	Mean of Ratio
SO_2	− 0·0864	0·2047	208	0·90
NO_2	− 0·0288	0·1475	200	0·99

Spirtas and Levin found a similar decline in particulate levels through a comparison of 1962–66 averages to 1957–61 averages, for 60 central cities and 20 non-urban sites [5].

We can infer that pollution regulation and control is having some impact.

3.3.1.2 *Other Scale Effects in the Physical Environment* [1]

Outdoor noise levels in central sections of larger cities are on the order of twice the perceived level in the residential areas of those cities, in turn twice the perceived levels in suburban areas or small towns. Solid waste disposal costs appear to increase much more with S.M.S.A. size than do money wages for homogeneous populations, as indicated by these rough orders of magnitude:

S.M.S.A. Population in 000	Money Wages for Homogeneous Populations	Solid Waste Disposal Cost per ton
100	1·0	1·0
2,000	1·1	1·6
10,000	1·2	1·8

Urbanisation (and density increase, in particular) causes an increase in the percentage of land area that is impervious, tending to increase the risk of flooding. Urbanisation also causes changes in local climate, with effects increasing approximately with log of S.M.S.A. population. There is creation of an urban 'heat island' with temperatures higher than in the surrounding countryside. Such may be beneficial, on net, for it primarily occurs at night. However, other effects (reduced sunlight, more fog, more precipitation) probably make the totality of climate effects negative on balance. Only in the case of water waste management is there evidence of scale economies in per capita cost: engineering data show declines in sewer cost with density and in water treatment cost with population size. However, if a stream standard is specified, i.e. if a minimum level of water quality must be attained, then it is likely that large urban areas will be forced to use high-cost tertiary treatment of sewage, making per capita costs U-shaped with urban size – first decreasing and then increasing.

3.3.2 THE SOCIAL ENVIRONMENT

3.3.2.1 *Journey to Work and Congestion*

A major factor in increasing cost-of-living with urban size is increasing rent per unit. We can expect corresponding increases in average transport cost, particularly in terms of time cost of the journey to work. Some available data conform to this hypothesis. Thus, a sample survey shows that daily work trips in the New York metropolitan area average about 70 minutes in total (to and from work). Within the next 12 largest S.M.S.A.s, total trip time averages about one hour, and for other S.M.S.A.s the total is 40 minutes. Outside metropolitan areas, the total is about 25 minutes [6]. Rough calculations yielded an estimate of the value of these time differences as about 1 per cent of income for each succeeding S.M.S.A. grouping, i.e. the difference between New York and non-metropolitan areas was estimated as equivalent to 4 per cent of income, assuming work trip time is valued at one-third the wage rate, on the basis of evidence developed by Beesley [7].

There is some evidence that congestion cost, as well as length of journey to work, increases with S.M.S.A. size. Voorhees *et al.* present data on a sample of 23 urban areas [8] which these results for average journey to work by automobile:

Urban Area Population, in 000	Trip Length in Miles	Miles per Hour
10–<100	3·0	28·6
100–<1,000	5·0	28·6
1,000+	6·2	23·1

The wage survey data employed for Table 3.4 contained information on weekly hours of work for female occupations; it turned out that hours of work declined with both S.M.S.A. population and density, the latter being the more important factor. It appears that compensatory payments may take non-money forms.

3.3.2.2 *Crime*

In earlier work relating crime rates to urban scale I used samples consisting of 50 large cities and 99 cities in California [1, 2]. In both cases rates for major crimes were regressed on population size and density, as well as a number of other explanatory variables. For some of the crimes, the urban scale factors had positive and statistically significant coefficients. However, there was some concern that the population at risk might be greater than the number of inhabitants, given commuting into cities by suburban workers. (Number of inhabitants is employed as the denominator in calculating crime rates.) To avoid the possible bias involved, a new set of regression equations were estimated, with the population unit now the S.M.S.A. Presumably, population at risk would now be much closer to number of inhabitants. There is a possible remaining source of bias if large S.M.S.A.s tend to have relatively more outside visitors (tourists, visiting businessmen) than do small; but, intuitively, this seems a relatively minor problem.

The sample for the S.M.S.A. regressions contained 137 observations, determined by number of cases common both to the F.B.I. *Uniform Crime Report* and *The Manpower Report of the President*, which contains data on S.M.S.A. unemployment rates, used as one of the variables.

Rates per 100,000 inhabitants for seven major crimes were each regressed on the explanatory variables exhibited in Table 3.12; Table 3.12 shows coefficient signs and statistical significance when all explanatory variables were included.

Table 3.13 presents results when explanatory variables entering the equations are limited to those with statistically significant coefficients.

The coefficient for log of S.M.S.A. population was always positive, and was significant in four of the cases in Table 3.13. The coefficient for central city density, on the other hand, was positive and significant only for robbery; it was significant but negative for rape. In all other cases, the effect of density was negative but not significant.

TABLE 3.12

SIMPLIFIED RESULTS, REGRESSION OF S.M.S.A. CRIME RATES ON ALL EXPLANATORY VARIABLES, 1970

Explanatory Variable, and Statistic	Coefficient Signs and Significance							Total Cases	
	Homicide	Rape	Robbery	Assault	Burglary	Larceny	Auto Theft	+	−
log S.M.S.A. population	+	+*	+*	+	+	+	+*	7	0
city density	−	−*	+*	−	−	−	−	1	6
per cent Black	+*	+*	+*	+	+	+	+	7	0
per cent Indian	−	+	−	−	+	+	+	4	3
per cent Japanese	−	−	−	−	−*	−	−	0	7
per cent all other non-white	+	+	+	+	+*	+**	+	7	0
per cent unemployed, 1969	−	+	+**	+	+*	+*	+*	6	1
average July temperature	+**	+	+**	+	−	+	+	7	0
Annual precipitation	−	−	+	+	+**	+	+	5	2
North-East Region	−	−	−	+	+	+	+	4	3
North Central Region	−	−	+*	+	−	+	+	4	3
South Region	+	−	+	+	−	−	−	3	4
per cent growth S.M.S.A. pop.	+	+	+	+*	+*	+*	+	7	0
Persons per household	−	−	−	−	−	−	−	0	7
per cent crowded housing	+	+	+	+	+	+	+**	7	0
R^2: Adjusted R^2	0·6244	0·3788	0·5944	0·3273	0·2323	0·1874	0·1579		

* Significant at 0·05 level; ** Significant at 0·10 level.

(Based on: Crime data from U.S. Federal Bureau of Investigation, *Uniform Crime Reports, 1970*; independent variables from U.S. Census Bureau, *U.S. Census of Population: 1970, Number of Inhabitants*, Final Report PC(1)-A1, U.S. Summary; *General Population Characteristics*, Final Report PC(1)-B1, U.S. Summary; Census of Population and Housing: 1970, *General Demographic Trends for Metropolitan Areas 1960 to 1970*, Final Report PHC(2)-1, U.S. Summary; *County and City Data Book, 1967*; and U.S. President, *Manpower Report of the President*, 1971.)

TABLE 3.13

RESULTS FOR REGRESSIONS OF S.M.S.A. CRIME RATES, SIGNIFICANT COEFFICIENTS

(Rates per 100,000 inhabitants)

Explanatory Variable and Statistic[a]	Homicide	Rape	Robbery	Assault	Burglary	Larceny	Auto Theft
			Coefficient Values and Significance[b]				
Constant	-14·060	-14·319	-467·837	429·937	285·374	356·235	-827·725
Log S.M.S.A. population (in 000)	1·548*	11·841*	113·536*	—	—	—	332·457*
City density (in 000)							
per cent Black	0·264*	-1·025*	9·354*	—	—	—	—
per cent Indian		0·368*	3·562*	3·642*	11·294*	5·773**	—
per cent Japanese		-5·622*	-29·806**	-8·656*	-209·535**	-167·271*	—
per cent all other non-white		4·836*	26·854**	—	201·684*	162·911*	—
per cent unemployed. 1969		—	13·278**	—	162·602*	103·503*	69·753*
Average July temperature, °F	0·190*	—	4·866*	—	—	—	—
Annual precipitation, inches			—				
North-East Region	-1·242**	—	—	—	—	—	147·997*
North Central Region		—	64·517*	—	—	—	—
South Region	2·075*	—	—	—	—	—	—
per cent growth in S.M.S.A. pop.	—	0·101**	0·707[c]	1·762*	13·370*	10·211*	—
Persons per household	—	—	-75·811**	-142·082*	—	—	—
per cent crowded housing	—						

Log S.M.S.A. population	2·180	—	5·147	—	—	—	—
City density	6·611	4·678	4·342	4·231	2·434	1·662	—
per cent Black	—	4·164	4·319	2·471	1·925	2·053	—
per cent Indian	—	4·616	1·762	—	2·138	2·307	—
per cent Japanese	—	—	1·843	—	3·597	3·057	2·574
per cent all other non-white	—	3·031	1·932	—	—	—	—
per cent unemployed, 1969	2·593	3·008	3·119	—	—	—	—
Average July temperature	1·859	—	—	—	—	—	—
Annual precipitation	2·217	—	4·237	—	—	—	2·252
North-East	—	—	—	—	—	—	—
North Central	—	—	—	—	—	—	—
South	—	—	1·335	3·364	4·142	4·225	—
per cent growth in S.M.S.A. pop.	—	1·676	1·681	—	—	—	—
persons per household	—	—	—	2·561	—	—	1·875
per cent crowded housing	—	—	—	4·161	—	—	—
$\bar{R}^2$: Adjusted R^2	0·6381	0·3758	0·6041	0·3364	0·2246	0·2091	0·1827

[a] All measures refer to S.M.S.A. except for city density.

[b] * indicates significant at 0·05 level; ** indicates significant at 0·10 level; — indicates t ratio less than 0·10 level.

[c] Not significant (t = 1·335), but exclusion of variable leads to lack of significance for unemployment and persons per household.

[d] Per cent of housing units with 1·01 or more persons per room.

Neglecting robbery, the generally negative result might be rationalised by the Jane Jacobs thesis that an increase in number of potential observers, with increasing density, tends to deter crime [9]. The results for density here run counter to those obtained using the samples of cities, for there the density coefficient was generally positive and often significant. Perhaps the presumed population-at-risk bias primarily affects density, rather than population size.

Results for other variables, though not bearing directly on the thesis of this paper, are of some interest.

Because black crime rates are well above those of whites, both in commission and victimisation, and because blacks tend to locate in large urban areas, there was concern about possible confounding of size and racial effect; hence, the percentage of blacks appears as explanatory variable. In addition, the percentage of American Indians, percentage of Japanese and percentage of all other non-whites were also included. The last group includes Chinese, Filipino, Hawaiian, Korean, other orientals, and people who marked 'other race' on Census questionnaires; the last group causes some over-statement of this category [10]. Because ethnic composition was often significant, future work might attempt to introduce other ethnic groups into the analysis.

The effect for the percentage of Japanese was always negative, and often significant; that for the other ethnic groups was generally positive, though the American Indian coefficient was sometimes negative and never significant. The coefficient for all other non-whites was significant in four of the cases, while that for the percentage of blacks was significant in six of the cases. It goes without saying that income, education and class effects may be important factors behind the ethnic composition results; future work ought to be directed to winnowing out such effects.

The percentage of unemployed for 1969 turned out to be a bit better as explanatory variable than the percentage of unemployed for 1970; it was a good deal better than percentage increase in unemployment between the two years. It is of interest that unemployment had positive and significant effects for the crimes of economic motive: robbery, burglary, larceny and auto theft. As an incidental note, the relation of unemployment and urban size was negative and significant, though the r^2 was very low (0·03). Inspection of the data showed that unemployment rates for individual urban areas possess a good deal of stability over time, suggesting that employment type may be a factor, e.g. some areas may have relatively more employment in seasonal occupations. This, in turn, may shake the obvious interpretation that unemployment causes some shift from legal to illegal activity; however, the concentration of the effect in economic crimes, noted earlier, supports the obvious interpretation.

The effect of both July temperature and precipitation was generally positive in Table 3.12, though the former was significant only for assault and robbery, and the latter was not significant in Table 3.13. It was hypothesised that increasing temperature might increase violent crimes because of presumed increase in irascibility with temperature; precipitation might work some effect through keeping people indoors. The temperature effect was in line with expectations, but the precipitation effect was not. Perhaps the variables really measured regional effects in a better fashion than did regional dummy variables. The effects for such regional dummy variables were not particularly pronounced, though the evidence of Table 3.12 suggests the West may be somewhat more crime prone, in terms of the effect of variables not included in the present equation. The results for temperature and precipitation, however, imply higher crime rates in the South.

Growth in S.M.S.A. population had a positive effect for all seven crimes, and was significant in four cases in Table 3.13. Explanations could include that of psychological stresses induced in high growth areas, or the more mundane explanation of better opportunities attracting those in criminal pursuits.

The effect of persons per household is always negative, and significant in two cases in Table 3.13. The explanation for this might be the simple one that both criminals and victims may be more likely to live in single-person or small-person households; for example, with more people at home there is probably a deterrent effect on crime committed by an outsider. But perhaps more involved sociological factors enter, in terms of ethnic group or life style associated with both the variable and the commission of crime.

The effect of crowded housing, measured as percentage of housing units with more than 1·01 persons per room, is always positive, and significant in assault and auto theft. This variable may be a proxy for poverty, but results for it can be interpreted to support the hypothesis (or myth) that crowded living conditions, *per se*, have negative consequences for behaviour. The density versus crowding results are very much in line with a Jane Jacobs argument distinguishing between the two variables [11].

A major reason for introducing the large number of explanatory variables used here was to avoid any confounding of presumed urban scale effect with that of the other variables. Their introduction does, in fact, generally lead to some reduction in impact of population size, as can be seen in the following set of comparisons of estimated coefficients for long S.M.S.A. population, in thousands. (In the three cases in Table 3.13 where log S.M.S.A. population size was not significant, it was added to the set of explanatory variables, for purposes of this comparison.)

	Coefficient when log S.M.S.A. Population is only Explanatory Variable	*Coefficient when other Significant Variables are Included*
Homicide	2·3	1·5
Rape	9·9	11·8
Robbery	188·2	113·5
Assault	51·3	22·8
Burglary	237·8	90·8
Larceny	173·7	55·4
Auto theft	290·8	332·5

Nevertheless, coefficient signs and t ratios strongly support the hypothesis that urban size is a factor in crime. It is not at all obvious why this is so. It may be that other variables are involved, e.g. ethnic composition effects not included here; or the existence of markets for narcotics, or the conditions for juvenile gangs, tending to occur only in large metropolitan areas. Or it may be that large areas intensify some factors involved in crime, e.g. anomie or anonymity. And it may be suggested – only in part facetiously – that criminals are faced with urban scale effects, too; they may obtain greater returns per criminal act, given higher income in urban areas; but perhaps more acts per criminal need be committed to achieve equivalent returns in criminal occupations.

Some additional probing into the urban size effect was carried out by examining the interaction of population size and percentage of blacks. Dummy variables for urban population size classes were formed using the size classes defined earlier (as in Table 3.1, for example), and in turn, each dummy variable was multiplied by the percentage of population that was black. In addition, regional interaction was examined by multiplying the southern region dummy by percentage black. Regression results, in terms of explained variance, did not improve for six of the seven crimes. However, in the case of robbery, substantial improvement occurred, with adjusted R^2 increasing from about 0·6 to 0·7; results appear as Table 3.14. With the interaction terms included, a number of explanatory variables, including population size, were no longer significant (compare Tables 3.13 and 3.14). The southern region – percentage of black interaction was negative, indicating lower black robbery rates in the South. (More generally, a negative coefficient for this variable was obtained for all of the crimes.) The effect of the population size-percentage of black interaction exhibits a general increase with urban size, which can be interpreted as indicating higher black robbery rates as urban size increases. (Population size dummies, *per se*, had no impact on robbery rates.) Perhaps part of the explanation for these results can be based on the hypotheses that (1) narcotics

TABLE 3.14

RESULTS FOR ROBBERY, INCLUDING INTERACTION VARIABLES IN EQUATION

Variable and Statistic	Coefficient	t ratio
Constant	− 189·22	1·90**
per cent Black	5·99	3·86*
per cent Japanese	− 35·44	2·65*
per cent all other non-white	30·99	2·68*
Average July temperature	3·39	2·52*
Southern region times % Black	− 4·74	3·95*
Pop. size dummy times % Black		
Population size in 000		
1. 0–<250 (omitted dummy)	0·00	—
2. 250–<500	− 0·47	0·42
3. 500–<1,000	1·86	1·53
4. 1,000 <2,500	8·71	6·56*
5. 2,500–<9,000	13·62	7·43*
6. 9,000 +(New York City)	27·87	6·86*

$R^2 = 0.7060$
* Significant at 0·05 level. ** Significant at 0·10 level.

addiction is greater for blacks than for whites, (2) the problem increases with city size, and (3) narcotics addicts are prone to robbery to support their habit.

Although much crime involves income transfer, it can be hypothesised that this is a wasteful process: the expected loss to the victim is greater than the gain to the criminal. Hence there is likely to be real utility loss, as well as income transfer, in the process.

Increased costs of crime with urban size include not only increased insurance premiums for insurable risks, and increased security costs for locks, alarms, police, etc.; there is also the disutility from increased perception of risk and concomitant internal apprehension and external restriction of activities. In particular, use of public space (parks, sidewalks, mass transit facilities) will be curtailed, causing less 'social return' on investment in such items than anticipated.

3.3.2.3 *Health and Welfare Effects*

There is a good deal of interest in, and controversy about, possible health and welfare effects of urban scale, but there is little hard evidence. The available evidence can be interpreted as indicating that some modest effect may exist (perhaps).

Robert C. Schmitt claimed to have controlled income and education, and yet he obtained close association between density measures and indicators of health and social problems for the Honolulu S.M.S.A. in 1950, with positive partial correlations above 0·5 for density and death rate, TB rate, mental hospital rate, and juvenile delinquency rate [12]. However, income and education were measured in terms of percentage above a specified level, and these may not be particularly sensitive measures.

Hallinan Winsborough used 1950 Census tract data for Chicago and found positive simple correlations between density and death rate, infant death rate, TB rate and public assistance rate; the introduction of a dozen other variables caused coefficients to become *negative* and significant for all effects save infant mortality [13]. But one wonders about possible multi-collinearity problems.

Galle, Grove and McPherson examined 'social pathology' and density using 74 community areas of Chicago for 1960 [14]. Controlling for social class and ethnicity, they found no significant relation between pathologies and density, measured as persons per acre. They then disaggregated density into four components: persons per room, rooms per housing unit, housing units per structure and structures per acre. Working with these variables, and the class and ethnic controls, they obtained results which they interpreted as indicating possibly significant density effects, after all, using the hypothesis that density is an intervening variable: class and ethnicity 'cause' density, which in turn causes pathology. Although regressions were carried out, no *t* ratios were presented. Persons per room was the major density variable explaining rates for mortality, fertility, public assistance and juvenile delinquency. But it is possible that persons per room is a better (negative) proxy for income than the social class variable that was used, which included median family income as a component. Admission to mental hospitals was explained best by a positive relation with number of rooms per housing unit; that is rather surprising, since that explanatory variable is probably positively correlated with income.

Jonathan Freedman examined mental illness and juvenile delinquency using data on 334 health areas in New York City [15]. These were related to a set of control variables and alternate measures of density (persons per acre and persons per room). Control variables included median income, median education, percentage of non-whites and age distribution measures. Statistical analysis indicated no relation between juvenile delinquency and either density measure, given inclusion of the control variables. The interpretation that density is an intermediate variable – i.e. low-income people have to live in high density areas, which in turn causes juvenile delinquency – was rejected because density had no effect within areas of low income and varying density. However, density in terms of persons per acre accounted for 6 per cent of a total explained variance of 65 per cent for mental illness, in an equation including a large number of control variables. Density in terms of persons per room had much less explanatory power. Controlling on income, Freedman found these positive correlations between mental illness and density:

	Median Income in Thousand Dollars				
	<5	*5–<6*	*6–<7*	*7–<8*	*8 +*
Density per acre	0·30	0·33	0·18	0·42	0·17
Density per room	0·13	0·25	0·26	0·29	0·56

Freedman concludes that density may well contribute a small amount to mental illness.

In all of these studies, intra-urban density was the key variable. There appears to be little attention in the literature to possible urban size effects. Such may be worth exploration. For example, Table 3.15 makes some comparisons of premature birth rates and fetal mortality

TABLE 3.15

PREMATURE BIRTH RATES, 1967 AND
FETAL MORTALITY, 1966

Race	Premature Birth Rates: Metropolitan Relative to Non-Metro. Counties[a]	Fetal Death Ratios: Ratio per 1,000 Live Births			
		Metropolitan Counties		Non-Metropolitan Counties	
		Urban		Urban	
		Places	Remainder	Places	Remainder
White	1·064	14·4	11·9	13·3	13·7
Non-white	1·256	26·5	22·6	25·9	26·3

[a] Premature birth rate: live births with a gestation period of 36 weeks or less, as a fraction of all live births.
(Based on: Premature birth rates: U.S. Public Health Service, *Vital Statistics of the United States 1967*, Vol. I – *Natality*, Washington, 1969, Table 1–43, pp. 1–41. Fetal death rates: *Vital Statistics of the United States, 1966*, Vol. II – *Mortality, Part A*, Washington, 1968, pp. 3–6.)

rates using some gross measures of urban scale. Prematurity is more common in metropolitan than in non-metropolitan counties. Relative to non-metropolitan counties, the fetal death rate in metropolitan counties is higher for urban places, but lower for areas outside. This might be explained by the hypothesis that health services are better in metropolitan areas, but that such is outweighed by environmental decline, particularly increased air pollution, within urban places.

Lave and Seskin [4] present some data implicating particulates in infant mortality, and Hickey *et al.* [16] present evidence associating nitrogen dioxide and sulphur dioxide with mortality rates for a number of diseases. All of these pollutants increase with urban size, as shown above. It would be of interest to relate mortality rates to all of these pollutants and measures of urban scale to see if there are residual effects for the latter variables.

3.4 *SOME IMPLICATIONS FOR RESEARCH AND POLICY*

A theme of this paper is that dollars are not the same between places: they yield different levels of utility, which can be estimated in terms of people's preferences revealed through an index of money wages for homogeneous populations. A variety of implications can be drawn from this argument. For example, the ratio of non-white to white median family income has shown an upward trend over time, as exemplified by these values:

Year	Ratio
1947	0·51
1960	0·55
1969	0·63

Such figures have been interpreted as 'indicating some movement toward more income equality for minority groups' [17]. But during the observed period, there has been a great migration of blacks from the rural South to the large urban North. It seems clear that deflation using a quality of life index would dampen the apparent movement towards equality. (It might be conjectured that there are some features of life in the North, not included in the index, that blacks might prefer to life in the South. But some might conjecture the opposite.)

The quality of life index can be used, as in Table 3.8, to estimate environmental deterioration over time. A variant of this approach can be applied to the problem Julius Margolis noted in 1954, when he wrote:

> ... without paying reverence to the image of our rural paradise lost, it is still true that much of our urban production (housing, public services, transportation, recreation) is the cost of maintaining our developed economies, and adds much less to consumers' satisfaction than is indicated in a production index [18].

Consider the data of Table 3.8 for 1969. If we first inflate Southern income to equivalent Northern levels by multiplying by the ratio of Northern to Southern indexes for each class, we obtain a personal income estimate of $595·7 billion. (The ratios for all classes were quite similar, ranging from 1·10 to 1·13; with inflation of the Southern component, aggregate personal income increases by 2·8 per cent.) Taking the Northern non-S.M.S.A. level as our base, we can deflate each class in turn by the Northern index; total deflated income is $516·5 billion, or 0·867 of the initial figure. Hence, the 'cost' of urbanisation is estimated as 0·133 of income. (This may contain a slight overstatement because some of the North-South differential may involve disequilibrium.)

Individual urban area deviations from the standardised money income relation can be interpreted as reflecting either (1) long-term local quality effects or (2) temporary disequilibrium, involving a V.M.P. shift of the kind shown in Fig 3.1. Evidence in the latter case might be useful in analysing and forecasting migration.

Work inputing money values to both amenities and disamenities of urban scale will allow comparisons with standardised money income figures. *If* there are marked divergences, it might be inferred that people are making a bad bargain. Policy at this point can range from making the information available to attempting to redirect people to other places 'for their own good'. This might be based on the argument that people are irrational (e.g. if insanity really were generated by high density) or that protection of the lives of minors were involved, e.g. if children are exposed to very dangerous levels of air pollution, but parents choose not to move. (For example, in Smeltertown, an El Paso community of 120 Mexican-American families, of 416 children between 3 and 8, 102 were found to have abnormally high levels of lead in their blood. The city of El Paso wants to remove the children from the environment, and is encouraging families to move out of Smeltertown, but most of the adults are opposed to moving [19].) Beyond this point, there is obviously conflict of values: free choice by responsible adults versus strictures against suicide, if such be extended to slow forms of suicide. The latter position is close to the argument that direct action on population distribution is the 'proper' way to avoid collective bads and internalise externalities. It has been argued here, in opposition, that compensation for such collective bads does occur through market mechanisms, but that improvement is likely through institutional rearrangement, including better pricing. Limiting entry to either large or pleasant places is seen as a form of monopoly. It involves assigning quasi-property rights, based on that monopoly, to people already in those places, at the expense of local landlords and prospective immigrants. Certainly there are many examples of similar forms of quasi-property: the benefits from rent control and zoning, for example. But if we insist on assigning such quasi-property rights, who not go all the way and make such rights marketable (full property rights) in the same way tobacco acreage allotments can be bought and sold? [20] This will optimise what I see as a suboptimal position; for limitation of entry does involve loss in real income as well as redistribution.

REFERENCES

[1] I. Hoch, 'Urban Scale and Environmental Quality', in R. G. Ridker (ed.), *Resource and Environmental Implications of U.S. Population Growth* (Government Printing Office, Washington, 1972).
[2] I. Hoch, 'Income and City Size', *Urban Studies* (1972).
[3] R. F. Muth, *Cities and Housing* (Univ. of Chicago Press, 1969).
[4] L. B. Lave and E. P. Seskin, 'Air Pollution and Human Health', *Science*, (1970), pp. 723–32.
[5] R. Spirtas and H. J. Levin, *Characteristics of Particulate Patterns 1957–1966* (National Air Pollution Control Admin., Pub. AP-61, 1970), p. 13.
[6] J. N. Morgan, I. A. Sirageldin and N. Baerwaldt, 'Survey Res. Center Monograph' 43 (Univ. of Michigan, 1966), Table S-3, 80.
[7] M. E. Beesley, 'The Value of Time Spent in Traveling: New Evidence', *Economica* (1965).
[8] A. M. Voorhees, *et al.*, 'Factors in Work-trip Lengths', *Highway Research Record* 141 (1966), pp. 24–6.
[9] J. Jacobs, *The Death and Life of Great American Cities* (Random House, N.Y., 1961), pp. 10, 203–5, 208–17.
[10] U.S. Bureau of the Census, Census of Population: 1970, General Population Characteristics. PC(1)-B1, App. B, 8.
[11] Jacobs, *op. cit.*, pp. 205–7.
[12] R. C. Schmitt, 'Density, Health and Social Disorganization', *J. Amer. Institute of Planners* (1966), pp. 38–40.
[13] H. H. Winsborough, 'The Social Consequences of High Population Density', in T. R. Ford and G. F. De Jong (eds.), *Social Demography* (Prentice-Hall, N.J., 1970), pp. 84–90.
[14] O. R. Galle, W. R. Gove and J. M. McPherson, 'Population Density and Pathology: What are the Relations for Man?', *Science* (1972), pp. 23–30.
[15] J. L. Freedman, 'Population Density, Juvenile Delinquency and Mental Illness in New York City', paper prepared for the Commission on Population Growth and the American Future, Commission research volume on population distribution, Gov. Printing Office, Washington (1972).
[16] R. J. Hickey, D. E. Boyce, E. B. Harner and R. C. Clelland, 'Ecological Statistical Studies Concerning Environmental Pollution and Chronic Disease', Institute of Electrical and Electronic Engineers Transactions on Geoscience Electronics, Vol. GE-8. No. 4 (1970), pp. 186–202.
[17] L. C. Thurow and E. B. Lucas, *The American Distribution of Income: A Structural Problem* (Joint Econ. Committee, Washington, 1972), p. 9.
[18] J. Margolis, review of S. Kuznets, 'Income and Wealth of the United States' *J. Pol. Econ.* (1954), pp. 443–4.
[19] *New York Times*, 17 May 1972, p. 49.
[20] M. Clawson. 'Why Not Sell Zoning and Rezoning?' (legally, that is), *Cry California* (1966/67), pp. 9, 39.

Discussion of Paper by Irving Hoch

Formal Discussant: Tulkens. Hoch's paper seeks to demonstrate two inter-related theses: (a) that with an increase in urban scale (the latter being measured, say, by the number of city inhabitants, N), there is a net decline in the quality of life Q, i.e. there exists a functional relation $Q = f(N)$ with $dQ/dN < 0$; (b) that this decline in the quality of life raises the equilibrium level of wages (w_E), for the same type of work, in the labour markets across cities of various sizes, i.e. $w_E = g(Q)$ with $dw_E/dQ < 0$ or, using the first relationship above, $w_E = g[f(N)]$ with $(dw_E/dQ)(dQ/dN) > 0$.

The second thesis is presented in Section 3.2, first in theoretical terms and then empirically (see Table 3.7). As regards the first thesis, no explicit theory is offered, but the hypothesis is put directly to statistical test in Section 3.3 of the paper. Here, various components of what one would intuitively call the quality of the environment (both physical and social) are confronted with urban scale parameters. While the author deals here with a *vector* of quality indicators, he alternatively looks (in Section 3.2) for a *scalar* measure of the quality of life: this is found indirectly in the presumed equilibrium wage effects of the urban environment, and it is used in Table 3.8 as a deflator for personal income data.

I shall concentrate the present discussion on methodological and theoretical aspects of the second thesis and of its corollary on the scalar indicator of quality of life. A final comment is concerned with the regressions on urban criminal behaviour.

The author's interesting thesis can be interpreted in terms of the classical supply and demand analysis of equilibrium wages – for a given profession in a given city – by specifying the labour demand function as

$$L_D = v(w,N), \text{ with } \partial L_D/\partial w < 0 \text{ and } \partial L_D/\partial N > 0,$$

(where L_D denotes the quantities of labour demanded), and the labour supply (L_D) function as

$$L_S = h(w,Q), \text{ with } \partial L_S/\partial w > 0 \text{ and } \partial L_S/\partial Q > 0.$$

The positive sign in the last partial derivative is meant to reflect the postulated reactions of the labour supply to the quality of life in the city. However, since it has been hypothesised before that $Q = f(N)$ with $dQ/dN < 0$, the supply function may take the form:

$$L_S = z(w,N), \text{ with } \partial L_S/\partial w > 0 \text{ and } \partial L_S/\partial N < 0.$$

In Fig. 3D.1, the co-ordinates of point E give the equilibrium wage and employment in the city considered, at a given time.

Consider now a larger city at the same time, where the labour market for the same profession exhibits the same general supply and demand characteristics. Under the above hypotheses, the supply and demand curves must now lie respectively to the left and to the right of their previous positions. The new equilibrium E' clearly results in a higher wage rate.

In his paper, the author is careful enough *not* to interpret any increase in the equilibrium wage rate as a reflection of the workers' reaction to the inter-urban difference in quality of life (which itself results from the change in city size). Indeed, in the framework sketched out above, there is an identification problem. This is clearly illustrated by comparing Fig. 3D.1 with Figs. 3D.2 and 3D.3. They show that the extent to which the curves L_D and L_S respond to changes in city size, determines whether any increase in the equilibrium wage is to be (mainly) attributed to the demand

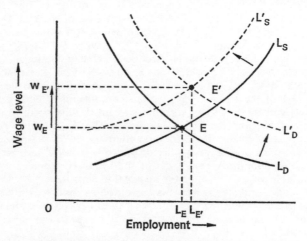

FIG. 3D.1   Relationship between Wages and Employment:
Both Demand and Supply as Important Determinants

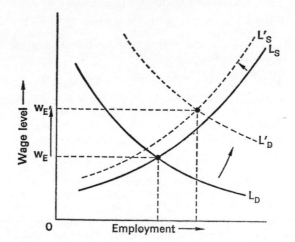

FIG. 3D.2   Relationship between Wages and Employment: Demand as Major Determinant for labour (Fig. 3D.2), or (mainly) to the supply of labour (Fig. 3D.3), or to *both* (Fig. 3D.1). By only observing the wage differences across cities, it is thus impossible to sort out the quality of life effects from any other effects (typically on the demand side) entailed by changes in city size.

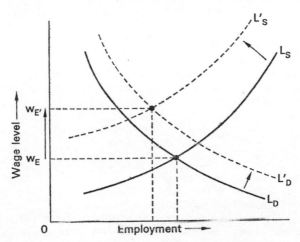

FIG. 3D.3   Relationship between Wages and Employment:
Supply as Major Determinant

In order to avoid this problem, the author makes two strong assumptions: (a) the labour supply is infinitely elastic with respect to the wage rate; (b) there is a minimum wage level, P_O, which is the same for all cities, and which corresponds to the equilibrium wage that would prevail under a 'perfect' environment, i.e. in the absence of any quality of life effects. It is clear that these assumptions enable all inter-city wage differences to be attributed to the suppliers' behaviour, irrespective of any shifts in demand. One should, however, question them. Assumption (a) clearly cannot be applied to all professions. The quality of life effect is estimated from the seven selected professions appearing in Table 3.4 and must thus be treated as a rather partial measure of society's overall reaction to urban disamenities. In other words, the effect that quality of life degradation is likely to have on labour behaviour might differ between professions. To adequately take this into account, the entire labour market in each city should be included, and then an infinite elasticity of supply could not hold simultaneously for all professions. As for assumption (b), which the author justifies on the grounds of a Ricardian hypothesis of population growth, it is difficult to maintain during the second half of the 20th century.

The validity of these assumptions can be further questioned on factual grounds (a labour economist's opinion would clearly be more informed than my own). However, there is also a methodological answer: this is to tackle the identification problem itself and thereby to dispense with these doubtful assumptions. We are indeed dealing here with a simultaneous model whose structural form is

$$\begin{cases} L_D = v(w, N) \\ L_S = h(w, Q) \\ L_S = L_D \\ Q = f(N). \end{cases}$$

Replacing L_S and L_D by L, we have three endogenous variables (L, w, Q) and one exogenous one N; the model is thus underidentified. In order to have it identified, two additional and independent explanatory variables, say A and B, could be introduced in some of the structural relations so that the reduced form

$$\begin{cases} L = a(N, A, B) \\ w = b(N, A, B) \\ Q = c(N, A, B) \end{cases}$$

could be estimated. Returning to the structural form, the ratio between the parameters of the variables Q and w in the supply function would provide the exact effect of the quality of life magnitude on the equilibrium wage, after due allowance for all other effects.

Although the author has performed an admirable task in his data collection, it is insufficient to enable the above procedure to be applied. However, the strength of the assumptions needed to avoid it make his current results at best exploratory. Without the use of more refined techniques, I doubt that we can recommend his quality of life index as a well-established measure.

At a more general level, one can now ask: is the labour market the best place to measure the effects of quality of life? The answer clearly depends upon the kinds of 'effects' that one is interested in. It is not only the price of labour that is affected by the same phenomenon, e.g. rents. But what do we want to infer from such measurements? In particular, suppose we had a 'quality of life' index estimated from rents rather than from wages; could we also use it as a deflator for personal income, interchangeably with the wage-based index used in Table 3.8? – or should one combine the two indexes? It seems that no well-founded welfare value can be inferred from these measurements of particular price effects; as suggested by the author, they reflect at best the compensation that labourers succeed in obtaining for the disamenities of this imperfect world. But this is probably not equal to (specifically, much less than) what society as a whole would be willing to pay for changing the quality of life. From that point of view, the correct alternative seems to be the one alluded to by the author elsewhere in his paper: to associate values (i.e. prices) directly to each of the components of the quality of life.

I would finally like to raise the question of private expenditure as an explanatory variable in the relationship between crime and health, and urban size. Such expenditure is alluded to in the text as a 'resulting implication' of the observed statistical relations. But does not the absence of those expenditures from the estimate introduce a bias in the urban scale variable? Their explicit introduction would, in addition, provide interesting indications of the substitutability between private expenditure and public-good variables (e.g. city size) – information that could be used in normative propositions about the optimal city size.

Hoch replied by saying that the major question raised by Tulkens was whether there was an identification problem in the empirical analysis. He noted, however, that wages were related to total populations and not to quantities in specific occupations, which would be the usual setting for an identification problem. Put in Tulkens' terms, the relation of w to *exogenous* N was seen as legitimate, reflecting long-term rather than short-term effects. He discerned a possible, relatively minor, problem of bias if there were a short-term systematic relation between population growth and wage increases on the one hand, and S.M.S.A. population size on the other. But this did not seem to be the case, empirically.

Beckerman remarked that it was not at all clear how the cross-section results obtained by the author, which seek to explain differences in the quality of life between cities, could be used to obtain any measure of the changes in the quality of life in cities over time. In an extreme case, for example, it was conceivable that the relative quality of life could be exactly the same in all the cities measured by the author's methods and could yet deteriorate uniformly over time. In such cases the author's measure would show nothing at all. It was not merely that the use of cross-section data was a bad approximation and was likely to underestimate the change in the quality of life over time; cross-section data really had no bearing at all on any inter-temporal changes in the quality of life.

Mills said that, although most people agreed that adjustments to equilibrium city size took a long time, the author's calculation of the costs of non-market disamenities would only be correct if the city was in equilibrium. The fact that there has been continuing net migration to cities clearly showed that they were not in equilibrium. It was the excess of urban wages and amenities over rural wages and disamenities that was inducing migration. This was evidence that the excess more than compensated for any urban disamenities. What was needed was an estimate of the speed at which city size adjusted to disequilibrium. It would then be possible to calculate the wage rates and populations in cities of various sizes just necessary to compensate for any urban disamenities.

Lave agreed with Mills and added that if the labour supply was not in equilibrium, the author's conclusions might represent a misinterpretation of the nature of the data.

Cameron pointed out that the paper suggested that high wages in large urban areas represented compensation for unwanted externalities. However, while that might be true to some extent, there were also other explanations. He suggested three possible causal factors.

(a) The nature of the product in a large urban centre was very different from that in a small urban centre. This made it extremely difficult to compare wages per unit of output for a given skill across city sizes. This was particularly true when the large centres were those in which risks were taken and where there were innovations in both products and in production processes. The large urban centre might then represent an investment in risk compared to the standard production processes used in smaller centres.

(b) If large cities have had persistently high wages this will probably have affected their production functions. They will substitute capital for labour and this will affect productivity and hence wages.

(c) Why do people in the U.K., particularly professionals, want to go to London? Many of them accept a wage which, after allowing for externalities, is lower than they could get elsewhere. He suggested that they might be investing in their future and that we should therefore recognise the possibility of investing in human capital thus maximising the individual's long run income.

He concluded by observing that the difficulty with explicitly and publicly selecting growth centres was that it often diverted attention from the solution of real problems as communities which had not been so selected 'fought it out' with central governments and attempted to justify why they should have been included. Something rather like this occurred in 1963–64 when the British Government specified particular growth centres in Scotland and the North-East of England. A more viable alternative might be for the central government to have no explicit policy but an implicit strategy which then guided the geographical allocation of public funds. This was profoundly undemocratic but might generate greater benefits in the long-run for any given region.

Prud'homme queried the author's usage of income data. A large part of his analysis had been conducted in terms of wages, yet a large part of his data had been given in terms of income. Wage income was clearly only a part of total income. Had the author explored the possibility of a relationship between non-wage income and city size?

Rothenberg added a final comment to the wages-city size controversy. He argued that if Central Place Theory was correct then centres of different size should specialise in different kinds of functions. Each centre would thus have a different mix of labour qualities and this might account for many of the observed differences in earned incomes.

On a more philosophical level *Machlup* wondered whether economists were not guilty of imputing their own tastes and preferences to the people who came into, stayed in or left a city because of its good or bad quality of life. He felt there must be a trade-off between physical and cultural suffocation: some people did not mind breathing bad air if only they could listen to an opera or watch a dirty peep show. The indifference curves for these goods and bads were different for different people. If, on the other hand, we did not impute our own preferences to the actual and potential workers in the city, but tried to derive their 'actual' preferences from those income differentials that are not explained by all the other variables which we choose to include in our equations, he was afraid we might mistakenly attribute our residuals to the so-called quality of life in the city.

Kolm raised the question of congestion taxes. He argued that taxing externalities (or congestion) within cities would not lead to the optimum city size when migration and the possibility of altering the number of cities were allowed for. He used the following model to illustrate this point.

He first of all assumed that there were N identical persons living in identical cities of population size n. There were therefore N/n such cities. He assumed that the total population N was given. It was city size n which we wished to optimise. Within a city, each citizen imposed on every other citizen an external cost v (congestion and external diseconomies of various kinds, net of any external economies that might exist). There were no technological externalities between cities. Each city provided public services (in the form of public goods, i.e. collective consumption) at a given cost c which was independent of city size.

Each person thus experienced external costs of $v(n-1)$. The total external costs within a city were clearly $v(n-1)n$. The total cost for a city was this plus c. Total social costs for the N/n cities were thus $[c + v(n-1)n]$ N/n. This was at a minimum when

$$c/n + v(n-1) \qquad (1)$$

was at a minimum.

The term n was spontaneously determined by individual choices of location (this was a long-run equilibrium). With no *ad hoc* personal taxation, individuals minimised $v(n-1)$ which was different from the social minimand given in Equation 1. Each individual *created* an external cost of $v(n-1)$. If asked to pay this amount, he faced a total cost of $2v(n-1)$, which was still different from the social minimand given in Equation 1. The result would be the same as if there was no tax; there would be a tendency for people to scatter ($a = 1$) if $v > 0$. If external economies were higher than any diseconomies, i.e. $v < 0$, the population would concentrate and form only one city, i.e. $n = N$.

However, there was a way to make individuals conform to the social optimum: this was to tax individuals, not for the external costs they produced but for the costs of public services. The tax would not be levied at marginal individual costs, which was zero, but at the average cost of public services c/n. Each individual would then face a total cost equal to Equation 1, the social minimand.

When Equation 1 was at a minimum c/n would be equal to vn (the minimum of a sum of two terms whose product was constant) which was none the less equal to $v(n-1)$ when n was large enough. But this was a property of the optimum; the way to reach it from a non-optimal point was to tax at the level c/n and not $v(n-1)$.

The result was the same whether the cost of public services depended upon city size, n, or congestion costs had another structure. For example, if c was replaced by $f(n)$, with some increasing returns to scale so that $f(n) - nf'(n) > 0$, and individuals experienced external costs of $g(n)$ in a city of size n, the total social cost becomes $[f(n) + n g(n)] N/n$, which will be at a minimum when

$$f(n)/n + g(n) \qquad (2)$$

is at a minimum.

The social cost caused by an individual thus seems to be equal to the marginal cost of public services $f'(n)$ plus any external costs $(n-1) g'(n)$. If individuals are faced with such a charge they will try to minimize $f'(n) +$

$(n-1) g'(n) + g(n)$. However, Equation 2 shows that the tax which makes individuals behave according to the social optimum consists of not taxing externalities but of taxing public services at their average cost $f(n)/n$. [1]*

Mills disagreed with Kolm's analysis. He felt that it relied on a public good which had been defined to exhibit very strong and very special increasing returns with respect to city size. His result thus simply showed that he had one dimension on which there were decreasing returns (e.g. some kind of pollution dimension), and one on which there were increasing returns, and that the tax should clearly take account of both.

REFERENCES

[1] S. C. Kolm, 'Laissez faire quand même', *Revue d'Economie Politique*, 4 (1972).

* Again, at the optimum $f(n)/n = f'(n) + ng'(n)$, and if n is large $f(n)/n + g(n) \simeq f'(n) + (n-1)g'(n) + g(n)$. But this is a property of the optimum, not an indication of the tax conducive to it.

4 Migration and Urban Change*

Lester B. Lave, Judith R. Lave and Eugene P. Seskin

4.1 *INTRODUCTION*

American cities continue to grow, but many are getting poorer fiscally and some face bankruptcy. People continue to migrate to urban areas, but many observers agree that the quality of life in major cities has been declining during the last decade. The problems of crime, housing, ghettoised blacks, declining tax bases, non-resident workers, education, and transportation have occupied many politicians, journalists and urban researchers.

There is no lack of suggestions for improving the state of our cities. The difficulty is that many of the policies which have been tried have contributed to the problem, instead of alleviating it. For example, the construction of limited access highways in the 1950s meant that the middle- and upper-income families could live outside the city and commute to work. Thus, this improvement in transportation tended to pull the city's tax base apart. Current proposals to construct mass transit systems with substantial subsidies threaten to complete this trend by stimulating even low-income people to leave the city in search of less expensive housing and more amenities.

It should be evident that goodwill and energy are not sufficient to stop the decay of the cities. Instead we must know the underlying causes of urban growth and migration. This research is focused on explaining some of the causes of the population change in major cities. Population change can be characterised as the sum of four processes. The first is (net) rural-urban migration. The second is movement from one city to another. The third is the relative birth and death rates in the city. The fourth is net movement from central city to 'ring' (the area within the Standard Metropolitan Statistical Area but outside the major city).

Here we will examine each of these four areas, citing relevant literature and exploring some of the models which have been developed to characterise the processes. Our primary attention will be given to the movement of people from the central city to the ring. A utility maximisation model for the household is used to motivate the

* This research was supported by grants from Resources for the Future, Inc. and the R. K. Mellon Charitable Trusts. Any opinions and errors are those of the authors.

empirical study of rates of migration from central city to ring for 71 S.M.S.A.s. This migration is important in the American context because of the different fiscal responsibilities and revenue raising capabilities that exist across the political boundaries.

4.2 *MIGRATION FROM OUTSIDE THE S.M.S.A.*

Important sources of population change within an S.M.S.A. are migration from one S.M.S.A. to another and from rural (outside any S.M.S.A.) to urban areas (within an S.M.S.A.). Migration resulted (by 1970) in 73 per cent of the population in the United States living within the boundaries of 243 S.M.S.A.s and 50 per cent of the population living within 50 miles of a sea coast (including the Great Lakes) [1]. Thorough knowledge of these population movements is crucial to our understanding the development of our cities. While it is not our purpose here to study them in depth, we would like to discuss briefly some of the models previously developed to study them.

Consider first the models developed to study urban-urban migration. Many of these studies employ variants of the gravity model in which movement between a pair of cities is hypothesised to vary with the product of the city populations and inversely with the distance between the cities (or the square of distance) [2, 3]. The gravity model is able to account for most of the transportation or migration between cities, but it is devoid of any suggestion as to why migration takes place or how to modify it. By knowing the population of various cities and the distance between them, one can predict movements, but the model has no information as to why these movements have increased over time or what can be done to influence them.

Recently attempts have been made to interpret gravity models in economic terms [3, 4, 5]. For instance, distance can be thought of as a measure of travel time and cost, while city size can be thought of as a measure of the interaction between cities (on a personal or business level), as well as an indication of the opportunity for finding employment in a city. However, these interpretations are not entirely satisfactory and do not translate directly into variables which increase our understanding of the structure of travel or of migration.

There have been a set of models developed by economists which view migration as the result of purposeful behaviour in that people migrate to improve their condition and their family's condition. Economists have tended to focus on income differentials and improved job opportunities as the basic reasons for migrating and have thus viewed migration as a response to geographically separate labour markets. (Age, sex, race and level of schooling are considered to be important in determining an individual's ability to take advantage of income differentials.) Distance is considered to be an important variable since it can stand as a surrogate for the cost of leaving friends and family as well as the ability to gain information about geographically distant labour markets. Migration can also be viewed as an investment in human capital in which the cost of movement and any new training costs are viewed as the major costs and expected increases in future earnings as the major return [6, 7]. This view is probably most appropriate for rural-urban migration.

Economic models of migration have been used to study migration across the 9 broad census regions [8]; interstate migration [9]; South-North migration [7]; and rural-urban migration in Colombia [10]. These models have explained a significant amount of the variation in migration rates, with a consistent result being that migrants respond positively to earning differentials and negatively to distance. Some of these studies have included environmental conditions as well as socio-economic variables to explain migration rates. In particular, Greenwood [9] found that a temperate climate is an important factor in attracting in-migrants.

In summary, there are a number of different models which can provide predictions of the magnitude of migration into an S.M.S.A. We prefer the economic models which have implications for public policy. These models show that migration into an S.M.S.A. is related to wage differentials, unemployment differentials and environmental factors. It is possible to extend these models into a utility maximisation framework in which other factors likely to affect a migrant's preferences, both economic and environmental, can be included explicitly.

4.3 BIRTH AND DEATH RATES

4.3.1 BIRTH RATES

Economic demographers have attempted to explain variations in the birth rate by variables such as desired family size, infant mortality rates and uncertainty [11, 12, 13, 14]. The underlying framework is one of utility maximisation by the parents. They are alleged to decide on desired family size after considering the opportunity income of the wife (what she would lose in order to have the child, including consideration of the cost of child care), the value of child labour, the family income (viewing the child as a consumption good), the costs of raising the child (including those associated with education, clothing, food, medical care and recreation), social institutions (including provisions for retirement, welfare payments for children, tax benefits, and inheritance laws), and the expense and ease of contraception and abortion. To attain the desired family size, they must take account of death rates, from the rate of stillborns to the mortality rate for older children; their decision is conditioned by the family's education and other factors influencing their non-economic perception of desirable family size. They must also account for uncertainty in the form of the actual realisation of mortality among their children (thus they might plan for more children than they would desire in the absence of uncertainty), uncertainty about the values of the factors influencing desired family size (such as income), and uncertainty in contraception.

There is empirical evidence that each of the factors described above does influence the birth rate. Models based on these factors are able to explain most of the variation in birth rates, as, for example, in Puerto Rico [11]. However, unexplained secular shifts in desired family size from time to time or from country to country do occur.

These rational models of fertility lead to conclusions that are quite different from simple extrapolations of population growth. Economic models have explained the majority of the variation in fertility rates, but there is no definite evidence differentiating between the economic rationalists and the population explosion pessimists. Little work has been done to estimate such models for the current U.S. population [14]. However, if one is interested in short-term forecasts of fertility, they can be approximated well by simple extrapolations of age-race-income specific birth rates. Such an extrapolation ignores the theoretical issues, but should predict well in the short tun.

4.3.2 DEATH RATES

Determinants of geographical mortality rates have been investigated extensively by epidemiologists [15]. Recently, Lave and Seskin [16, 17] have examined factors affecting mortality in 117 United States S.M.S.A.s in 1960. They hypothesised that the total mortality rate (number dying divided by total population) will depend upon characteristics (both present and past) of the individuals in the study population, including their habits and exposures, and on the characteristics of the environment. Important factors include age, sex, genetic factors, nutrition, smoking, exercise habits, income, race, quality of medical care, occupation, population density, weather, housing and air pollution.

4.3.2.1 *Total Deaths*

The initial result of regressing the total mortality rate (MR) on the arithmetic mean of 26 biweekly suspended particulate readings (for each city) (*Mean P*), the smallest of 26 biweekly sulphate readings (*Min S*), the population density of the S.M.S.A. (P/M^2), the proportion of the population which is non-white ($\%NW$), and the proportion of the population which is 65 and older ($\% \geq 65$) is shown below. Eighty-two point six per cent of the variation in the mortality rate across S.M.S.A.s is explained by the regression

$$MR = 19 \cdot 376 + 0 \cdot 039 \text{ } Mean \text{ } P + 0 \cdot 069 \text{ } Min \text{ } S + 0 \cdot 001 \text{ } P/M^2 +$$
(total)   (2·43)   (3·06)   (1·41)
$$0 \cdot 041 \text{ } \%NW + 0 \cdot 696 \geq \%65 \tag{1}$$
   (5·77)   (18·98)

and each of the coefficients (except population density) is statistically significant. The figures in parentheses are the *t* statistic (the estimated coefficient divided by its standard error).

Since the estimated coefficients depend directly on the measurement units, it is useful to state the implications of the estimated coefficients as elasticities (in unit-free terms). A 10 per cent decrease in the mean level of particulate pollution is associated with a 0·53 per cent decrease in the total death rate (a decrease of 11·81 micrograms per cubic metre in the annual mean level of particulate pollution is associated with a decrease of 0·48 deaths per 10,000). A 10 per cent decrease in the minimum level of sulphate pollution is associated with a reduction in the total mortality rate of 0·37 per cent (a decrease of 0·47 micrograms per cubic metre in the biweekly minimum sulphate reading is associated with a decrease of 0·33 deaths per 10,000). A 10 per cent decrease in the population density is associated with a 0·08 per cent decrease in the total death rate (a decrease of 75·62 P/M^2 is associated with a reduction in total deaths of 0·08 per 10,000). A 10 per cent decrease in the percentage of non-whites in the population is associated with a reduction of 0·56 per cent in the total death rate (a 1·25 percentage point decrease in the proportion of non-whites is associated with a reduction in total deaths of 0·51 per 10,000). A 10 per cent decrease in the percentage of people 65 and older in the population is associated with a reduction of 6·32 per cent in the total mortality rate (a 0·84 percentage decrease in the proportion of older people is associated with a reduction in total deaths of 5·77 per 10,000). These results show that the mortality rate is significantly related to air pollution and that a 10 per cent increase in air pollution is estimated to increase the mortality rate by 0·90 per cent (0·53 per cent + 0·37 per cent).

Also shown in Table 4.1 is an expanded regression where seven 'urban' variables which reflect some of the available medical resources and some of the additional socio-economic aspects of the S.M.S.A. are added as explanatory variables. The coefficient of determination rises slightly (from 0·826 to 0·866) and there is little effect on the previous estimated coefficients. Pollution variables do lose some importance. The number of hospital beds in the S.M.S.A. per capita is positively associated with the death rate; this is presumably

TABLE 4.1

DEATH RATE ANALYSIS

Regression	1	2	3	4	5	6
Dependent Variable	Total	Total	<1 Year	<1 Year	<28 Days	<28 D:
R^2	0·826	0·866	0·544	0·626	0·276	0·3?
Independent Variables:						
Constant	19·376	46·949	184·410	153·572	148·538	103·9?
Min P			0·356 (2·69)	0·322 (2·53)		
Mean P	0·039 (2·43)	0·026 (1·73)			0·081 (1·59)	0·05 (1·05
Min S	0·069 (3·06)	0·032 (1·43)			0·107 (1·53)	0·13 (1·79
Mean S						
P/M^2	0·001 (1·41)	0·000 (0·36)	0·001 (0·45)	0·003 (1·37)	0·001 (0·54)	0·00 (1·55
% NW	0·041 (5·77)	0·029 (3·86)	0·184 (6·42)	0·189 (5·84)	0·096 (3·86)	0·08 (3·01
%≥65	0·696 (18·98)	0·653 (17·82)				
% Poor			0·165 (3·46)	0·178 (2·54)	0·064 (1·58)	0·08: (1·35)
Beds		1·093 (1·95)		5·195 (2·35)		4·00? (2·07)
MDs		− 0·515 (− 0·24)		− 31·848 (− 3·75)		− 18·247 (− 2·45)
% Urban		− 0·004 (− 0·60)		0·037 (1·33)		0·049 (1·98)
% Rural		− 0·084 (− 2·62)		− 0·199 (− 1·58)		− 0·141 (− 1·28)
% Rich		0·011 (0·67)		0·039 (0·46)		− 0·020 (− 0·27)
% Ed		− 0·044 (− 3·58)		0·042 (0·94)		0·038 (0·91)
Med		− 0·918 (− 0·64)		− 3·748 (− 0·68)		0·373 (0·08)

a demand phenomenon. Physicians per capita is insignificant, as is the proportion of the population living in urban areas, the proportion of the population with high incomes, and whether the S.M.S.A. has a medical school. The proportion of the population living in rural areas within the S.M.S.A. is an extremely significant variable and, as expected, is negatively associated with the death rate. The proportion of people with a high school education is also a significant variable and, as expected, is negatively associated with the death rate.

4.3.2.2 *Infant Deaths*

Data were analysed for two classes of infant mortality rates (per 10,000 live births): the rate for infants under one year, and the rate for infants under 28 days.

Equation 2 regresses the under-one-year infant death rate on one measure of pollution (the minimum particulate level), the percentage of non-whites in the population and the percentage of poor families in the population.

$$MR = 185 \cdot 060 + 0 \cdot 369 \ Min \ P + 0 \cdot 186 \ \%NW + 0 \cdot 160 \ \% \ Poor \quad (2)$$
$$(<1 \ \text{Year}) \qquad (2 \cdot 86) \qquad (6 \cdot 55) \qquad (3 \cdot 45)$$

Just over half (54·3 per cent) of the variation in the mortality rate is accounted for across the 117 S.M.S.A.s. The coefficient of the pollution variable indicates that a decrease of 4·55 micrograms per cubic metre (10 per cent) in the biweekly minimum level of particulate pollution is associated with a decrease of 1·64 (0·65 per cent) deaths per 100,000 live births in the under-one-year category.

Equation 2 is shown as Regression 3 in Table 4.1; Regression 4 adds the 'urban' variables. R^2 rises from 0·544 to 0·626 and the previous coefficients are little changed. Hospital beds per capita is still positively associated with the less-than-one-year death rate, although physicians per capita is significant and negatively associated. The proportion of the population living in urban and rural areas within the S.M.S.A. have the expected signs, although neither is significant. High income, a high school education and the presence of a medical school appear to have no effect.

Equation 3 regresses the under-28-day infant mortality rate on mean particulates, minimum sulphates, and the proportion of non-whites and of poor

$$MR = 149 \cdot 054 + 0 \cdot 083 \ Mean \ P + 0 \cdot 120 \ Mean \ S + 0 \cdot 098 \ \%NW +$$
$$(<28 \ \text{Days}) \qquad (1 \cdot 64) \qquad (1 \cdot 82) \qquad (4 \cdot 04)$$
$$0 \cdot 058 \ \% \ Poor \qquad\qquad\qquad\qquad\qquad (3)$$
$$(1 \cdot 50)$$

families. The R^2 of 0·274, while statistically significant, is less good than in the previous regression. The coefficients of the pollution variables indicate that a decrease of 11·81 micrograms per cubic metre (10 per cent) in the annual mean level of particulate pollution is associated with a decrease of 0·98 (0·52 per cent) deaths per 10,000 live births in the under-28-day infant group; a decrease of 0·47 micrograms per cubic metre (10 per cent) in the biweekly minimum level of sulphates is associated with a decrease of 0·56 (0·30 per cent) deaths per 10,000 live births in this category.

The less-than-28-day mortality rate is shown as Regression 5 in Table 4.1. The estimated coefficients are changed little by adding the 'urban' variables, while R^2 rises from 0·276 to 0·378. The estimated urban variables are similar to those for the under-one-year mortality rate.

4.3.3 CONCLUSION

Both birth and death rates depend on the structure and characteristics of cities and their citizens. The utility maximisation framework for fertility rates focuses on income, employment opportunities for the mother and the cost of raising the child; the birth rate is closely related to economic conditions in the city. The equivalent formulation for death rates would be a utility maximisation framework for decisions concerning health care. This formulation is too complicated to be included here (for a discussion see 'A Model for the Delivery of Medical Care to the Urban Poor' [18]). The function relating death rates to income and population characteristics demonstrates the close relation between urban structure and mortality rates. Thus, it is apparent that changes in urban attributes, family income and population characteristics will influence population trends through both birth and death rates.

4.4 *THE MIGRATION FROM CENTRAL CITY TO RING*

The American people are very mobile. Approximately 20 per cent of them change residences each year. While most of these moves are within the same or adjacent neighbourhoods, some of them are between the central city and the suburbs and a few are movements into other S.M.S.A.s [19]. The result of this mobility has been not only the urbanisation of America that we pointed out in Section 2, but also the suburbanisation of America. By 1970, of all people living within the boundaries of an S.M.S.A., 64 million lived in the central city and 76 million lived in the ring [1]. In this section we will try to explain some aspects of this suburbanisation. First, we will examine movements from central city to ring. Then we will look at the two-way flows of movements from city to ring and from ring to city by attempting to explain the net migration rate. Finally, we will examine the location decision of those moving into the S.M.S.A. in an effort to find those factors that induce them to locate in the ring instead of the central city.

The basic theoretical framework for studying these decisions is a modification of Alonso's model where the location decision depends on place of employment, income, family size and the structure of taxes and prices [20]. The family is seen to behave as if it were maximising its utility subject to a budget constraint. Arguments in the utility function are public goods (some of which are environmental and some of which are supplied by the city), private goods whose prices are a function of the distance from the central business district (C.B.D.), private goods whose prices do not change with distance from the C.B.D., and commuting time. The budget constraint is that income (presumably permanent income) is spent on taxes, both types of private goods and commuting. In this formulation public goods include air pollution, population density and other environmental variables as well as government supplied services, such as education, police protection and parks. Many of these public goods change with the distance from the C.B.D.: air pollution decreases and governmental services depend on the political subdivision. Housing, attendance at theatres and sporting events and some services are examples of private goods whose price depends on the distance from the C.B.D. Commuting time and expense are directly related to distance from the C.B.D.

Since many of the goods in the utility function change with distance from the C.B.D. and since the prices of some of the private goods change with distance from the C.B.D., one output of the conditional maximisation process is determination of the distance of residential location from the C.B.D. This formulation simplifies many of the complexities of the urban environment by making the variables and prices continuous functions of distance from the C.B.D. It has some obvious advantages in simplifying the maximisation and in enabling a deterministic solution of equilibrium residential location.

This formulation supposes the existence of only a single C.B.D. where employment and shopping are concentrated. This is no longer a reasonable approximation for major U.S. cities. There is no conceptual problem in incorporating a number of C.B.D.s, although the algebra gets quite complicated. The complication does not illuminate the theoretical analysis, nor does it seem essential in modelling city to ring migration. At this point little is gained from a formal treatment of this utility maximisation problem. The first- and second-order conditions have the usual implications concerning the equality of the ratio of marginal utility to price across goods and services. The problem is sufficiently large that one must know the size of the various partial derivatives of the function in order to get unequivocal statements about signs. Some of the partial derivatives are contained in sociological investigations, while we uncover others in our analysis of migration below.

4.4.1 URBAN EXTERNALITIES

Rothenberg [21] and Mills and de Ferranti [22] have emphasised the negative externalities that arise when additional people locate in a large city. Congestion and air pollution eventually offset the economies of agglomeration and establish an upper limit on city size. Congestion has been treated extensively in economic literature [21, 23].

Air pollution is caused by industry and the concentration of people, i.e. by the existence of the city itself. Stationary emitters include electricity generating plants, incinerators, heating units (either industrial or residential) and other industrial processes, such as smelting. Mobile emitters consist of automobiles, trucks, buses and other transportation vehicles (such as airplanes and motorcycles). With the exception of the industrial base of a city, the effects of the other factors generating pollutants should be roughly proportional to city population and population density.

Elaborate diffusion models have been constructed which predict the air quality at a point in the city from the quality of air entering the city, the location of city emitters and meteorological factors, such

TABLE 4.2

AIR POLLUTION ANALYSIS

Regression	1	2	3	4
Dependent Variable:	Mean P	Mean P	Mean S	Mean S
R^2	0·352	0·358	0·408	0·429
Independent Variables:				
Constant	284·147	281·044	7·350	8·485
Pop_o	0·010	0·010	0·002	0·002
	(2·13)	(2·10)	(2·68)	(2·56)
P/M^2_o	− 0·000	− 0·000	0·000	0·000
	(− 0·38)	(− 0·27)	(1·01)	(1·02)
Mfr. VA	6·763	7·578	1·931	2·123
	(0·99)	(1·05)	(2·16)	(2·30)
Humid.	− 1·778	− 1·748		
	(− 3·34)	(− 3·11)		
Wind	− 0·637	− 0·634	− 0·073	− 0·091
	(− 2·65)	(− 2·38)	(− 2·34)	(− 2·68)
Rain			0·038	0·040
			(1·85)	(1·73)
Cold	0·319	0·341	0·027	0·032
	(3·19)	(3·03)	(1·97)	(2·17)
Oil		− 7·298		1·414
		(− 0·45)		(0·63)
Coal		− 14·728		− 5·055
		(− 0·42)		(− 1·11)
Elec.		24·846		− 4·062
		(0·40)		(− 0·50)

as wind speed. We have analysed the relationship between air pollution and city characteristics as shown in Table 4.2. This might be thought of as a crude diffusion model or as a rough relationship between current city characteristics and the level of air pollution for that city. These relationships provide one more feedback loop relating city growth to undesirable environmental attributes, and thus to out-migration.

Table 4.2, Regression 1 shows the results of regressing the mean level of suspended particulates on certain urban and climatological characteristics of an S.M.S.A. Regression 2 adds three categories of fuels used for home heating. About one-third of the variation in the mean suspended particulate level in the 71 S.M.S.A.s is explained in the two regressions. Central city population is an important variable which positively affects the level of suspended particulates. However, neither population density nor manufacturing value added are significant variables (although the sign of the latter is 'correct'). Humidity and wind tend to lower the level of pollution, presumably by washing it out of the air or by blowing it away, and both are statistically significant. The number of days when it is cold raises the pollution level, probably because additional fuel must be used for heating. The characteristic home heating fuels are not significant variables affecting this type of pollution.

Regressions 3 and 4 are parallel regressions for the mean level of sulphates. About 40 per cent of the variation in the level of sulphates across the 71 S.M.S.A.s is explained in the regressions. Central city population continues to be an important variable. Here, population density has the 'correct' sign, but it is statistically insignificant. Manufacturing value added is statistically significant. The negative sign for wind indicates that it blows away the pollution, while the positive signs for rain and cold indicate that more fuel is burned under these conditions. Again, none of the heating fuels is significant.

These results indicate that air pollution is not closely related to general urban characteristics. Population is always an important variable, as are some of the climatological characteristics. However, it would be difficult to forecast the air pollution in a city from knowing only its urban characteristics. No doubt much better models will be developed in which the specific characteristics of an S.M.S.A.s manufacturing base and the existence of air pollution control laws (which were not terribly prevalent or effective in 1960) will be included.

4.4.2 CITY-RING MIGRATION

Between 1955 and 1960 many families moved their residence from the central city to suburb. With the 1960 central city population as a base, 14·3 per cent of total whites moved to the ring, 3·2 per cent of total non-whites (these are approximately the same proportions as the corresponding categories of males 14 years and over moving), 7·1 per cent of poor families (incomes less than $4,000), 16·1 per cent of rich families (incomes greater than $10,000), and 25·3 per cent of white males aged 25–34. These are substantial shifts and with the absence of compensating changes in the relative birth and death rates, movements from the ring to the central city, and in-migration from outside the S.M.S.A., the population of the central city became increasingly poor, old and non-white. This general trend was accompanied by substantial variation among cities. For example, in Miami 32·7 per cent of total whites moved to the ring while only 1·2 per cent did in El Paso.

4.4.2.1 *Sociological Models*

Intra-urban migration can be dichotomised into two decisions: (a) when to move and (b) where to move. Aspects of mobility have been studied intensively by sociologists. Their most important finding is that the desire to move is a function of family size, age of household head, current tenure (renter or owner), tenure preference and attitudes towards existing accommodations. Since these variables follow a natural pattern over the life cycle of the family, the 'life cycle' has become the focus of sociological investigations [24, 19, 25]. In addition, Wolpert [26] has conjectured that families move in response to environmental stresses.

Although 'when' (and also 'why') families move has been the subject of many studies, 'where' they choose to locate has not received much attention. Gravity models have been developed, but they have neither behavioural nor policy implications [19]. It has been hypothesised that people who move to the suburbs have chosen 'familism' over career or consumership as the most important aspect of their life style [27].

4.4.2.2 *Economic Models*

We argued above that the family can be thought of as employing a utility maximisation framework in choosing whether to move and, if so, where to locate. Changes in a family's age, size (and composition) and income as well as changes in the environment will alter the relative costs and benefits of moving. However, residential location is subject to neighbourhood externalities and is not a random process. Instead of finding expensive houses located next to shanties and wealthy families living next to poor ones, one finds not only neighbourhoods which are characterised by income and ethnic factors, but also neighbourhoods which tend to be homogeneous with respect to occupation, family size, age and the presence of small children. Since the homogeneity is the result of neighbourhood externalities and also implies similarity in other preferences, one might expect great gains if the neighbourhood were able to control the quality and level of governmental services (from education to garbage collection). In the absence of economies of scale in producing these government services, one would expect to find neighbourhoods forming their own political subdivisions, as Ellickson [28] has argued.

From 1890 to World War II small cities tended to merge with larger ones to form our major cities. Apparently, there were significant economies of scale in the production of government services (from police protection to recreation) so citizens of smaller cities benefited from mergers even though they lost control over the exact government services to be performed.

We investigate the decision to move from central city to ring, focusing on economic and environmental factors. The sociological results cited in the previous section are unlikely to be important in our investigation, since life-cycle variables should be approximately constant across cities and are unlikely to account for the variation in the migration rate to the ring. That migration rate is likely to be more sensitive to family income and environmental variables. In our empirical work, we investigate the migration rate for white males, aged 25–34 (a homogeneous group from a life-cycle viewpoint), and find results almost identical to those for all white migrants.

We have formulated two basic models of suburbanisation. In the first model we assume that the negative attributes of the central city push people to the ring; this is our 'city-push' model. The negative attributes of the central city might be thought of as irritating the family to the point where it migrates in desperation. A more rational family will consider both ring and city attributes in deciding to move. In our 'ring-city' model we represent the decision to move to the ring as a function of the difference in attributes between the ring and the central city.

The relevant categories of variables are easily specified. However, there are no clues as to the exact form of the function or the relative importance of the variables. The census contains information on a number of these variables and on others which are approximations of important variables. Unfortunately, still others are not measured. A major difficulty with the data is that for many variables only ten-year census information is collected. One would prefer to have observations on the variables at the time families were about to migrate. Instead, only the decennial characteristics are observable. The most important problem arises in computing the relevant population base, as discussed below. It is useful to deal with some of these problems in context so we turn to the 'city-push' models.

City-Push Models. The proportion of a group that chooses to move to the ring is assumed to depend upon the level of city air pollution, population density, crime rates and the proportion of non-whites. Taxes and job opportunities are important, but we specify these as differentials between ring and city, rather than as city variables. Particularly for taxation, the relative level must be the one entering into a family's decision. Unmeasured factors include the family size and composition (life cycle), the price of housing in the ring and in the city, public amenities and the availability of certain services in the ring. Those variables at our disposal are used to explain migration rates for seven groups: total whites, total non-whites, white males 14 years and older, non-white males 14 years and older, poor families, rich families, and white males aged 25–34. (This latter group is included because of its high mobility and because, as noted above, the variation in the stage of the life cycle for these men should not be large across S.M.S.A.s.) Results for all of these groups are shown in the tables, but we limit our discussion almost entirely to total whites and total non-whites. We will discuss two 'city-push' models for both whites and non-whites, respectively.

City-Push Models: Total Whites. The first regression is shown in Table 4.3 and reproduced below in Equation 4, where TW is the total number of whites moving from central city to ring divided by the central city population of whites; *Mean S* is the annual mean of sulphate pollution, a measure of air pollution in the city; $D1_c$, $D2_c$ and $D3_c$ are measures of population density (entered in a piecewise linear fashion); $\%NW_c$ is the proportion of the central city population which is non-white; $Crime_c$ is the 1960 city crime rate, Mfr_{r-c} is the difference between ring and city growth rates for jobs in manufacturing from 1954 to 1958; Tax_{r-c} is the difference in taxes per capita between ring and city for 1957; and $\bar{Y}_c$ is the median income of the central city. To take account of a possibly non-linear relationship between migration and population density, the density variable was split into three variables. The first includes the population density of all cities with fewer than 2,600 people per square mile (its value is zero for other cities), the second includes the density for all cities with 2,600 to 12,000 people per square mile (and is zero for other cities), and the third includes the density for all cities with more than 12,000 people per square mile (and is zero for other cities). The purpose of breaking up a variable in this way is to estimate a series of slopes of the relationship over the three intervals. If the fundamental relationship were really linear, the three variables would have identical coefficients; different coefficients indicate the shape of the underlying association.

$$TW = -2\cdot095 + 0\cdot135 \; Mean \; S + 0\cdot006 \; D1_c + 1\cdot014 \; D2_c + 0\cdot052$$
$$(1\cdot05) \qquad (0\cdot00) \qquad (3\cdot98) \qquad (0\cdot49)$$
$$D3_c + 0\cdot151 \; \%NW_c + 0\cdot227 \; Crime_c + 0\cdot009 \; Mfr_{r-c}$$
$$(2\cdot52) \qquad (2\cdot73) \qquad (0\cdot85)$$
$$-0\cdot030 \; Tax_{r-c} + 0\cdot141 \; \overline{Y}_c \qquad\qquad\qquad (4)$$
$$(-4\cdot13) \qquad (1\cdot44)$$

Air pollution is a negative attribute of the city, as is crime, and we expected their coefficients to have positive signs, i.e. the higher the level of air pollution in the central city, the greater the migration to the ring. Population density can be thought of as a measure of privacy or space; the higher the population density, the greater the reason for moving to the ring (and to lower population density). We expected that for cities with low population density, the effect would not be important and that the coefficient would be small and insignificant. For cities of middle and high density, we expected that the coefficient would be positive and significant. Non-whites are viewed as being undesirable neighbours so we conjectured that the sign of this variable would be positive and significant, contrary to the results of Muth [29] and Bradford and Kelejian [30]. As manufacturing jobs grow in the ring, relative to the city, people will be induced to move; the sign of the estimated coefficient should be positive, indicating that people are being drawn to the ring by employment opportunities. We viewed people as moving to the ring to escape taxes; the greater the difference in tax rates, the more people should migrate. However, this variable is complicated by the fact that ring taxes are actually higher than city taxes, on average, due to the higher incomes of ring residents. If the difference between per capita taxes in ring and city is small, migration will be encouraged; thus the estimated coefficient should be negative. We conjectured that the higher the median income of the city, the greater would be the migration rate since families with high incomes could better afford to move.

As shown in Equation 4, these predictions are largely borne out. The regression accounts for 62·0 per cent of the variation in the proportion of total whites migrating to the suburbs from the central cities across 71 S.M.S.A.s. Air pollution and city crime rates were factors pushing whites to the suburbs. Migration was also highly associated with the percentage of non-whites in the central cities and to a lesser extent with median income. Tax rates acted as expected; other things equal, relatively high taxes in the ring discouraged migration. The density variables contained unanticipated results: whereas low density rates did not have any effect on migration, medium density acted as a positive push, and very high density was unimportant. The first two results are not surprising, but the third is unexpected. One possible explanation is that very dense cities may be surrounded by relatively dense suburbs. Hence the benefit of low density can be obtained only by moving a great distance and incurring substantial travel costs. Finally, a high growth rate of manufacturing jobs in the suburbs relative to the central city was not a significant factor in drawing white migrants.

It is clear that one can think of other factors not included in Equation 4 which are likely to affect the suburbanisation process. We selected a number of these variables and re-estimated an expanded regression for total whites as shown in Equation 5:

TABLE 4.3 CITY-PUSH MODEL

Regression	1	2	3	4	5	6
Dependent Variable:	TW	TW	TNW	TNW	MW	M⎸
R^2	0·620	0·657	0·276	0·563	0·624	0·
Independent Variables:						
Constant	− 2·095	− 4·853	4·223	− 41·266	− 0·551	− 0·
Mean S_c	0·135	0·143	− 0·058	− 0·046	0·131	0·
	(1·05)	(1·01)	(− 0·73)	(− 0·63)	(1·08)	(1·
Dl_c	0·006	0·151	− 0·421	− 0·250	− 0·097	0·
	(0·00)	(0·11)	(− 0·54)	(− 0·37)	(− 0·08)	(0·
$D2_c$	1·014	1·049	− 0·005	0·069	0·928	0·
	(3·98)	(3·93)	(− 0·03)	(0·51)	(3·84)	(3·
$D3_c$	0·052	0·136	− 0·049	0·061	0·030	0·
	(0·49)	(1·01)	(− 0·74)	(0·90)	(0·30)	(0·
% NW_c	0·151	0·183	− 0·047	− 0·054	0·139	0·
	(2·52)	(2·80)	(− 1·27)	(− 1·62)	(2·44)	(2·7
$Crime_c$	0·227	0·175	0·135	0·027	0·214	0·1
	(2·73)	(1·53)	(2·62)	(0·47)	(2·71)	(1·6
Mfr_{r-c}	0·009	0·005	0·016	0·008	0·008	0·0
	(0·85)	(0·41)	(2·37)	(1·33)	(0·79)	(0·3
Tax_{r-c}	− 0·030	− 0·024	− 0·006	− 0·003	− 0·029	− 0·0
	(− 4·13)	(− 3·05)	(− 1·45)	(− 0·80)	(− 4·32)	(− 3·2
$\bar{Y}_c$	0·141	0·134	− 0·014	0·492	0·119	0·0
	(1·44)	(0·39)	(− 0·22)	(2·86)	(1·28)	(0·2
JS		0·130		0·170		0·1
		(1·10)		(2·84)		(1·1
JC		0·019		− 0·006		0·0
		(0·49)		(− 0·29)		(0·49
SS_r		0·013		0·027		0·01
		(0·83)		(3·42)		(0·6
ΔS.M.S.A.		0·013		0·015		0·01
		(0·34)		(0·79)		(0·34
% $Poor_c$		− 0·023		0·683		− 0·05
		(− 0·05)		(3·20)		(− 0·15
Pop_c		− 0·001		− 0·001		− 0·00
		(− 1·50)		(− 2·48)		(− 1·47

$$TW = -4 \cdot 853 + 0 \cdot 143 \; Mean \; S_c + 0 \cdot 151 \; D1_c + 1 \cdot 049 \; D2_c + 0 \cdot 136$$
$$\qquad\qquad (1 \cdot 01) \qquad\quad (0 \cdot 11) \qquad\quad (3 \cdot 93) \qquad (1 \cdot 01)$$
$$D3_c + 0 \cdot 183 \; \%NW_c + 1 \cdot 75 \; Crime_c + 0 \cdot 005 \; Mfr_{r-c}$$
$$(2 \cdot 80) \qquad\quad (1 \cdot 53) \qquad\quad (0 \cdot 41)$$
$$-0 \cdot 024 \; Tax_{r-c} + 0 \cdot 134 \; \overline{Y}_c + 13 \cdot 039 \; JS + 1 \cdot 898 \; JC$$
$$(-3 \cdot 05) \qquad\quad (0 \cdot 39) \qquad (1 \cdot 10) \qquad (0 \cdot 49)$$
$$+1 \cdot 305 \; SS_r + 0 \cdot 013 \; \Delta SMSA - 0 \cdot 023 \; \%Poor_c - 0 \cdot 001$$
$$(0 \cdot 83) \qquad\quad (0 \cdot 34) \qquad\qquad (-0 \cdot 05) \qquad\quad (-1 \cdot 50)$$
$$Pop_c \tag{5}$$

Here *JS* (journey to the suburbs) represents the proportion of people who commuted to the suburbs for work in 1960. This is a

MIGRATION FROM CITY TO RING

7 MNW	8 MNW	9 Poor	10 Poor	11 Rich	12 Rich	13 25–34 MW	14 25–34 MW
0·288	0·551	0·363	0·535	0·548	0·591	0·623	0·642
5·474	−40·541	11·788	−44·216	1·845	6·341	−1·653	28·471
−0·071	−0·055	−0·134	−0·100	0·296	0·300	0·449	0·439
(−0·95)	(−0·79)	(−1·52)	(−1·15)	(1·56)	(1·43)	(1·71)	(1·48)
−0·540	−0·301	−1·642	−1·013	−0·140	−0·113	1·285	1·018
(−0·73)	(−0·46)	(−1·90)	(1·24)	(−0·08)	(−0·06)	(0·50)	(0·36)
0·028	0·105	0·091	0·197	1·501	1·537	2·218	2·193
(0·19)	(0·81)	(0·52)	(1·20)	(3·99)	(3·89)	(4·26)	(3·92)
−0·039	0·064	−0·089	0·034	0·184	0·269	0·033	0·159
(−0·63)	(0·98)	(−1·23)	(0·42)	(1·17)	(1·35)	(0·15)	(0·56)
−0·049	−0·059	−0·127	−0·133	0·133	0·175	0·238	0·305
(−1·41)	(−1·84)	(−3·11)	(−3·31)	(1·51)	(1·81)	(1·95)	(2·22)
0·130	0·022	0·055	−0·052	0·426	0·311	0·453	0·572
(2·69)	(0·40)	(0·97)	(−0·74)	(3·47)	(1·84)	(2·66)	(2·39)
0·013	0·006	0·005	0·001	0·011	0·004	0·016	0·011
(2·06)	(1·06)	(0·70)	(0·08)	(0·67)	(0·22)	(0·73)	(0·46)
−0·007	−0·004	−0·018	−0·011	−0·021	−0·014	−0·062	−0·058
(−1·74)	(−1·02)	(−3·61)	(−2·37)	(−1·94)	(−1·18)	(−4·27)	(−3·54)
−0·029	0·487	0·019	0·655	−0·053	−0·164	0·160	−0·245
(−0·52)	(2·95)	(0·29)	(3·15)	(−0·37)	(−0·33)	(0·80)	(−0·34)
	0·151		0·190		0·117		0·210
	(2·63)		(2·62)		(0·67)		(0·85)
	0·002		0·024		0·042		−0·059
	(0·10)		(1·02)		(0·73)		(−0·73)
	0·024		0·013		0·025		0·009
	(3·11)		(1·33)		(1·09)		(0·28)
	0·012		0·000		0·031		−0·000
	(0·67)		(0·02)		(0·56)		(−0·01)
	0·695		0·828		−0·141		−0·585
	(3·39)		(3·20)		(−0·23)		(−0·66)
	−0·001		−0·001		−0·002		−0·003
	(−2·25)		(−2·12)		(−1·11)		(−1·33)

surrogate for those who commuted in 1955 and it is assumed to have a positive effect on migration as people seek to move nearer to their their jobs. *JC* (journey to city) represents the proportion of people who commuted from the suburbs to the city in 1960. The inclusion of this variable was motivated by Rothenberg's argument that this could be used as a surrogate for externalities imposed upon city dwellers by suburbanites as they use city services [31]. We expected that its coefficient would be positive as people move to the ring to escape this burden, although we are aware that a number of biases are introduced by using 1960 values for *JS* and *JC*; SS_r represents the value of selected services per capita in the ring. This variable is a surrogate for various amenities available in the ring such as theatres and other cultural activities. $\Delta SMSA$ is the growth rate of the total S.M.S.A. We are hypothesised that higher growth rates are accompanied by higher property turn-over and an easier housing market. $\%Poor_c$ represents the percentage of the 1960 population with incomes less than \$3,000. This variable was included in an effort to separate the effects of non-whites and poor on migration. Pop_c is the size of the central city.

The introduction of the new variables does not increase the power of the regression very much for total whites (R^2 increases from 0·620 to 0·657). While most of the signs are as hypothesised, only two of the coefficients border on significance. The sign of *JS* is positive and its implication is that people tend to move towards their jobs. The negative sign of Pop_c indicates that, other things equal, people tend to migrate less out of large cities. One possible explanation is that the larger the population, the larger the geographic area of the city and hence movement is more likely to take place within the limits of the city. In general, the introduction of the new variables does not have an appreciable effect on the coefficients of the previous ones.

City-Push Models: Total Non-whites. We also used Equations 4 and 5 to explain the variation in the rates of migration by non-whites to the suburbs. We expected that, with the exception of the percentage of non-whites in the city population, all of the variables would affect non-white rates of suburbanisation in the same direction as they affected white rates. The results are also presented in Table 4.3.

Consider first the simple model (regression Table 4.3, column 3). The results for non-whites differ in some interesting respects from those for whites. The R^2 is much lower (0·276) and neither population density nor air pollution acted to push non-whites out of the city. The higher the crime rates, however, the more non-whites moved to the suburbs. Non-whites reacted as did whites with respect to relative tax differentials between the ring and the city. Employment opportunities (the growth rates of manufacturing jobs in the ring relative to the central city) were much more important for non-whites, while median income was unimportant for them. The higher the proportion of non-whites in the central city, the less non-whites were likely to migrate. This result can be used either to support the argument that non-whites prefer homogeneous societies or to support the argument that non-whites face discrimination in finding housing in the ring.

For non-whites, the introduction of the additional variables increases the power of the regression significantly (from 0·276 to 0·563). Comparing regressions Table 4.3, columns 3 and 4, one notes crime (as a positive factor) and taxes (as a negative factor) both decrease in importance. The importance of relative changes in manufacturing jobs also decreases slightly. Median income becomes very important. Of the new variables both JS and SS_r are strong factors affecting non-white migration. A possible explanation for the relative weight of selected services is that, for non-whites, they represent not so much the availability of amenities as the availability of jobs. The higher the percentage of poor in the central city, the more non-whites are likely to migrate to the ring – a result that was also found by Bradford and Kelejian [30].

City-Push Models: Other Subgroups. The two migration models developed above also explain much of the migration to the suburbs by the other groups. The regression results for white males 14 years older, white males between 25 and 34 and rich families are very similar to those for total whites. The regressions do less well in accounting for the migration of the poor. Unfortunately data were not available which would allow one to separate poor whites from poor non-whites.

Discussion of Possible Biases. Before drawing any conclusions from this analysis we should discuss some of the problems with respect to biases and identification in the regression coefficients and in the data. (This discussion is relevant to all of our empirical results.) As noted above, we could not obtain 1955 data on the percentage of non-whites, income or the journey to work variables. Consequently, as these variables are observed after the migration has taken place, there is a possibility that we may be confounding cause and effect. The cities in which a high proportion of white migration has taken place will (after the migration has taken place) have a higher proportion of non-whites. Hence the statistical relationship between white migration and the proportion of non-whites may be picking up the results of the migration not the cause. In addition the base of the dependent variable is incorrect.

The dependent variable in regression Table 4.3 column 1 (TW), is

divided by the total number of whites in 1960. If there were no
migrants into the S.M.S.A. and no births and no deaths, it is evident
that there would be fewer whites in 1960 than in 1955, since the net
migration flow was to the ring. While there is some migration into
the S.M.S.A. and while the birth rate is higher than the death rate,
it is still true that we are dividing by too small a number for most
cities. Little can be done to correct this difficulty, but its effect
should be noted. Those cities with the greatest migration to the ring
will have their migration rate proportionally overstated, and *vice
versa* for cities with very small migration rates. Thus the estimated
coefficients will be biased towards overstating the effect of variables
characterising cities with high migration rates. A similar problem
comes about because the white migration rate is greater than the
black migration rate. This means that even if non-whites had no
effect on white migration rates, we would expect the non-white
variable to have a positive sign. As whites leave the city more rapidly
than non-whites, the proportion of non-whites must increase. It is
difficult to determine what part of the coefficient is due to the
inappropriate base and what part is due to a disinclination of whites
to live with non-whites. One can test whether the effect is a non-
behavioural one by examining the magnitude of the estimated
coefficient.

An example will help to clarify the problem. Suppose a city has a
1955 population of 850 whites and 150 non-whites (there are 15·0
per cent non-whites). If 150 of these whites move to the ring along
with 5 of the non-whites, the correct migration rates are 17·7 per cent
for the whites and 3 per cent for the non-whites. Assuming there are
no births or deaths or in-migration, this means that the 1960 city
population will consist of 700 whites and 145 non-whites or 17·2 per
cent non-whites. Using the incorrect 1960 base, the white migration
rate is 21·4 per cent and the non-white migration rate is 3·5 per cent.
Since the estimated coefficient of $\%NW_c$ for total white migration is
0·151 (regression Table 4.3, column 1) the incorrect proportion of
non-whites (17·2 per cent instead of 15·0 per cent) leads to a predicted
increase in migration of 0·33 per cent. Since the total estimated
effect of non-whites on white migration is estimated to be 2·6 per
cent, 28 per cent of the estimated effect of non-whites on white
migration is due to an incorrect population base, rather than to the
estimated effect of the non-whites on white migration.

This example also illustrates the bias in the migration rates. If 150
whites move to the suburbs, the estimated migration rate is 21·4
per cent (it is 3·7 per cent too high). If 200 whites move to the ring,
the estimated migration rate is 33·3 per cent, which is 15·6 per cent
too high. This tendency to overstate more, the greater the migration

rate, will bias the estimated coefficients. The same will be true for non-whites if the non-white population in the city is falling. However, since the non-white population has been rising in central cities, the non-white migration rate is understated by using the 1960 population base, and the estimated coefficients will be biased downward.

Conclusion. The variables hypothesised to affect migration from city to ring tend to have the expected sign and explain, at least in the expanded models, more than half of the variation in the migration rates for all of the seven groups. For whites (who presumably have relatively high incomes), environmental variables (including crime, the population density and air pollution) are the more important determinants of movement to the ring. For non-whites (who presumably have relatively low incomes), employment-related factors are the more significant considerations. These results which, in general, confirm our expectation must, however, for reasons given above, be taken with some caution.

The Ring-City Model. In the city-push model it was assumed that a potential migrant would focus on city attributes and move if, for example, crime rates were high. A more rational potential migrant would consider what was to be gained by moving and so would compare ring to city values of the variables. The next group of models are estimated using the differences between ring and city characteristics. The results for all groups are presented in Table 4.4 although the following discussion is again limited to the models for total whites and total non-whites.

Ring-City Model: Total Whites. The ring-city models are similar to those presented in Equations 4 and 5. The new variables are as defined above, except that they are noted as '*r–c*' or ring minus city. The one exception is air pollution, since no measures of ring air pollution were available. If ring air pollution were a constant fraction of central city air pollution (across S.M.S.A.s), the variable would be proportional to the difference. The other variable that should be discussed is population density. $D1_{r-c}$ consists of those S.M.S.A.s where the ring and central city had a similar population density; $D2_{r-c}$ consists of those S.M.S.A.s where there was a medium difference in population density, and $D3_{r-c}$ consists of those S.M.S.A.s where there was a large difference in population density. The first ring-city model is shown in Equation 6:

$$TW = 12.724 - 0.035 \ Mean \ S_c + 0.694 \ D1_{r-c} - 0.688 \ D2_{r-c}$$
$$(-0.26) \qquad\qquad (0.50) \qquad\quad (-1.98)$$
$$- 0.101 \ D3_{r-c} - 0.184 \ \%NW_{r-c} - 0.092 \ Crime_{r-c} + 0.008$$
$$(-0.088) \qquad (-1.71) \qquad\qquad (-0.91) \qquad\qquad (0.76)$$
$$Mfr_{r-c} - 0.028 \ Tax_{r-c} + 0.184 \ \bar{Y}_{r-c} \qquad\qquad\qquad (6)$$
$$(-3.94) \qquad\quad (1.27)$$

This model explains slightly less of the variation in the migration of whites to the suburbs than did the city-push model (0·599 compared to 0·620). In particular the importance of both crime and air pollution as factors contributing to suburbanisation diminishes substantially significant. Of the three density differentials, only the middle range is statistically significant. The effect of taxes and of non-whites on white migration to the ring is the same as that in the city-push model. The higher the median income in the ring relative to the central city, the more whites are likely to migrate.

The fact that two of the environmental variables diminish in importance in this formulation is interesting. Air pollution generally has a negative coefficient, which is never significant. (We speculate that air pollution has become a more significant factor in the last decade, as evidenced by increasing public attention.) Since we believe that crime rates are important in affecting a person's decision to leave the central city, it may well be that it is in fact the absolute and not the differential crime rates that are important.

TABLE 4.4 RING MINUS MODEL

Regression	1	2	3	4	5	6
Dependent Variable:	TW	TW	TNW	TNW	MQ	MW
R^2	0·599	0·618	0·305	0·531	0·611	0·628
Independent Variables:						
Constant	12·724	10·268	4·965	1·148	12·380	10·251
Mean S	− 0·035	− 0·016	− 0·041	− 0·019	− 0·029	− 0·010
	(− 0·26)	(− 0·11)	(− 0·51)	(− 0·27)	(− 0·23)	(− 0·08)
$D1_{r-c}$	0·694	1·273	0·076	0·732	0·662	1·214
	(0·50)	(0·87)	(0·09)	(1·00)	(0·51)	(0·88)
$D2_{r-c}$	− 0·688	− 0·675	− 0·139	− 0·191	− 0·651	− 0·625
	(− 1·98)	(− 1·89)	(− 0·67)	(− 1·08)	(− 1·99)	(− 1·86)
$D3_{r-c}$	− 0·101	− 0·139	0·068	0·025	− 0·078	− 0·113
	(− 0·88)	(− 1·17)	(1·00)	(0·43)	(− 0·72)	(− 1·01)
% NW_{r-c}	− 0·184	− 0·216	0·124	0·069	− 0·175	− 0·201
	(− 1·71)	(− 1·96)	(1·94)	(1·26)	(− 1·73)	(− 1·94)
$Crime_{r-c}$	− 0·092	− 0·089	− 0·095	− 0·087	− 0·090	− 0·088
	(− 0·91)	(− 0·87)	(− 1·57)	(− 1·71)	(− 0·95)	(− 0·91)
Mfr_{r-c}	0·008	− 0·000	0·017	0·007	0·007	− 0·000
	(0·76)	(− 0·01)	(2·69)	(1·06)	(0·71)	(− 0·04)
Tax_{r-c}	− 0·028	− 0·028	− 0·008	− 0·009	− 0·028	− 0·028
	(− 3·94)	(− 3·89)	(− 2·01)	(− 2·47)	(− 4·20)	(− 4·13)
$\bar{Y}_{r-c}$	0·184	− 0·130	0·045	− 0·200	0·174	− 0·139
	(1·27)	(− 0·45)	(0·52)	(− 1·38)	(1·28)	(− 0·51)
SS_r		0·019		0·031		0·016
		(1·19)		(3·98)		(1·06)
% $Poor_{r-c}$		− 0·350		− 0·174		− 0·366
		(− 1·03)		(− 1·02)		(− 1·14)
$\Delta S.M.S.A.$		0·024		0·035		0·022
		(0·72)		(2·11)		(0·70)

We augmented Equation 6 with a subset of the variables added to the city-push model. The two journey to work variables and the central city population variable are not included in this model since they cannot be defined as a difference, although we did include $\Delta SMSA$ and SS_r. The expanded regression is shown in Equation 7:

$$
\begin{aligned}
TW = {}& 10{\cdot}268 - 0{\cdot}016 \; Mean \; S + 1{\cdot}273 \; D1_{r-c} - 0{\cdot}675 \; D2_{r-c} \\
& \phantom{10{\cdot}268} (-0{\cdot}11) (0{\cdot}87) (-1{\cdot}89) \\
& - 0{\cdot}139 \; D3_{r-c} - 0{\cdot}216 \; \%NW_{r-c} - 0{\cdot}089 \; Crime_{r-c} \\
& (-1{\cdot}17) (-1{\cdot}96) (-0{\cdot}87) \\
& - 0{\cdot}0001 \; Mfr_{r-c} - 0{\cdot}028 \; Tax_{r-c} - 0{\cdot}130 \; \overline{Y}_{r-c} + 0{\cdot}019 \; SS_r \\
& (-0{\cdot}01) (-3{\cdot}89) (-0{\cdot}45) (1{\cdot}19) \\
& - 0{\cdot}350 \; \%Poor_{r-c} + 0{\cdot}024 \; \Delta SMSA \qquad\qquad (7) \\
& (-1{\cdot}03) (0{\cdot}72)
\end{aligned}
$$

The inclusion of the new variables adds little to the power of the regression but it does affect the magnitude of some of the previous

OF MIGRATION

7 MNW	8 MNW	9 Poor	10 Poor	11 Rich	12 Rich	13 25–34 MW	14 25–34 MW
0·316	0·511	0·313	0·361	0·582	0·618	0·582	0·602
5·499	2·144	11·331	9·353	10·882	6·907	21·436	18·032
−0·054	−0·037	−0·093	−0·088	0·005	0·020	0·105	0·134
(−0·71)	(−0·55)	(−0·99)	(−0·92)	(0·03)	(0·11)	(0·37)	(0·46)
0·381	0·930	1·873	2·131	−0·056	0·802	−0·284	0·802
(0·50)	(1·32)	(1·96)	(2·13)	(−0·03)	(0·40)	(−1·10)	(0·26)
−0·102	−0·153	−0·182	−0·227	−1·182	−1·144	−1·718	−1·591
(−0·53)	(−0·89)	(−0·76)	(−0·93)	(−2·45)	(−2·37)	(−2·36)	(−2·13)
0·066	0·029	0·044	0·024	−0·138	−0·210	−0·120	−0·199
(1·03)	(0·50)	(0·55)	(0·29)	(−0·86)	(−1·31)	(−0·49)	(−0·80)
0·118	0·070	0·058	0·028	−0·025	−0·079	−0·250	−0·288
(1·97)	(1·31)	(0·78)	(0·38)	(−0·17)	(−0·53)	(−1·11)	(−1·25)
−0·099	−0·093	−0·034	−0·030	−0·154	−0·154	−0·166	−0·167
(−1·76)	(−1·90)	(−0·49)	(−0·44)	(−1·10)	(−1·11)	(−0·78)	(−0·78)
0·014	0·005	0·005	−0·000	0·015	0·002	0·015	0·000
(2·34)	(0·82)	(0·60)	(−0·05)	(0·97)	(0·09)	(0·64)	(0·01)
−0·009	−0·010	−0·015	−0·015	−0·026	−0·025	−0·063	−0·061
(−2·39)	(−2·82)	(−3·02)	(−3·07)	(−2·64)	(−2·55)	(−4·27)	(−4·14)
0·033	−0·185	−0·106	−0·207	0·594	−0·129	0·456	−0·428
(0·41)	(−1·32)	(−1·06)	(−1·04)	(2·96)	(−0·33)	(1·50)	(−0·70)
	0·028		0·018		0·037		0·027
	(3·74)		(1·68)		(1·76)		(0·83)
	−0·154		−0·046		−0·867		−1·152
	(−0·94)		(−0·20)		(−1·88)		(−1·61)
	0·028		0·013		0·017		0·024
	(1·76)		(0·58)		(0·37)		(0·35)

coefficients. For example, the importance of median income differentials diminishes. The higher the proportion of poor in the central city, relative to the ring (% $Poor_{r-c}$), given the non-white differential (% NW_{r-c}), the more whites are likely to migrate. The availability of selected services in the ring is also positively associated with white migration.

The Ring-City Model: Non-whites. Both Equations 6 and 7 were estimated for non-whites. The simple ring-city model accounts for slightly more of the variation in the rate at which non-whites move to the suburbs than did the simple city-push model (30·5 per cent compared to 27·6 per cent). In general the results obtained from this specification do not differ from those obtained from the city-push model: the faster the growth of manufacturing jobs in the ring relative to the central city, the more non-whites migrated; the greater the difference in the percentage of non-whites in the ring relative to the central city, the less non-whites migrated. High crime rates in the ring relative to the central city encouraged non-white migration. We can only speculate as to why crime differentials should be important in explaining non-white migration but not white migration; non-whites may be victimised proportionately more than whites.

The introduction of the additional variables once again significantly increased the power of the non-white regression. One result of the new variables was that the coefficient of $\bar{Y}_{r-c}$ became negative and more significant; the implication is that the higher the income in the ring (relative to the central city) the less non-whites are likely to migrate. This result is consistent with the estimated effect for the percentage of poor (where a high proportion of poor in the ring relative to the central city stimulates non-white migration). The coefficient of $\Delta SMSA$ is positive and significant; the faster the total S.M.S.A. is growing, the more likely the non-whites are to move to the ring. One possible explanation for this is that discrimination is likely to break down under the impetus of rapid growth. (In the city-push model, however, the changing S.M.S.A. population did not affect non-white migration.)

4.4.3 NET MIGRATION

The migration rates studied in the city-push models and the ring-city models were one-way migration rates; that is, the dependent variable was the proportion of people in a given group who moved to the ring from the central city relative to the 1960 central city population of that group. While people were moving out of the central city to the ring, others were moving from the ring to the central city. It is the net effect of the intra-S.M.S.A. migration that will affect the characteristics of the central city, not merely the one-way flow of the out-migration.

We estimated models identical to those presented in Equations 6 and 7 to study the factors affecting net migration within an S.M.S.A. We believed that the same factors that encouraged out-migration, other things equal, would discourage in-migration to the central city. Since ring residents would be motivated by ring variables or by ring minus city variables, the latter were most appropriate for examining net migration. We defined net migration as the number of people who left the central city for the ring minus the number of people who left the ring for the central city (during 1955–60) divided by the relevant city population in 1960. The results of this estimation for total whites and total non-whites are presented in Table 4.5.

The net migration model for whites is very similar to the ring-city

TABLE 4.5

NET MIGRATION FROM CITY TO RING AND LOCATION CHOICE OF NEW MIGRANTS

Regression	1	2	3	4	5	6	7	8
Dependent Variable:	TW^*	TW^*	TNW^*	TNW^*	TW^{**}	TW^{**}	TNW^{**}	TNW^{**}
R^2	0·650	0·659	0·419	0·555	0·530	0·564	0·496	0·500
Independent Variables:								
Constant	0·060	0·048	− 0·000	− 0·023	76·280	72·426	60·829	58·468
Mean S	− 0·000	− 0·000	− 0·000	− 0·000	0·203	0·093	0·318	0·332
	(− 0·13)	(0·17)	(− 0·44)	(− 0·68)	(0·57)	(0·26)	(0·95)	(0·95)
$D1_{r-c}$	0·004	0·005	− 0·000	0·001	6·895	6·066	3·718	4·075
	(0·28)	(0·38)	(− 0·01)	(0·22)	(1·92)	(1·61)	(1·09)	(1·11)
$D2_{r-c}$	− 0·007	− 0·007	− 0·004	− 0·004	1·195	0·919	1·898	1·844
	(− 2·07)	(− 2·01)	(− 2·21)	(− 2·77)	(1·32)	(1·00)	(2·22)	(2·06)
$D3_{r-c}$	− 0·002	− 0·002	− 0·000	− 0·000	0·186	0·138	0·898	0·877
	(− 1·45)	(− 1·62)	(− 0·00)	(− 0·61)	(0·62)	(0·46)	(3·16)	(2·96)
$\% \, NW_{r-c}$	− 0·002	− 0·002	0·001	0·000	0·223	0·131	1·158	1·123
	(− 1·87)	(− 2·00)	(1·05)	(0·34)	(0·80)	(0·46)	(4·37)	(4·07)
$Crime_{r-c}$	− 0·001	− 0·001	− 0·001	− 0·001	− 0·104	− 0·118	− 0·042	− 0·036
	(− 0·98)	(− 0·99)	(− 1·89)	(− 2·11)	(− 0·39)	(− 0·45)	(− 0·17)	(− 0·14)
Mfr_{r-c}	0·000	0·000	0·000	0·000	0·030	0·030	0·064	0·058
	(1·68)	(1·20)	(3·88)	(2·97)	(1·04)	(0·96)	(2·39)	(1·87)
Tax_{r-c}	− 0·000	− 0·000	− 0·000	− 0·000	− 0·102	− 0·099	− 0·097	− 0·098
	(− 3·28)	(− 3·13)	(− 1·12)	(− 1·06)	(− 5·56)	(− 5·46)	(− 5·62)	(− 5·50)
$\bar{Y}_{r-c}$	0·003	0·000	0·000	− 0·002	0·435	− 0·008	0·318	0·265
	(1·97)	(0·03)	(0·63)	(− 1·69)	(1·16)	(− 0·01)	(0·89)	(0·36)
SS_r		0·000		0·000		0·080		0·019
		(1·08)		(4·14)		(2·00)		(0·47)
$\% \, Poor_{r-c}$		− 0·003		− 0·002		− 0·328		0·038
		(− 0·95)		(− 1·65)		(− 0·38)		(0·04)
$\Delta S.M.S.A.$		− 0·000		− 0·000		− 0·102		0·025
		(− 0·21)		(− 0·50)		(− 1·20)		(0·30)

migration model; slightly more of the variation in the migration rates is accounted for by this model (65·0 per cent compared to 59·9 per cent). The rate of net migration to the suburbs is now significantly influenced by the relative rate of growth in manufacturing jobs in the ring.

For non-whites, the results are also similar to the corresponding ring-city model and R^2 is also a bit higher for the net migration (0·419 compared to 0·305). The middle population density difference is extremely significant in the net model; thus for medium differences in population density, non-whites choose to locate in the less densely populated ring. The crime rate is also more significant and seems to provide a strong motivation for non-whites to locate in the ring. As before, the availability of jobs in the ring is a strong factor determining location. The concentration of non-whites is no longer a significant variable in determining net migration rates, which is somewhat surprising. Finally, the growth rate of the S.M.S.A. is no longer a significant factor in spurring net migration to the ring.

4.4.4 LOCATIONAL PREFERENCES OF MIGRANTS ARRIVING IN THE S.M.S.A.

The central city population is changed not only by net migration from the central city to the ring, but also by migrants arriving into the S.M.S.A. who decide to locate in the central city. If arriving migrants had the same characteristics as those moving to the ring, no disequilibrium forces would be set in motion by migration. Of 1,000 migrants arriving in a representative S.M.S.A. in 1960, 497 were whites from other S.M.S.A.s, 425 were whites from non-metropolitan areas, 36 were non-whites from other S.M.S.A.s, and 42 were non-whites from non-metropolitan areas. These figures emphasise the greater mobility of whites (taking account of their greater proportion of the entire population) and the fact that relatively more whites come from other metropolitan areas while relatively more non-whites come from non-metropolitan areas.

The locational choices of these arriving migrants is shown in Table 4.6. Over one-half of the white migrants choose to locate in the ring, while only 28 per cent of the non-white migrants choose the ring. These results suggest that arriving migrants do not counterbalance the net migration from central city to ring. Migrants view the ring as being more attractive than do people currently located in the S.M.S.A., since the proportion locating in the ring is much greater than the five-year migration rate from city to ring. Thus, from 1955 to 1960, almost one-half of the families in the S.M.S.A. changed residence; of these, roughly one-third decided to locate in the ring rather than the central city as compared to over one-half of the arriving migrants. Non-whites arriving in the S.M.S.A. found the ring even more attractive (compared to non-whites in the central city)

TABLE 4.6

LOCATION CHOICE OF MIGRANTS ARRIVING IN
THE S.M.S.A.

Demographic Characteristic	Location Choice (per cent)	
	Central City	Ring
All whites	43·2	56·8
All nonwhites	72·4	27·6
White males	43·7	56·3
Nonwhite males	69·3	30·7
Poor	52·0	48·0
Rich	39·7	60·3
White males, 25–34	43·7	56·3

than did arriving whites. Only about 5 per cent of the non-whites in the central city who changed residence chose to move to the ring whereas 28 per cent of arriving non-whites chose the ring (compared to 28 per cent and 57 per cent, respectively, for whites).

The effect of migration on the composition of the central city can also be investigated by looking at the sum of the net migration from central city to ring and the migration from non-metropolitan areas to the central city. The assumption is that net migration from one S.M.S.A. to another is negligible and that migration from S.M.S.A.s to non-metropolitan areas is very small. The average across central cities from 1955 to 1960 is a net loss of 18,438 whites and a net gain of 3,283 non-whites. One can disaggregate these data to point out that there was a net loss of 5,820 white males older than 14, a net loss of 2,161 white males aged 25–34, and a net gain of 1,166 non-white males older than 14. Finally, there was a net loss of 8,453 rich and a net gain of 14,606 poor. It is evident that central city populations became progressively more non-white and poor from 1955 to 1960. This evidence confirms the earlier conjecture that using 1960 population as the base in computing migration understates non-white migration rates and overstates white migration rates.

We now turn to an examination of the factors most critical to the location decision of these new arrivals into the S.M.S.A. by an analysis similar to the ring-city model. We have re-estimated Equations 6 and 7 with the new dependent variable being the proportion of whites (or of non-whites) from outside the S.M.S.A. who decide to locate in the ring. These results are presented in regression Table 4.5, columns 5 to 8.

For whites arriving in the S.M.S.A. who decide to locate in the ring, the results are similar to white migration results in the ring-city model. The coefficient of determination is a bit smaller (R^2 has dropped from 0·599 to 0·530), but tax rates and selected services continue to be important variables. The concentrations of non-whites and of the poor appear to be less important to the new arrivals than they were for whites moving from the city to the ring. The implications of the population density differentials are quite different for new arrivals, since they seem to regard population density as a good thing and tend to locate in the ring more often when it has a density comparable to that of the city.

The coefficient of determination for non-white deciding to locate in the ring is a bit lower than for non-whites deciding to move from central city to ring ($R^2 = 0·496$). The new arrivals are more sensitive to jobs and taxes and less sensitive to selected services, the S.M.S.A. growth rate and concentrations of the poor. They strongly prefer to locate with concentrations of non-whites and in rings with population densities comparable to those of the central cities.

4.5 SUMMARY AND IMPLICATIONS

It is more important to note that the processes we have examined are sensitive to economic variables and can be modelled theoretically and explained empirically by maximising behaviour. Birth rates and migration patterns appear to be guided by utility maximisation, given the opportunities and constraints of the individual. It is important to stress the apparent rationality of this behaviour since it means that we gain insight into the policies which will influence these processes.

The migration data make it clear that large cities are losing whites and upper-income families while they are gaining non-whites and lower-income families. Since about one-half of the families changed residence during 1955–60, the urban population is highly mobile and likely to react rapidly to the changing environment.

We have investigated the movement from central city to ring across cities as well as the factors which determine where new arrivals into the S.M.S.A. will locate. Movement to the ring is influenced by the urban environment (including crime rates, air pollution and population densities). Economic factors, such as job opportunities and tax rates, are also important. Whites tended to be motivated more by environmental variables and taxes, while non-whites responded more to job opportunities and crime rates. The concentration of non-whites was an important factor in explaining residential location. Whites moved away from non-whites, while non-whites tended to move towards other non-whites. This phenomenon could be explained either by systematic discrimination or by people choosing to live in neighbourhoods with others of similar backgrounds and tastes.

The fact that city populations are changing (becoming relatively poorer and more non-white) is estimated to set further migration into motion. The rising concentration of non-whites should serve to increase white migration to the suburbs. One would expect a continuation of the rise in crime rates in the central city and a general deterioration of the environment as a result of the out-migration of the middle classes. This, in turn, is estimated to lead to further migration of whites and of upper-income families. Cities are likely to change even more rapidly in the future than they did from 1955–60. This is a testable hypothesis for the 1965–70 data, when they are available (our preliminary examination of the data which have been released support this proposition).

An analysis of this sort characterises the processes changing central city population at a point in time. Even granting that it is an accurate characterisation as of that time, there is no reason to believe that one can extrapolate these processes into the indefinite future. Underlying factors shift as more and more people migrate to the ring. For example, the ring's advantages in terms of low population density, low crime rates, and other environmental factors will be eroded as migration continues. There is also the fact that the first people to migrate have the strongest preference for the amenities the ring offers, while those who remain behind have less preference. These considerations imply that a constant or increasing rate of migration is not a reasonable assumption.

If the rings maintain relative homogeneity, they will continue to enjoy an advantage over the central city (especially for those preferring homogeneous neighbourhoods). Homogeneity enables a suburb to supply services tailored precisely to the tastes of its citizens. It also minimises income redistribution since there will be fewer welfare programmes and non-taxpaying citizens. However, suburban attempts to maintain homogeneity (such as by zoning for large lots and only single-family dwellings) are being attacked by the Federal Government and other groups. Indeed, examples come to mind of older suburbs of New York and Chicago which have not preserved a high degree of uniformity.

It is evident that migration will continue to be an important force shaping cities. Although an analysis of this sort cannot be used to predict final equilibrium (or even the rate of adjustment very far into the future), it can be utilised to study the underlying factors affecting the path towards equilibrium. Our analysis shows that migration will add to central city problems by increasing the number of lower-income families (and of non-whites) and by decreasing the number of upper-income families (and of whites). The short-run forecast is a gloomy one.

APPENDIX

VARIABLES USED IN DEATH RATE ANALYSIS*

	Mean	Standard Deviation
Air Pollution ($\mu g/m^3$)		
Min P (minimum particulate reading for biweekly period)	45·47	18·57
Mean P (arithmetic mean particulate reading)	118·14	40·94
Min S (minimum sulphate reading for biweekly period; ×10)	47·24	31·28
Mortality		
Total (per 10,000)	91·26	15·33
<1 Year (per 10,000 live births)	254·03	36·44
<28 Days (per 10,000 live births)	187·29	24·52
Socio-economic		
P/M² (persons per square mile)	699·65	1354·43
%NW (per cent of population non-white; ×10)	124·81	104·10
%≥65 (per cent of population≥65; ×10)	83·87	21·07
% Poor (per cent of families with incomes<\$3,000; ×10)	181·12	65·24

VARIABLES USED IN MIGRATION ANALYSIS*

	Mean	Standard Deviation
Migrants		
TW (per cent of migrants from central city to ring, total whites)	14·31	7·69
TNW (per cent of migrants from central city to ring, total non-whites)	3·24	3·45
MW (per cent of migrants from central city to ring, white males≥14)	13·63	7·34
MNW (per cent of migrants from central city to ring, non-white males≥14)	3·28	3·27
Poor (per cent of migrants from central city ro ring, incomes<\$4,000)	7·07	4·05
Rich (per cent of migrants from central city to ring, incomes≥\$10,000)	16·06	10·41
25–34MW (per cent of migrants from central city to ring, white males 25–34)	25·34	15·78
TW* (per cent *net* migrants from central city to ring, total whites	0·10	0·08

* Based on observations for 117 S.M.S.A.s.

	Mean	*Standard Deviation*
TNW* (per cent of *net* migrants from central city to ring, total non-whites)	0·01	0·03
TW** (per cent of in-migrants locating in ring, total whites)	56·77	18·44
TNW** (per cent in-migrants locating in ring, total non-whites)	27·58	16·84
Central City Variables		
$D1_c$ ($\leq$ 2,600 persons per square mile;/1,000)	0·21	0·63
$D2_c$ ($>$ 2,600 and $\leq$ 12,000 persons per square mile; /1,000)	4·69	3·39
$D3_c$ ($>$ 12,000 persons per square mile;/1,000)	2·41	7·92
%NW_c (per cent of population non-white)	18·57	12·72
$Crime_c$ (total crimes per 1,000 inhabitants)	17·16	8·05
$\bar{Y}_c$ (median income;/100)	57·22	7·26
%$Poor_c$ (per cent of families with incomes $<$ \$3,000)	19·55	6·18
Pop_c (population;/1,000)	609·47	1061·23
Mean S (arithmetic mean sulphate reading)	10·94	5·71
Ring-City Variables		
$D1_{r-c}$ (difference $\geq$ – 2,500 persons per square mile;/1,000)	– 0·20	0·61
$D2_{r-c}$ (difference $<$ – 2,500 and $\geq$ – 9,000 persons per square mile;/1,000)	– 3·28	2·68
$D3_{r-c}$ (difference $<$ – 9,000 persons per square mile; /1,000)	– 3·36	8·01
%NW_{r-c} (per cent of population non-white)	– 11·93	10·76
$Crime_{r-c}$ (total crimes per 1,000 inhabitants)	– 8·70	7·04
$\bar{Y}_{r-c}$ (median income;/100)	5·27	8·60
% $Poor_{r-c}$ (per cent of families with incomes $<$ \$3,000)	– 4·04	6·03
Mfr_{r-c} (relative growth in manufacturing, 1954–58)	17·67	63·04
Tax_{r-c} (total general revenue per capita)	165·69	108·21
Additional Variables		
JS (journey to suburbs)	12·44	6·60
JC (journey to city)	18·76	23·61
SS_r (selected services receipts per capita;/100)	0·81	0·48
S.M.S.A. (per cent population increase or decrease, 1950–60)	32·51	24·82

VARIABLES USED IN POLLUTION ANALYSIS*

	Mean	*Standard Deviation*
Air Pollution ($\mu g/m^3$)		
Mean P (arithmetic mean particulate reading)	10·94	5·71
Mean S (arithmetic mean sulphate reading)	129·07	41·75

* Based on observations for 71 S.M.S.A.s.

	Mean	Standard Deviation
Socio-economic		
Pop$_c$ (population; $\times 1/1,000$)	609·47	1061·23
P/M^2$_c$ (persons per square mile)	7309·28	6970·17
Mfr. VA (per capita value added by manufacture, adjusted, 1958) ($1,000's)	1·04	0·68
Climatological		
Humid. (relative humidity; 1:00a E. S. T.)	76·27	8·09
Wind (average hourly wind speed; $\times 10$)	92·54	19·25
Rain (number of days precipitation $\geq 0·01$ inch)	88·45	51·50
Heating Fuels (per cent per 100 homes)		
Oil (fuel oil, kerosene, etc.)	0·27	0·27
Coal (coal or coke)	0·11	0·15
Elec. (electricity)	0·03	0·08

REFERENCES

[1] C. Taeuber, 'Population Trends of the 1960's', *Science*, 176 (1972).
[2] G. K. Zipf, 'The P1P2/D Hypothesis: On the Intercity Movement of Persons', *Amer. Sociological Rev.*, 11 (1946).
[3] J. Niedercorn and B. Bechdolt, Jr., 'An Economic Derivation of the "Gravity Law" of Spatial Interaction', *J. Regional Science*, 9 (1969).
[4] J. Niedercorn and B. Bechdolt, Jr., 'A Further Reply and a Reformulation', *J. Regional Science*, 12 (1972).
[5] W. Allen, 'An Economic Derivation of the "Gravity Law" of Spatial Interaction: A Comment on the Reply', *Reg. Science*, 12 (1972).
[6] L. A. Sjaastad, The Costs and Returns of Human Migration, *J. Political Economy*, 70 (1962).
[7] S. Bowles, 'Migration as Investment: Empirical Tests of the Human Investment Approach to Geographic Mobility', *Rev. Econ. Stat.*, LII (1970).
[8] L. E. Gallaway, 'Industry Variations in Geographic Labor Mobility Patterns', *J. Human Resources*, 2 (1967).
[9] M. J. Greenwood, 'An Analysis of the Determinants of Geographic Labor Mobility in the United States', *Rev. Econ. and Stat.*, LI (1969).
[10] T. P. Schultz, 'Rural Urban Migration in Colombia', *The Review of Economics and Statistics*, LIII (1971).
[11] T. P. Schultz, 'An Economic Model of Family Planning and Fertility', *J. Political Economy*, 77 (1969).
[12] G. Becker, 'An Economic Analysis of Fertility, in National Bureau of Economic Research', *Demographic and Economic Change in Developed Countries* (Princeton University Press, Princeton, 1960).
[13] J. Mincer, 'The Labor Force Participation of Married Women', in National Bureau of Economic Research, *Aspects of Labor Economics* (Princeton University Press, Princeton, 1962).
[14] G. Cain and A. Weininger, 'Economic Determinants of Fertility: Results from Cross-Section Aggregate Data' (University of Wisconsin, Discussion Paper, 1967).
[15] B. MacMahon, T. Pugh and J. Ipsen, *Epidemiologic Methods* (Little, Boston, 1960).
[16] L. B. Lave and E. P. Seskin, 'Air Pollution and Human Health', *Science*, 169 (1970).

[17] L. B. Lave and E. P. Seskin, 'Does Air Pollution Cause Ill Health', Working Paper, Carnegie-Mellon University, August 1971.

[18] J. Lave, L. Lave and S. Leinhardt, 'A Model for the Delivery of Medical Care to the Urban Poor', Working Paper, Carnegie-Mellon University, 1972.

[19] J. W. Simmons, 'Changing Residence in the City, A Review of Intraurban Mobility', *Geographical Rev.*, 58 (1968).

[20] W. Alonso, *Location and Land Use* (Resources for the Future, Inc., Washington, 1961).

[21] J. Rothenberg, 'The Economics of Congestion and Pollution: An Integrated View', *Amer. Econ. Rev.*, 60 (1970).

[22] E. Mills and D. de Ferranti, 'Market Choices and Optimum City Size', *Amer. Econ. Rev.*, 61 (1971).

[23] L. B. Lave and J. DeSalvo, 'Congestion, Tolls, and the Economic Capacity of a Waterway', *J. Political Economy*, 76 (1968).

[24] P. Rossi, *Why Families Move* (The Free Press, Glencoe, Illinois, 1955).

[25] D. Friedland, *Residential Mobility and Choice of Tenure*. Unpublished Doctoral Dissertation, Harvard University, October 1970.

[26] J. Wolpert, Behavioral Aspects of the Decision to Migrate, *Papers of the Regional Science Association*, 15 (1965).

[27] W. Bell, 'The City, the Suburbs and a Theory of Social Choice', in S. Greer *et al.* (ed.), *The New Urbanization* (St. Martin's Press, New York, 1968).

[28] B. Ellickson, Jurisdictional Fragmentation and Residential Choice, *Amer. Econ. Rev.* 61 (1971).

[29] R. F. Muth, *Cities and Housing* (University of Chicago Press, Chicago, 1969).

[30] D. Bradford and H. Kelejian, 'An Econometric Model of the Flight to the Suburbs' (Princeton University, Working Paper, 1971).

[31] J. Rothenberg, 'Strategic Interaction and Resource Allocation in Metropolitan Intergovernment Relations', *Amer. Econ. Rev.* 59 (1969).

A Biologist's View of the Consequences of Urban Change

Tibor Bakács

INTRODUCTION

The technological revolution of our age has been accompanied by an ever increasing process of urbanisation. In the economically developed countries this process has almost reached a saturation level. Some countries have even reached this level, with urban populations amounting to 90 per cent of the total population. This process of urbanisation has furthermore widened the gap between man and his environment. Man now lives in towns under increasingly artificial conditions. He has gradually moved away from the natural environment in which he has lived in harmony for millions of years. The whole pattern of biological evolution has thus been interrupted.

Man has adapted to this new environment. However, the former equilibrium has been upset with the result that the urban environment, and its changes, has led to more and more noticeable conflicts. This disequilibrium is causing the progressive biological degeneration of urban man. This degeneration is usually termed the health hazards of urbanisation.

The changes in the pattern of urbanisation are now so rapid and dramatic that biological adaptation by itself is no longer sufficient. Reconciliation becomes more and more difficult and even impossible. Such difficulties can only be overcome by a careful biological analysis of the underlying causes of biological degeneration. We have to study the health hazards of urbanisation to identify their biological causes so that we can monitor carefully the relevant processes in the ecosystem which lead to the long-term denudation of the environment.

THE BACKGROUND TO URBANISATION

Before man started any social organisation the earth had been populated by a number of natural, self-regulating ecosystems dependent on the climate. Within these ecosystems man existed surrounded by an intact, undamaged environment. Some development clearly did take place within these systems but only at a very slow pace. The animal and plant kingdoms (the flora and fauna) which developed alongside the natural ecosystem likewise underwent slow changes over long periods of time. These changes were regulated by the existing feed-back mechanism of population density and by the short-term and long-term assimilative capacity of a given area. The ecological equilibrium was thus dynamic although in this initial model of the ecosystem the changing balance of forces was much slower than in the accelerated life of the present.

All patterns of life followed this slow but continuous process. In the long past cold (ice age) and warm climatic periods interchanged even more slowly than they have done in the recent past. As a result the assimilative capacity of an area has also changed producing changes in the number of existing species, in their inner proportions, and has sometimes even led to the extinction of a species. This was how animals like the mammoth, the cave-bear, the sabre-toothed tiger and other species disappeared (natural catastrophes often gave the final impetus to such changes).

Man, evolving one to two million years ago in limited numbers with a short life expectancy, was an insignificant part of the first natural ecosystem. Man thus hardly affected the fate of this ecosystem. His influence on the ecosystem began much later and it was only gradually that he started to accumulate knowledge and experience as he emerged from this natural environment.

Man's emergence naturally had repercussions on the ecosystem. The ecological equilibrium was upset and the rate of change increased. Man monopolised more and more of the natural environment for agricultural purposes, he domesticated wild animals and established settlements in which to live.

This stage of development produced a transitory model of the ecosystem. In contrast to the previous model where natural forces predominated and the natural feed-back mechanism was able to operate unhindered, in this type of ecosystem the natural feed-back mechanism was upset as a direct and conscious result of man's activities. The natural ecological self-regulatory mechanism was affected as the short-term effects gradually diminished at the expense of long-term ones.

In due course this intermediate agricultural model of the ecosystem developed into a new ecosystem characteristic of our age. In this artificial ecosystem man's activities gradually resulted in a further denudation of the natural environment. Genuine environments can now only be found in tropical jungles, in nature conservation areas or in reservations. A completely artificial environment, a 'culture' environment, has now become dominant. This is characterised by cities, by industrialisation and by a surrounding agricultural area overloaded with biologically active substances. In this new environment the most important change is the process of urbanisation harnessed to a pattern of agriculture based on the use of chemical fertilisers and pesticides.

In the cities the natural environment is almost completely lacking and has been replaced by an almost wholly artificial one. Man, by transforming nature, has apparently eliminated the natural feed-back mechanism and has replaced it by his own will. In the course of this process, the short-term environmental effects have been almost completely abolished but – contrary to man's intention and will – the number of negative long-term effects have increased. It is only recently that we have begun to realise this and to understand the implications of these unexpected consequential effects. This explains why everyone engaged in analysing the problems of urbanisation (engineers, physicians, local government officials and economists) has to employ biological methods to analyse the overall effects of urbanisation.

Until recently the process of urbanisation took place spontaneously without due regard to the biological requirements of the population. This has led to the biological basis of the environmental deprivation caused by urbanisation. Man has made substantial progress since the Industrial Revolution, i.e. in little more than 200 years. In the short run it seemed that man had succeeded in controlling his environment. However, in the long run, the diagnosis was quite different. The increased disruption of the biological feed-back mechanism has led to irreversible biological damage. It has not taken thousands of years for this to become apparent: the accelerated pace of recent decades has resulted in noticeable damage within the recent past. The last 200 years have supplied unequivocal evidence of environmental deprivation.

Since the end of the 18th century, man has effectively been able to control epidemics. This has had ecological implications. Jenner's discovery, at the end of the 18th century, soon resulted in the production of an effective smallpox vaccine able to control this apparently intractable disease that usually accounted for a large number of fatalities. During the last 30 years of the 19th century new knowledge in the field of microbiology rendered the control of infectious diseases even more successful.

Among the results achieved were the following: fatal diseases like smallpox, plague, typhus and cholera – which were fatal in 25 to 30 per cent of cases and seriously disrupted the pattern of urban life – were reduced to a fraction of their former occurrence. Even polio-myelitis and measles are now effectively controlled.

With scientific progress man also succeeded in overcoming a number of other environmental factors which had also indirectly affected population densities. Insects like mosquitoes, ticks, etc., which transmitted infectious diseases in many parts of the world, were successfully brought under control. The net result was that infant mortality rates were considerably reduced. In some developed countries it has fallen to less than 2 per cent, a figure that many people thought was impossible to attain. Indeed, the control of infectious diseases is now so efficient that in the developed countries they only account for a seventh or an eighth of the mortality figures; only 40 years ago they were the single most important cause of death. Today it is traffic accidents, killing people like a 'sweeping guillotine', that now precede infectious diseases as the principal cause of death.

Development has become so rapid that man's most dangerous enemy is man himself. Although he has effectively conquered most of his traditional enemies, his hasty and unconsidered action has upset the natural balance, creating new hazards to life and to its qualitative enjoyment. These unexpected side-effects are mainly attributable to the impact of urbanisation which is cumulatively affecting man's entire life cycle.

The disequilibrium resulting from urbanisation has manifested itself during the latter part of the 20th century. Scientific and technical progress contributed to this pattern. Life expectancy slowly began to increase and foreshadowed the demographic explosion, illustrated in Fig. 4D.1, that we are presently witnessing. The prolongation of man's life span was hardly noticeable at the start. The figure of

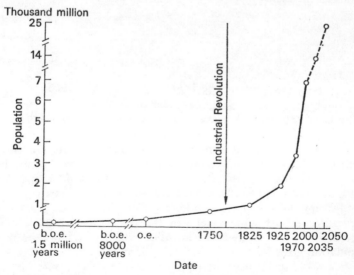

FIG. 4D.1   Growth of World Population

30–33 years in the 18th–19th century was little higher than the 22–24 years of the migration period. The difference was small enough to leave the ecological equilibrium undisturbed. During the last 50 years, however, life expectancies have doubled in the economically developed countries (see Fig. 4D.2). In several of them it has reached an average level of 70 years.

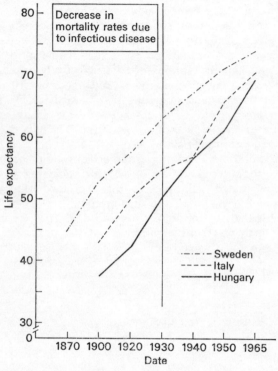

FIG. 4D.2   Life Expectancy in Some European Countries between 1870 and 1965

During this period a similar process started in the developing countries. In India, for example, average life expectancies have increased during the past 20 years from 27 to 44–45 years. While overpopulation due to increased longevity has been partly compensated for by family planning in the developed countries, this has not been done to the same extent in the developing countries. This pattern is well illustrated in Fig. 4D.3 which compares the recent population growth in the United Kingdom and India.

On a world scale, the number of births is thus increasingly exceeding the number of deaths. The former balance between births and

deaths has been upset and has seriously disturbed the previous eco-
gical equilibrium. Population increases have assumed the proportions
of a demographic explosion. The situation is even worse in most
cities. Quite apart from the demographic explosion most cities are
experiencing massive population migration from countryside to

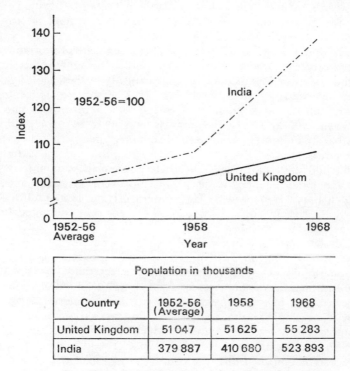

Population in thousands			
Country	1952-56 (Average)	1958	1968
United Kingdom	51 047	51 625	55 283
India	379 887	410 680	523 893

FIG. 4D.3   Population Growth in India and the U.K.

town. In the countryside, on the other hand, this trend has mitigated
the consequences of the demographic explosion.

The explosive growth of population was first experienced in those
countries undergoing an industrial revolution. It thus first appeared
in Europe and in the United States. It is not difficult to find an
explanation. Prior to the Industrial Revolution and even after this
period, a considerable proportion of the population was employed
in agriculture. The technology of agriculture was fairly primitive.
Modern large-scale farming was initiated much later than large-scale
industrial production.

Lacking mechanisation, the farm workers had to increase their
output by employing more labour; large farming families thus

became the pattern rather than the exception. Modernisation of agricultural production clearly led to a great deal of redundancy. Family planning thus became 'a social necessity' which rapidly broke through most impediments (e.g. the interdicts of religion).

In the developed Western countries population growth slowed down between 1900 and 1950 as family planning started to have an effect. After 1950 it became so 'successful' that their annual increase in population hardly reached 1 per cent. The population of Hungary will be doubled only in 224 years at the present rate of reproduction.

The centre of gravity of the demographic explosion has thus shifted to the underdeveloped countries. The majority of these states gained their independence after World War II. The shift in the centre of gravity of the demographic explosion is a recent phenomenon. Between 1900 and 1950 the population growth in these countries was hardly more than 1 per cent. The underlying cause was not the low birth rate but the poor health conditions and the extremely high child and infant mortality rates. After these countries had become independent, the situation improved, bringing about a sudden population growth. In the period from 1950 to 1965, the yearly increase in population reached 2·1 per cent compared to 1·2 per cent in the developed countries.

This breath-taking increase in population has severely upset the ecological equilibrium with all its direct (short-term) and indirect (long-term) implications. First, as a direct effect, there were quantitative and qualitative shortages of food. Food production could not cope with the increasing requirements of the population – particularly in developing countries. Let me illustrate this by means of an example. The developing countries, which comprise 70 per cent of the world's population, only produce 11 per cent in the world's total food production. In India, the country most afflicted by the demographic explosion, the per capita food consumption is now believed to be lower than it was during the last decades of the Great Mogul Empire – in spite of the efforts made by the progressive Indian Government. The per capita daily intake of calories in India is much less than a healthy body requires and is considerably less than it is in Europe.

THE RESULTS OF URBANISATION

It was on the above basis that the process of urbanisation started and has continued to develop at an increasing speed. Urbanisation is actually a consequence of the Industrial Revolution and its effect on environmental hygiene. During the last 150 years (1800 to 1950) the number of cities with a population of 20,000 to 100,000 inhabitants increased twenty times and the number of people living in cities increased from 16 million to 314 million.

In 1800 only 2·4 per cent of the world's population lived in cities with more than 20,000 inhabitants. In 1960 some 20 per cent of the world's population, i.e. 600 million people, lived in cities with more than 100,000 inhabitants and by 2000 this figure will probably reach 3,000 million or 50 per cent of the world's estimated population (some authors suggest it might be as high as 60 per cent of the world's population).

This is clearly the most important event in the present environmental-ecological situation. The trend of urbanisation, with its progressively destabilising effects, is further undermining the ecological equilibrium. The number of city inhabitants is increasing more rapidly than the world's total population. The former is increasing at an annual rate of 2 to 3 per cent (in the tropics, Latin America, Africa and in some parts of Asia the rate is as high as 5 to 7 per cent); the latter is only increasing at a rate of 1·7 to 2·0 per cent (see

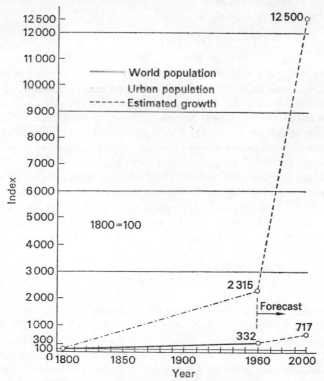

FIG. 4D.4   Index of World and Urban Populations

Fig. 4D.4). The number of people living in a natural environment is consequently decreasing in both relative and absolute terms. This points to the heart of the urban problem and to its hazards for human health.

What ecological implications has the urban environment for urban man? People living in an urban environment have become irreversibly detached from their natural surroundings, from the environment with which – as we have seen – man interacted during thousands of years of evolution (before he moved into settlements and cities) as a stable and balanced biological entity. The artificial urban environment is a distinctly unnatural one composed of modified hygienic factors which may represent a long-term health hazard to urban man. Considering the complexity of these factors, the damage may be irreversible if no attempt is made to eliminate them. The unnatural factors are: polluted urban air, lack of sunshine and ultra-violet radiation, inadequate drinking water – both in quantity and quality, lack of foliage and other complex factors upsetting the ecological equilibrium (e.g. stress effects, noise, accident hazards, the pace of life, urban overcrowding, etc.).

CONCLUSION

Summing up, the cumulative long-term effects of environmental deprivation are related to those points of the natural feed-back mechanism which defy more and more human activity and which prevent man from taking entire possession of his environment. Urban man lives in this environment under self-inflicted dangers which are characterised by combustion products, polluted urban air, quantitative and qualitative limitations on water supply, the constant danger of accidents, noise and other stress effects, and a host of other environmental constraints. These are not problems which can be overcome by architectural interventions and town planning alone. All the related disciplines (engineering, medicine, etc.) must join hands to reconstitute the natural environment. It will not be an easy task.

The recognition of the biological implications of environmental deprivation has already been partly achieved. But that only deals with the biological side of the problem. Man is the only member of the ecosystem who is able to create a social environment independent from the biological one. And as a result of the interaction between dynamic, ever-changing social factors, the social environment – in a similar way to the biological one – is also subject to continual change. However, the discussion of these relationships goes well beyond the scope of this review.

Discussion of the Paper by
Lester B. Lave, Judith R. Lave and
Eugene P. Seskin

Formal Discussant: Evans. Very little work has gone into the study of the direction of intraurban migration, even by geographers. This paper is useful in that it indicates a possible line of approach. However, there are several ways in which the authors' methodology may yield incorrect results and I shall attempt to point these out in my comments.

In the first place it is surprising that in the equations which are used to explain migration from the central city to the ring of the S.M.S.A.s there is no variable indicating the proportion of the population (or the area) of the S.M.S.A. within the central city. Using a development of Alonso's [1, 2] theory of land rent it can be shown that, even in a city in long-run equilibrium, there will be considerable migration towards the centre as young people move from the parental home to their own flat and away from the centre as they grow older, marry and have children. In a city in which the central city constitutes a small portion of the S.M.S.A. it is inevitable that a large part of this normal migration will involve movement out of the central city; where the central city is a larger part of the S.M.S.A. most migration will occur within the central city and in any one period a smaller proportion of the population of the central city will migrate to the ring.

This point may not be merely a technical one, since other variables which are included as explanatory variables in the authors' regressions may well be highly correlated with the proportion of the S.M.S.A. which lies within the central city. An example might be the proportion of the central city's population which is non-white. If the proportion of the population of the S.M.S.A. which is non-white were approximately the same in all S.M.S.A.s, and all the non-whites lived near the centre of the city, the proportion of the population of the central city which is non-white would be negatively correlated with the proportion of the population of the S.M.S.A. which is in the central city and would therefore be positively correlated with the proportion of the central city population migrating to the ring. Another variable which should be included in their equations is one indicating the state (or the rate of improvement) of the transport system in each city. As they themselves mention in the introduction to the paper, an intuitive explanation for migration to the suburbs is that it is caused by improvements to the transport system, particularly the construction of limited access highways. It is therefore surprising that they do not use as an explanatory variable some measure of the transport system such as miles of limited access highways per square mile of the S.M.S.A. However, the major difficulty with their methodology and their results is that if the city were in long-run equilibrium they would not obtain significant results. Suppose that the S.M.S.A. were initially in equilibrium but that for some reason taxes and/or pollution were to increase in the central city relative to the ring. The initial result would be a migration from the

city to the ring but this migration, because it would result in an increase
in the demand for property in the ring relative to the central city, would
lead to an increase in property values in the ring relative to property values
in the central city. Now it may be that this equilibrating mechanism works
only slowly and inefficiently but, since several empirical studies have shown
that property in areas with low air pollution is valued more highly than
that in areas with high pollution (Nourse [3], Ridker and Henning [4],
Anderson and Crocker [5]) and at least one study has shown that property
values are inversely related to the level of local taxes (Oates [6]), it seems
certain that it does work at least partially. These changes in relative
property values will damp down the rate of migration and in equilibrium
will eliminate it entirely. Two conclusions follow from this; firstly, the
non-significant variables in the authors' analysis may be those with respect
to which equilibrium has been reached in the property market; secondly,
where the authors' explanatory variables have significant correlation coefficients it follows that the property market is not in equilibrium and
hence that variations in property values do not fully reflect the differences
in pollution levels, etc. Therefore the attempts which have been made to
measure pollution costs by differences in property values underestimate
these costs. This is, I think, an important point.

Mills did not believe that this model captured the dynamics of metropolitan decentralisation. Research by Colin Clark [7], Richard Muth [8],
himself [9] and others showed that decentralisation had been pervasive
since the 19th century in cities throughout the industrialised world. This
strongly suggested that the basic causes were not the peculiarities of post-
war U.S. life that the paper was concerned with. Race, local government
fragmentation, etc., were undoubtedly contributing factors, but could
hardly be very important.

Kolm warned against generalising too much from the present U.S.
situation since other countries, other cultures, other historical experiences
and other periods in time had resulted in different city structures. One
could not claim to have produced a general theory of urban structure on
the basis of explaining why the rich left the central cities or why buildings
were higher at the centre. In France, for example, it was the poor who
left the city centre and went to live in the suburbs. City centres also usually
had safer streets than the suburbs (but this was much less of an issue than
in the U.S.). Commuting congestion was more a low-income activity in
France than it was in the U.S. Or consider the height of buildings. Hoch's
and Mills' papers (Chapters 3 and 7) showed cities with higher buildings
close to the centre. This structure was not typical of most French cities.
The French city generally had four-storey buildings in the central areas,
which increased to 10 or 15 stories further away from the centre. They
finally fell to one story or zero (countryside) at the perimeter.

Albers, speaking as a physical planner, observed that economists
tended to treat space as a homogeneous commodity subject to the workings
of market forces. To some extent this had changed at the national and
regional level, e.g. Central Place Theory, but had not really affected
thinking at the urban level. This was particularly true in the U.S.A. where
city structure had developed almost solely under the influence of market

forces, and city phenomena were interpreted within this framework. It was no accident that Europe (whose cities were more determined by historical forces and – in the last decade – by planning decisions) had produced no theories like those of Burgess [10] and Hoyt [11], on land use structure in cities. But if Bakács was right in saying that urbanisation could not be stopped but could only be controlled, then the physical arrangement of urban land uses at the micro-scale would assume added importance. Economics could contribute to the solution of these questions if only it would extend its interest to the location of human activities – equivalent to the allocation of spatial resources – at the micro-scale as an aid to planning.

Silver thought that the investigation of the environmental adjustments made by the household through the residential move were extremely worth while. Their pursuit represented one of the lines of research which promised to enhance our understanding of the dynamics of urban growth. However, the empirical approach used by the authors was not very promising. Evans had very skilfully summarised its shortcomings. One now had to ask what gross or net population flows from the central city to the suburbs really represented. Surely they reflected a great diversity of motives and responses. By examining the phenomena over a cross-section of metropolitan areas, the authors had introduced additional heterogeneity by way of differing spatial patterns, etc., which could not be easily captured by any of the summary measures likely to be available to the investigators.

While the authors had discussed some of the problems of the particular data set they had employed, there were also additional considerations which should at least have been mentioned. First, the decade of the 1950s was one of substantial annexation of peripheral areas to the central city. These annexations were especially prominent outside the North-Eastern U.S. where central cities tended to be surrounded by incorporated municipalities. In metropolitan areas, such as Phoenix and Albuquerque, the 1960 population of areas annexed to the central city was comparable to the 1960 population within the 1950 central city boundaries. Much of the movement from older, centrally-located neighbourhoods to newer neighbourhoods of stereotypical 'suburban' character would therefore have been recorded as moves within the central city. Households which in 1955 resided in areas annexed to the central city between 1955 and 1960, and which moved to the area defined as the ring in 1960, would have been counted as movers within the ring. Both of these facts biased the numerator of the dependent variable downwards in the gross migration equations, a bias which varied directly with the proportional increase in central city populations through annexation. Inclusion of the 1960 central city population in the denominator tended to counteract this bias, but to an indeterminate extent.

Another kind of problem resulted from the particular form of the dependent variable which included in the denominator total numbers of the class (whites, non-whites, etc.) residing in the central city. If departures from the average mobility rate were stochastic, i.e. accounted for by influences outside the models, included variables which were correlated with the denominator, and hence with the size of the metropolitan area, might appear significant. Variables positively correlated with size would display a negative regression coefficient, and *vice versa*.

Few of the variables included in the regressions actually displayed significant parameter estimates. Examination of Equation 5 in the text, for instance, indicated that only central city density in the medium range, percentage of non-whites in the central city, and the tax rates in the ring relative to the central city were significant at the one per cent level. Even for these there were some plausible alternative explanations along the lines of the previous objections. Higher densities were associated with older Eastern areas where extension of the central city was likely to be constrained by the existence of incorporated municipalities surrounding it. The percentage of central city residents non-white may appear to be related to the out-migration rate of whites because in the older central cities of the South, where non-white proportions were high, intra-metropolitan mobility was much more likely to be inter-municipal mobility than it was in the West, where central cities had a greater tendency to expand to keep pace with the rate of urban settlement (or even more simply because the proportion of non-whites was negatively correlated with city size). The influence of tax rate differences might also be of interest, but since they did not represent a price for services but a proxy for the level of service, their influence was difficult to interpret. It seemed plausible that there were very different preference orderings for various public and private goods among different types of households, so that the effect of a divergence between tax rates in the ring and the central city would presumably depend upon the composition of the central city population. The authors' willingness to waive consideration of differences in household characteristics other than race, particularly stage in the life cycle, therefore seemed difficult to rationalise. Again, including a measure of city size in the denominator of the dependent variable might account for the apparent significance of the tax-rate variable, since larger central cities were more likely to be surrounded by very urbanised municipalities which were obliged to provide high levels of public service.

While a number of additional specific observations about the analysis might be made, it was clear that the phenomena which the authors were attempting to explain were disparate and complicated, but that their analysis bordered on the simplistic. In particular, it seemed that in their empirical work the level of aggregation was such that any positive results were likely to be spurious and misleading. A potentially more fruitful – though also more arduous and costly – approach lay in analysis at the micro level, so that differences both in household and in environmental variables could be accounted for.

Lave thanked the discussants for some helpful observations, but reserved the right to argue that virtue was predominantly, if not entirely, on the authors' side. Evans pointed out that the city could not be in static equilibrium when there was migration. This was correct, but rather than reason from a model where a structural change occurred at a single point with all subsequent changes being adjustments to it, they had viewed the city as constantly experiencing minor structural changes that gave rise to migration and other adjustments. While they wouldn't quarrel with Mills' observation that migration had been with us for a long time, and that their model was hardly an adequate representation of dynamic forces, they would argue that it tended to isolate the important factors affecting migration in the U.S. from 1955 to 1960.

Finally, they had a fundamental disagreement with Silver about the relative merits of theoretical and empirical work in looking at urban adjustment. Of course there was a diversity of reasons for migration, just as there was for individual purchases of tea. Economists hardly claimed to estimate demand functions by looking at the individual motives of every tea purchaser, but rather gained extremely useful information by ignoring these 'details' and concentrating on simple, aggregate, price-quantity observations. In any empirical work there were an indefinitely large number of places where the data were inadequate. The task of good empirical work was to incorporate suggestions for dealing with inadequacies, to provide a sensitivity analysis of the results and to replicate the analysis. Quantitative estimates required empirical work and one often gained great insight from simple analysis.

REFERENCES

[1] W. Alonso, *Location and Land Use* (Harvard University Press, 1964).
[2] Alan W. Evans, *The Economics of Residential Location* (Macmillan, 1973).
[3] H. O. Nourse, 'The Effect of Air Pollution on House Values', *Land Economics*, Vol. 43, No. 2 (1967).
[4] R. G. Ridker and J. A. Henning, 'The Determinants of Residential Property Values with Special Reference to Air Pollution', *Review of Economics and Statistics*, Vol. 49, No. 2 (1967).
[5] R. J. Anderson and T. D. Crocker, 'Air Pollution and Residential Property Values', *Urban Studies*, Vol. 8, No. 3 (1971).
[6] W. E. Oates, 'The Effects of Property Taxes and Local Spending on Property Values', *Political Economy*, Vol. 77, No. 5 (1969).
[7] C. Clark, 'Urban Population Densities', *J. Royal Statistical Soc.*, CXV, Pt IV (1951).
[8] R. Muth, *Cities and Housing* (University of Chicago Press, 1969).
[9] E. Mills, *Studies in the Structure of the Urban Economy* (Johns Hopkins Press, 1972).
[10] R. E. Park, E. W. Burgess and R. D. McKenzie, *The City* (University of Chicago Press, 1925).
[11] H. Hoyt et al., *The Structure and Growth of Residential Neighbourhoods in American Cities* (U.S. Printing Office, Washington, 1939).

Part II

Urban Transportation

5 An Introduction to Urban Transportation Problems*

Robert Mossé

5.1 INTRODUCTION

Before 1914 there were very few urban transportation problems, except in a few large cities like Paris, London and Tokyo where congestion had been the rule for more than a century. The great bulk of the population lived in towns or villages, seldom larger than 50,000 inhabitants, and of more or less regular shape with a diameter of something like 1 or 2 kilometres. To go from one place to another in the town usually involved distances of less than 1 km, which could easily be walked in ten minutes or less. There was little traffic congestion (as we know it today) and there were to traffic lights. Pedestrians were not therefore forced to stop *en route*. The introduction and spread of the bicycle in the first half of the 20th century allowed towns to grow to twice, or even three times their former size, since people could cycle at 15 k.p.h. instead of walking at 5 k.p.h. This development had, of course, already occurred to some extent with the limited use of horses and horse-drawn carriages.

The real revolution in urban transport came during the inter-war period with the growth of private motoring. Thanks to the speed of the private motor car it became possible to enlarge the area of cities very considerably. However, the longer distances soon started cancelling the advantages of greater speed. The growing number of vehicles led to the need for controls, e.g. traffic lights and one-way streets, or to obstacles like a shortage of parking places, which soon reduced the speed of cars to that of the bicycle and hansom cab. Moreover, a larger proportion of the population now lived in towns, so that the inconvenience of urban traffic affected far more people than it did during the 19th century. As a result the problem of urban transport has become one of major importance. Travelling is not only tiring, it also wastes a great deal of time and causes so much air pollution that it destroys many of the benefits associated with shorter working hours. The working week declined from roughly 70 hours in 1900 to 40 hours in 1970 but, allowing for travelling and other similar wastes of time, people are still away from home for 55 to 60 hours a week. Real progress is therefore now more a matter of reducing travelling time than of further increasing productivity at work.

* Translated from the French by Elizabeth Henderson.

It should be added that transport difficulties have reduced the attractiveness of large towns. Indeed they have often destroyed their very *raison d'être*, A city used to be a place that provided entertainment; but what good are theatres if poor transport facilities make them inaccessible? A city also used to be a place for meeting people, as on the Spanish *paseo* or the Rue de la République of any French town – but this is of little use if one has to travel for two hours to be able to walk up and down the *paseo* for half an hour!

The problem of urban transport is thus rightly considered one of today's most important practical problems. To understand it we must first analyse journeys, or rather the need for mobility, according to their nature, frequency and the preferred mode of travel. In the broadest sense, this may be regarded as defining the demand for transport services. It is a multi-dimensional demand and the first question is whether it can be moulded or modified to enable it to be satisfied in the easiest way. Once we have a thorough knowledge of this demand, and of its human and social characteristics, we can then turn our attention to the technical problems of urban passenger transport. This should clearly include a consideration of new modes of urban transport.

There remains the problem of finance. There is little reason to expect that the present imperfect market mechanism could balance supply and demand. The user is probably unwilling – and is very rarely asked – to pay, even ovei a long period, for the enormous investment necessary to improve an urban transport system. There may also be social arguments (e.g. income distribution) for requiring the charge for transport services to be kept below their average cost and perhaps even below their marginal cost. It follows that urban transport must generally be treated as a public service involving government intervention in financial matters, as well as in the fields of control and regulation.

5.2 *TRANSPORT NEEDS*

From the point of view of journey purpose, a distinction can be drawn between two categories of journey external to the urban agglomeration and five wholly internal to it.

(1) *Transit traffic*. This represents vehicles which merely pass through the town on their way to a place outside it and this often causes considerable congestion on main streets (e.g. Valence and Nîmes). The physical planning in this case is well known and is already applied on a large scale: construct a by-pass. No transit traffic needs to go through towns like Lyon, Montelimar and other cities. By-passes are, incidentally, an old solution, witness the

circonvallazione of medieval Italian towns. The technical question is simply one of counting the traffic and then deciding whether the by-pass – which may be an urban motorway or a ring road – should have two, three, four or more traffic lanes. There is also the financial question of working out the cost of the project and of finding a suitable means of funding it. This is not always easy, since it is often a matter of political decision.

(2) The second 'external' traffic category consists of journeys entering or leaving the town. I shall call this *secant* or *radial traffic*. It requires access roads and these may create congestion at their interchanges. It may be expensive to build such roads in old towns, although it is often possible to use, or reserve, some existing major roads. In any event, journeys of this kind are often made by rail or by air. The former requires a set of suitable railway lines connected to one or more stations inside the town. While it is difficult at this stage to plan for new radial railway lines, except below ground level and at great expense, something needs to be done about giving more space to urban stations and to improving their interchange facilities, e.g. parking lots, and connections with city transport. Airports in their turn need to link-up with several central points or, at the very least, with one well-equipped town terminal.

(3) The category of traffic with which the public is most familiar are daily *commuter trips*, between home and work. They involve a large number of people at the rush hour and consume a great deal of time. Public authorities generally favour a public transport solution (subway, bus, etc.), but a large number of users prefer to travel by private car, and this causes peak-hour congestion which slows down traffic. In theory, public transport is preferable because it occupies less space and is much cheaper, in total as well as to the user. If demand could be modified so that a much larger proportion of travellers used public transport, the latter could be speeded up and overall travel times could be reduced. This solution is unfortunately not very promising since, given the absence of any road pricing mechanism, most people prefer to use a car no matter how much congestion there is. There are a number of indirect incentives which could be used to induce people to use public transport, e.g. parking fees, tolls on access roads, or a car tax, while another possible remedy might be to encourage, for town traffic, the use of smaller cars which create no noise, pollution or congestion, e.g. electric mini-cars. The greatest obstacle to the latter solution lies in the vested interests of car manufacturers and the trade unions.

In the longer term, commuter travel depends on the relative location of residential areas and of places of work (factories, offices, etc.). Where each of these is grouped around one end of a traffic corridor, public transport is easier; where homes are scattered and places of work are not, travel routes tend to be so complicated that each person prefers an individual means of transport. One way of getting results fairly quickly and cheaply is to stagger working hours as a means of reducing peak-hour traffic. For the mid-day hours this has already been done very successfully by the simple expedient of works canteens and restaurants in business districts; this development could be encouraged by a policy of government subsidies for canteens where there were shortages. Rush-hour traffic could, furthermore, easily be spread over two hours instead of one by staggering working hours in each district. For instance, the peak demand for transport along the boulevard Saint Germain in Paris could easily be spread by staggering the working hours, by only a few minutes either way, of the War Ministry, the Ministry of Public Works and the Ministry of Education. If urban transport is closely connected with location patterns, it is equally closely connected with location patterns and it is equally connected with time patterns. This suggests that all three should be controlled by one co-ordinating authority.

(4) *School travel*, at all levels of education, must be dealt with separately. In France primary schools are well dispersed throughout residential areas, so that the children can walk to school. In new housing developments and in new towns, primary schools have also been suitably located near homes. But for secondary and higher education the problem is more difficult. One way of reducing transport needs would be to introduce more boarding schools, or to attach student homes and hostels, together with canteens and restaurants, to schools and universities so that the young student's life could be organised within a relatively small geographical area. This would reduce overall travel demands. In other cases buses could be used and this would reduce the number of individual trips required.

In the United States, the situation is entirely different. There many students of universities live in dormitories at their institution and, thus, have no transport needs (except for week-end trips). Children at primary schools, however, are, in most communities, transported by bus from their homes to their schools and back again. In recent years, policies to achieve racial integration or desegregation have increased the 'school-bus problem'. In some places 85 per cent of the school children are transported by bus. Such policies clearly increase the demand for transport.

(5) Journeys from home to work and school take place at regular times each day. By contrast, *business and commercial journeys* are of uncertain frequency and can be influenced fairly easily. This category includes shopping trips, trips by shopkeepers to get their supplies,

those by commercial travellers and commercial business trips. All these take place at irregular times and cannot easily make use of public transport. The people often need door-to-door transport and this creates a strong need for an individual means of transport. Public transport is not precluded, of course, for it can be used during the off-peak.

Trips in this category can probably be fairly easily reduced without involving any hardship. With the increased availability of refrigerators and deep-freezers, shopping trips need to be less frequent; telephone ordering in conjunction with shop deliveries has the same effect. Many business appointments could likewise be eliminated altogether by using more single and multiple telephone connections. It may sound surprising to suggest that traffic conditions could be improved by introducing more telephones and reducing telephone charges, yet using a telephone is often a very convenient way of replacing a journey. This again suggests the need for one co-ordinating agency able to handle both transport and telephone problems.

(6) The sixth category consists of journeys providing access to *entertainment*. In the old days, the city offered convenient access to entertainment facilities. This was probably one of the major reasons for the rural exodus. But nowadays we are moving into a situation where many people prefer not to live in towns. The development of television, radio, motor cars, local festivals, etc., has meant that many small townships and rural villages can now offer a wide range of local entertainment. In big cities, on the other hand, distances have increased to such an extent that many people are now no longer able to take advantage of what the city has to offer. Although trips of this kind often take place in the evening when public transport is not crowded, this usually coincides with lower frequencies and even with the total cessation of public transport services. If one wants to go to a theatre, for example, this might mean two journeys; one to get home from work, and another to get from home to the theatre. This is another example which illustrates the advantage of co-ordination. In London, for instance, shows start fairly early and are generally concentrated in a limited area around Leicester Square. It is thus easy to get there straight from the office, either on foot or by taxi. The use of private cars, on the other hand, is most inconvenient because of the formidable parking problems this concentration creates. However, to the extent that Londoners go straight to the theatre from their places of work, rush-hour traffic is relieved and part of the evening peak is shifted to between 11 o'clock and midnight when travelling is easier.

(7) Finally, there is a *catch-all* traffic category to cover *miscellaneous* and *occasional* journeys. They may consist of a journey to the

dentist, to purchase a pair of shoes or to visit an art exhibition. They might also include periodic trips by old people or invalids needing special care and attention. In all these cases the user usually requires an individual means of transport, possibly with a professional driver.

5.3 *CONCLUSIONS TO PART ONE*

The above analysis of traffic demand leads to three conclusions:

(a) There is no such thing as a single demand for urban transport. There are a variety of needs, many of whose characteristics are only indirectly responsive to changes in price (e.g. the overall demand for home–work commuting). Some of these characteristics can be influenced, however: e.g. their timing can be influenced by staggering working hours; their frequency by increasing telephone facilities; and their nature by incentives to use certain modes of transport (e.g. public instead of private transport, or small cars instead of large ones). But to regulate demand in these ways is an extremely complex matter and requires co-ordination by one central authority empowered to act in a variety of fields, many having no direct connection with transport as such.

(b) The second observation concerns public transport. This is a tempting, and relatively cheap, solution to the problem of urban transport congestion. However, there will always remain some need for individual means of transport. This need rests not only on user attitudes, but also on objective necessity, e.g. the need for door-to-door transport for an invalid, for someone who has to travel with a heavy suitcase and for people who live some distance from the nearest public transport station. The problem of choice is to determine the optimum proportions of public and individual transport, and to achieve these proportions by non-discriminatory incentives. But policy makers should guard against opting for too much public transport. There is thus a case for trying to adapt the remaining private car traffic by trying to encourage manufacturers to make the cars smaller, less noisy and less apt to cause pollution.

(c) Finally, there is the relationship between transport and land-use patterns. In recent years, urban development programmes have been subordinated to the needs of public transport. Dwellings, factories, offices and shops are clustered around public transport terminals (railway and subway stations, bus terminals, etc.). It might be better to get rid of these restrictions and to utilise each different method of transport (including private cars) to preserve, or encourage, decentralisation and thus to reduce the existing congestion in urban areas. In other words, transport must no longer be conceived of as a constraint but must be seen as part of the solution. This does not of course preclude the use of lifts, moving stairs, funicular or cable railways, etc., to solve the problems of mobility in densely inhabited areas that do not readily lend themselves to solution by decentralisation. It is also worth noting that town-centre traffic congestion afflicts both old and new cities. In old cities, congestion at first causes paralysis and then decline, although revival might be possible by introducing pedestrian zones, etc. In new towns, on the other hand, attempts could be made to place the administrative centre, the business centre, the entertainments district, and a promenade, all within a small enough area to be within easy walking distance of parking garages and public transport terminals. Another solution might be to have more than one centre.

5.4 *THE MEANS*

The traditional distinction between individual and public transport is both confused and sterile. It is confused because it is not clear whether the words 'individual' and 'public' refer to ownership, management or the use or type of vehicle. It does not, furthermore, account for the ambiguous and complex cases where, for example, an individual vehicle is used successively by several individuals (e.g. taxi cabs). The distinction is sterile because both forms of transport are still needed so that the problem, in any given case, is simply one of deciding on the optimum balance between them. In some cities public transport will need to be developed; in others it might be better to plan for more individual transport. There thus seems to be no point in retaining this distinction. Each mode of transport will thus be discussed from four points of view: legal aspects, method of traction, capacity and type of vehicle.

(1) *Legal Aspects*

A method of transport may be owned by individuals, by private companies, or by public authorities. There ought to be no political or social bias in favour of one or the other category of owner. In some cases it is fairly clear that ownership needs to be individual (e.g. a bicycle), in others that it needs to be public (e.g. the subway). But there is more to it than that. We must ask who is responsible for management and who uses the vehicle or transport system. A fleet of buses may be entrusted to a technical management company with the public authorities merely controlling such matters as safety, fares, etc. Legal arrangements will also vary from one country to another. To any specific case an attempt must thus be made to work out a system which will optimise management and use. Private cars should not be unduly penalised, unless they lead to the underutilisation of transport capacity and to an excessive demand for road space. Instead of encouraging the expansion of public transport, it might thus be better to encourage the better use of individual vehicles for door-to-door transport (e.g. by the collective use of taxi cabs).

(2) *Method of Traction*

Human traction (or portage) was used until the end of the 18th century in Europe and rickshaws are still used in Asia. Animal traction became common in the 19th century, while the internal combustion engine is a relatively new development. Let us not forget that twenty years ago the normal means of transportation in Copenhagen was the bicycle. Next, no doubt, we shall go over to electricity, and then possibly to nuclear power. The ubiquitous and, to us, normal engine that drives our motor vehicles is thus a comparatively recent innovation and may well be superseded.

The choice of the method of traction is generally based on production costs, both of which depend on the state of technology. Technology and production costs depend also on the supply of raw materials and the size of their reserves. We are perhaps not thinking enough about the dangers of exhausting oil reserves, nor about the political risks involved on having to rely on imports. Calculations on the basis of private costs are therefore not good enough. The petrol engine causes pollution and noise. This imposes a serious social cost on the community, which can only be removed at great expense. Correct economic calculations should internalise these external costs, i.e. they should make the user bear them. Electricity-driven vehicles would do away with pollution and noise, but would probably be more expensive; to penalise petrol-driven cars and to enforce the use of electric vehicles in certain zones would thus be tantamount to internalising external costs. If a special tax were levied on petrol-driven cars, users would have an incentive to choose electric-driven ones. Consumers' choices could similarly be influenced by a reduction in vehicle taxes on electric cars.

(3) *Capacity*

The capacity of vehicles cannot simply by measured in terms of their carrying capacity. Other relevant factors are the daily or annual utilisation and the mileage covered. A better unit of measurement is the number of passengers per km per hour. A commuter train carrying 1,000 passengers at a speed of 60 km per hour has thus a capacity of 60,000 passengers per km per hour. A motorway carrying 5,000 vehicles per hour at a speed of 60 km per hour, each carrying four passengers, has a corresponding capacity of 600,000 units. If ten trains per hour are run on the commuter line, its capacity increases to 600,000. This elementary calculation should make it clear that the theoretical superiority of trains cannot be taken for granted. Clearly, one also needs to take account of the respective operating costs of 5,000 cars and x trains, as well as of the respective fatigue of n railway mechanics and 5,000 car drivers.

However, in actual fact, individual cars are generally underutilised, and it is this underutilisation which reduces their efficiency. We need to devise a system which will allow longer and continuous use of individual vehicles. This is the idea behind the scheme of introducing fleets of self-service taxis in certain towns; operated by dropping a coin or token into a slot machine to obtain a special key. These taxis could then be driven by anyone from one rank to another.

(4) *Type of Vehicle*

We cannot avoid the conclusion that during the last fifty years there has been no breakthrough in new means of transport. Subways go back to the end of the 19th century and, since then, have only undergone secondary improvements, e.g. longer trains, better lighting at stations, automatic doors, etc. The motor bus is certainly an improvement over the horse-drawn omnibus or an electric tram, but its average speed is no higher and the rolling stock is often obsolete (the average age of Paris buses is more than 30 years). It is hardly surprising, therefore, that the proportion of journeys made by public transport has remained rather low (about 55 per cent in Paris, and far less in most other towns). In any case, public transport is chiefly used for daily trips from one place to another. It is also difficult to adjust schedules to take account of daily variations in traffic. Public transport services are also usually infrequent and, worst of all, only serve a limited number of strategic points at the expense of adjacent areas. Public transport networks of relatively low density have led to an urban development pattern in which a number of central clusters are separated by large empty zones. But it bears repeating that urban patterns must not be subordinated to the requirements of public transport, however useful the latter may be in cases where large numbers of travellers need to be transported over long distances.

At present, experiments are going on with two great innovations. The first is overhead transport by vehicles suspended from a cable or monorail. This could greatly reduce road congestion, but requires access stations spaced out at a fair distance from each other. Another innovation is moving sidewalks. These could carry a lot of people and could have numerous access points, but their speed is bound to remain low until engineers have devised a system to enable people to step over from a slow to a fast track. Such a system, combined with automatic escalators, could be extremely useful in city centres and pedestrian zones. In the meantime public transport remains indispensable and, in many towns, should be encouraged. Its investment cost per passenger per km is much lower in terms of both vehicles and infrastructure. So is its operating cost, and it needs much less room both for circulation and for parking. For example, a bus occupying about 25 square metres of surface area carries 50 passengers; on the same area there is room for only about four cars carrying ten passengers. Finally, for an equal number of passengers, private cars create more noise and more exhaust gas. However, if public transport is to be expanded, it must be made relatively more attractive. It must be made to move faster, either by a reduction in the number of cars by the introduction of reserved bus lanes. Buses must become more comfortable, their frequency must be stepped up and their routes diversified to reflect more closely existing settlement patterns. Future developments will no doubt be of two kinds. We shall have fast and spacious coaches serving busy, long-distance routes, in conjunction with mini-buses running frequently on more varied routes in densely populated areas.

Whenever users have a real choice they nevertheless seem to prefer individual means of transport. A car takes a person from door-to-door. If offers the widest choice of departure and arrival times and thus adjusts flexibly to traffic variations during the course of the day. It can be used on motorways as well as on ordinary roads. At the same time it has two major disadvantages:

(a) it is expensive, both for the individual user and for the community, in terms of noise, pollution, etc.
(b) it creates congestion and thereby slows down traffic sometimes to the point of a complete standstill.

Whatever scheme is adopted for public transport, ample room will always have to be left for individual transport as well. With rising living standards, users will have more chance to satisfy their well-known preference for individual transport. But major improvements will be needed both in the road network and, above all, in parking facilities. Equally, we need an entirely new generation of cars, as regards their shape, performance and method of traction. We must develop, and bring into general use, a small car with a very small turning circle and an electric motor which causes neither pollution nor noise. And of course such a vehicle must be cheap enough to be used as a private car and leave enough purchasing power over for family journeys.

Studies have already been conducted along two lines, the 'beetle' (hanneton) and the electric mini-car.

5.5 *GENERAL CONCLUSION*

The problem of urban transport is one of the fundamental economic and social problems of our age. The benefits of half a century of economic progress are being all but wiped out by the inconvenience of urban transport. Given the complex nature of the questions involved, there is a cogent case for each city having a public co-ordinating agency which can effectively intervene in all the fields concerned, from road works and the purchase of vehicles to the expansion of the telephone system and the staggering of working hours. There must also be adequate financial arrangements for providing the necessary funds. In other words, urban transport must be considered as a public service.

Discussion of the Paper by Robert Mossé

Formal Discussant: Lady Hicks. As this is a very short paper I do not propose to discuss it in detail. I will merely emphasise a few points which seem to be especially important. The paper asserts that:

1. The transport problem, including congestion, is essentially a modern phenomenon for which the motor car is mainly responsible.
2. Since he cannot be expected to pay for it, it is socially necessary for the user (polluter) to be given what he wants at very concessionary rates.
3. Six categories of transport demand are identified (but several are closely interrelated and in fact overlap).
4. There is need for a central authority to 'manipulate' demand for road transport, i.e. to equilibrate it (to bring it to equality with available supply). Various experimental devices are suggested to *improve demand management* such as electric cars, monorails and moving sidewalks. (Note that the emphasis is concentrated on *demand* not on supply adjustment.)

A great deal could be said on all this, but there is neither the time nor the space to do so here.

In the first place traffic congestion is by no means a new phenomenon; it existed in certain cities long before the motoring age, especially where the site was cramped, e.g. Naples. The problem is now more general, but equally there are now more ways of dealing with it. The 19th- and early 20th-century method of improvement was to get the excess population off the streets into suburban trains and subways. This made very good sense before the generalisation of motoring, and it still makes sense where there are large numbers of low-income commuters to be transported for sizable distances. But every means should be used to ameliorate this position; for the modern world the suburban train/underground system is no longer an optimum solution. It is extremely rigid, entails under capacity usage of rolling stock and personnel for most of the day, and creates the need for additional means of locomotion from home to station and from town terminal(s) to place of work. Where an underground network has long been in existence, and where the conditions which made its establishment desirable are still in existence, it will no doubt continue to be useful. Additional lines filling in the system may be useful even if expensive. But to attempt to establish a new underground *system* is almost always a mistake (one or even two lines are of little use). The construction is very expensive and the disruption to traffic during construction may be very heavy. The underground system suffers from all the rigidities of the suburban surface system.

To my mind we have to accept as part of the data two propositions: (1) that large cities (Metro areas) will continue to expand both in size and population, notwithstanding tendencies (as yet relatively weak) for out-migration and decentralisation; (2) that the preferred means of transport is, and will remain, the private car. It far exceeds, in both flexibility and in potential capacity usage, any sort of public transport. (Buses are less wasteful of equipment than trains, but more wasteful of personnel.)

If these propositions are accepted the problem divides into (a) one of making optimum use of road possibilities, (b) making the road system capable of bearing an optimum circulation of traffic (the optimum naturally varying with location and stage of development); the overriding objective being to secure a steady flow of traffic with a minimum of congestion, although naturally speed will be reduced at peak hours. (Steady circulation minimises pollution.)

Making optimum use of existing street networks. I hazard that there is no city in the world which could not quickly increase the usefulness of its streets by a number of methods requiring little investment. In the longer run substantial street realignment, creation of inner and outer ring roads, and in many Metros in the less developed countries a doubling or trebling of street area in relation to built-up area will also be required. I am not concerned with these here.

Adapting the road network for better circulation. In the more short-run situation, many improvements suggest themselves: better maintenance both of main and of alternative route traffic segregation with limited access (for instance of lorries) on certain streets, better control at intersections (linked traffic lights, more roundabouts), and so on. The best of the minor improvements is probably underpasses at intersections, with escalators for pedestrians. Shopping plazas underground could help to pay for their construction. An idea which is popular with the authorities is to encourage the use of buses, which are certainly space saving if full. If streets are broad enough one traffic lane can be reserved for buses; this however reduces the space for general traffic, and may increase the degree of congestion. In the longer run custom built (probably elevated) bus lanes can be constructed, also express ways for general traffic. But if buses are to be really competitive they need to be both comfortable and frequent. There is some danger of overproduction to meet a market which does not exist.

The other side of adapting the road system for better circulation is improvement of parking facilities. It is necessary to distinguish (a) short-period (say up to 2 hours) parking, (b) all-day parking, (c) all-night parking (in lieu of domestic garage space). Item (a) can be dealt with by parking meters in side streets and discs in inner suburbs. The aim is drastically to reduce on-street parking and to forbid it in essential through ways. Item (b) calls for more parking blocks in multi-storey buildings and the compulsory inclusion of parking spaces (at ground level or below) in new buildings. Discs can be charged for, and all night parking could be subject to registration and charge.

Enforcement of controls is essential, particularly of parking rules. This calls for a substantial police and traffic warden force who are sufficiently well paid to be unbribable, and who are fully reliable. (For wardens, character counts more than training.) The whole force must clearly be under strict control.

Finance of street improvement is essentially a local responsibility and should be met from local resources, including charges, fines and taxation. Correct valuation and assessment of the local tax on land and buildings is very important. These sources should cover maintenance and minor investments. For large investments capital funds are needed from general capital funds or road bonds (which are popular with business interests which appreciate the advantages of increased speed). Higher level governments may be induced to help, e.g. by grants to cover debt service; but they should follow local policy and refrain from making the problems in the city harder, e.g. by insisting on concessionary bus fares and rent controls which drive the population out and swell the commuter tide. (Planned decentralisation of factories, housing and shopping centres is another matter. This tends to reduce the commuter tide.)

The adaptation of the street infrastructure for better circulation cannot sensibly be separated from other aspects of planning: location, housing and construction policy, and the relation between public and private activity. When short-term investments are being made it is very important to have a long-term programme concerning the shape of the future city at hand. Investments once made are difficult to alter. This is eminently a field where short-term mistakes can get in the way of the long-term optimum.

The planning process for the whole metropolitan area is much easier if there is a general planning (or administrative) authority for the whole area.

Hoch suggested that other transport innovations should also be noted. There was an express bus lane experiment in Washington, D.C. (Shirley Highway); there was work under way on computerised traffic signals and on stacked car parking. In the Washington area, it had also been suggested that parking be taxed to reduce traffic and pollution; this had met with a great deal of opposition. In general, in the U.S. parking access was often a function of status in the work organisation. People far enough up in the status hierarchy were granted subsidised parking spaces, i.e. the fees charged were well below the market price. This was probably an implicit way of avoiding income taxes on the imputed income involved. But it did constitute an incentive for private car use.

Kolm said that approximately one-third of the cars parked in Central Paris were parked illegally. Since the enforcement rate was low – indeed some of the illegal parking even seemed to be tolerated – the cost of illegal parking was similar to a random price. The probability of enforcement was highest where, and when, the nuisance caused by the illegal parking was highest. This system might be optimal. Part of the random nature of the enforcement system, was, however, avoided by means of 'clubs' in which the members collectively insured themselves against being fined. A similar system was used for vehicle licences which, in France, did not have to be displayed.

Lady Hicks replied that equity considerations demanded efficient enforcement and that this was true of most traffic management measures.

Müller commented that the author and Lady Hicks seemed to accept the assumption that consumers preferred an individual means of transport. But which consumers had this preference? In Denmark about 40 per cent of the population were either too young or too old to have a driver's licence. The two-car household was still very rare so that many people, including those who had no car at all, had to rely on public transport services. When Mossé therefore claimed that by stimulating individual transport he was making it a liberating factor, he was clearly only thinking of the affluent male. His liberating factor would cause a decline in public transport services and this would virtually imprison the rest of the population. He also disagreed with the author who argued that the distinction between public and private transport was both misleading and confusing. The author interpreted this distinction in terms of ownership: a much more useful interpretation distinguished between modes that could only be used by the owners and those which were available to everyone. This distinction argued strongly in favour of stimulating public rather than private transport.

Foster said that even in the San Francisco area, where car ownership rates were among the highest in the world, surveys of transit users showed that a very high proportion of these users, even in families with two, three or more cars, stated that they used public transport because no car was available. The redistribution effects of urban highway improvements often imposed severe losses on a comparatively small number of people through the decline of public transport. The chain of events was often as follows:

1. Car ownership increased. The male head of the family was most likely to drive and a proportion of them would motor to work. The wife and family would use public transport for local journeys.
2. Radial public transport would decline as more users diverted to car travel; as a result the quality and use of the public transport system would deteriorate further.
3. City public transport systems are commonly financed by the radial services which cross-subsidise the local services. The decline in the profitability of the former clearly encourages the closure of the latter.
4. The city family, especially in the suburbs, tends to acquire more cars. However, the cost of this, and the inability of many families to afford a car, revives interest in public transport.
5. The most profitable, or least unprofitable, public transport service that is able to help the suburban family is a radial one – the very service whose decline began the process.

It had been suggested that there were few short-run solutions which cities could implement as an alternative to capital expenditure. However, besides the introduction of efficient parking charges, there were a large number of traffic management measures available, particularly those designed to improve flows at intersections. One extremely interesting possibility was the use of temporary flyovers or overpasses. Because they were relatively cheap, more could be installed for a given cost. Because they were quickly assembled and taken down, they could be used experimentally in various configurations. This was especially useful since it was almost impossible to anticipate the resulting traffic flows analytically or by simulation. One could thus experiment until a successful configuration was found. The temporary flyovers could then be replaced by permanent ones while the temporary ones were moved somewhere else.

Albers sympathised with the way the discussion had shown that a multi-disciplinary approach was required which linked the economic to the traffic engineering aspects of urban traffic. However, as a physical planner, he was concerned with the apparent contradiction between individual preferences (the desire to use a private car) and the consequent loss of social amenities which everyone enjoyed. There seemed to be a problem of social accounting. The individual was unwilling to change his preferences because isolated action would almost certainly leave him worse off. One way of solving this dilemma seemed to be by influencing collective preferences; another was by manipulating land-use patterns. This was why planners favoured placing physical limitations on city size; although they tended to overlook the wide range of economic choice which a big city provided. Land-use planning should nevertheless be regarded as an alternative to solutions involving new transport technologies.

Seskin, replying to an earlier point made by Lady Hicks suggesting that urban transport problems could be reduced by providing low-cost housing in city centres, questioned the long-term effects of such a policy. The findings presented by Lave, Lave and Seskin (Chapter 4) regarding U.S. migratory habits from the central cities to the suburban rings, suggested that it was possible, if not probable, that such new housing would result in further out-migration by higher income groups. It may thus simply result in a trade-off between the modes of transportation serving the city. There would be less public transportation for the low-income groups now residing in the city and more private vehicles to transport the newly transplanted suburban residents. The final consequences on the environment of the city might be quite undesirable.

Hansen suggested that one way of increasing the utilisation of cars was to operate them as a self-drive car hire service. Cars could then be picked up from any one of a number of designated terminals and used to make journeys which would clearly have to end at another terminal.

Münnich pointed out that this method only worked when the demand for vehicles was scattered in both time and space. It could not work for commuter trips because all the cars would end up in the same place.

Evans said that the author had twice referred to the benefits of staggering office hours. However, most transport authorities had the greatest difficulty in persuading employers to stagger hours, and it was only now that we were studying the economics of cities that we could see why this should be so. The reason why the Central Business District existed was that firms wished to be in close proximity so that information could be passed quickly between them. The firms had to be in the same place *at the same time* to achieve these benefits. Differences in working hours would therefore be resisted. A relevant example was the pressure by London businessmen for Britain to synchronise its clocks with those of the Western European countries so that the London financial market would be at work at the same time as its European counterparts.

Decentralisation was likely to be more successful than staggering hours because the firm which decentralised gained some benefit through reductions in rent and wage costs, while the firm which staggered its hours benefited very little.

Lave observed that, since transportation in a large city required a great deal of capital, one could trade-off labour for capital by substituting buses and cabs for trains and trolleys. The latter were more flexible than the former and also saved capital by being used more intensively during the day.

The classical city, with its C.B.D. for working and shopping, was not adjusted to the automobile. The much more decentralised city (such as Los Angeles) is. A number of shopping and working centres would then be scattered throughout residential areas. He also noted that Los Angeles had a number of dense 'sub-cities', such as Santa Monica and Century City, with about 100,000 to 200,000 inhabitants. They contained both shopping and work areas. They also had good public transportation systems so that all normal activities could be carried on conveniently without cars. People who did not want to drive could easily take expensive cabs for those occasional activities outside their area (theatres or sports events).

Hoch raised two further points. First, there was a great deal of monopoly in local transit operations, particularly in taxi cabs (e.g. the prohibition of jitneys in most U.S. cities). Such monopoly was likely to generate opposition to any innovations like dial-a-bus systems.

Secondly, there had been some discussion of the underutilisation of capacity. The author referred to individual cars being underutilised and Lady Hicks noted less underutilisation for buses than for railroads. However, in the private sector, if people were willing to pay the price for a little used item (summer homes, snowshoes), he saw no real problem. The transport capacity problem was really an institutional problem connected to the use of non-compensatory prices.

Münnich observed that the urban transportation problem could not be solved without reference to the rest of the transport system. Cars were not only used for commuting. They were also used for short-term and long-term recreational trips. They were used in the evening or on week-ends to make inter-city trips, trips to the countryside and trips around the urban environs; on long vacations they were used to travel even further afield. A car therefore had to serve a variety of needs and a car suited to commuting was unlikely to be suitable for making long inter-city trips and *vice versa*. One could thus only solve the particular problems of the urban area by considering them in terms of the transportation system of the area as a whole.

6 Transport and the Urban Environment *

Christopher D. Foster

No completely comprehensive list can be made of the kinds of environmental effect urban transport has. A satisfactory urban transport decision which tried to allow for significant environmental effects might cover:

noise
vibration
air pollution
dirt
visual intrusion
loss of privacy
changes in the amount of light
neighbourhood severance, both physical and sociological
relocation
disruption during planning and construction
accident experience
pedestrian journeys
congestion and other benefits to vehicles [1].

Much longer lists have been made but one would expect that, if they could be valued, these would be widely accepted as a factual basis for decision-making. The effects under each head may in any given case be negative or positive compared with the *status quo ante* except, one supposes, those of disruption during planning and construction, which will be negative.

Because of institutional arrangements there is no easy general distinction possible between externalities and internal costs and benefits. Under most highway regimes the only properly internal factors are construction, maintenance and possibly costs of highway operation, traffic control and management. Probably, throughout the world, the vast majority of decisions on urban highway improvement, capital or operational, are still taken on a highly arbitrary basis, recognising little more than congestion at the point of improvement as relevant to the decision to improve. Even where more sophisticated studies are made, one still finds that what actually gets done is often

* Thanks are due to D. Bayliss, A. D. J. Flowerdew, I. Heggie, P. J. Mackie, H. L. I. Neuberger, and D. Wright, for comments on an earlier draft.

decided in old arbitrary ways. The more sophisticated procedures often require that agencies consider some categories of externalities – e.g. benefits to traffic and relief of accidents – but debar them from considering others. It is often easier to draw a distinction between internal and external for public transport undertakings, but normally not as clearly as for a private firm, because of the public service obligation, usually rather vaguely expressed, these undertakings frequently have. Nevertheless the principle that urban transport decisions should be taken as if all significant environmental effects were internal to the decision-making agency would seem sensible.

Some of these environmental evaluation problems may not be best considered in the immediate context of urban transport planning. An efficient policy on noise, vibration, dirt, accidents and congestion will affect the design characteristics and performance of vehicles. Pollution policy will affect the characteristics of vehicles and the fuel they use, but the effects of vehicle pollution are not fully separable from those of other pollution in as much as the consequences of much pollution are progressive with the concentration of pollutants [2]. Neither can some measures to improve the environment of transport be adopted by a city on its own – either because they involve changes in national law or because of economies of scale which fix the optimum at a level of activity greater than that of the city. The introduction of methods of metering to achieve efficient road charges which reflected the state of congestion would normally require changes in the law. It would be costlier for a city to adopt on its own because of economies of scale in the supply and use of the necessary equipment.

There is also the choice of criterion. Marglin [3] draws a useful distinction between redistributive policies to be ranked by social welfare functions that give explicit weights to the interests of defined groups, policies to achieve redistributive goals subject to efficiency constraints and those intended to achieve efficiency subject to constraints in their redistributive effects. A distributively weighted social welfare function is as yet almost certainly outside our experience but sometimes the main purpose of transport policies is to benefit certain groups (subject to constraints on efficiency). This paper will concentrate on the problems as they seem from the aspect of the city. In recent years far more attention has been paid to the redistributional effects of urban transport decisions. Sometimes this is to achieve distributional aims. In many large cities in underdeveloped countries, many of the poor can only afford to live at the periphery far from their job opportunities so that they have to accept the real cost to them of a long walk or bicycle ride to work. Subsidised public transport – probably through the adoption of a single fare irrespective of distance on the bus system – will increase their real income substantially. The distributional effects of policies or investment undertaken to improve efficiency are often of concern, however well or ill the goal of efficiency is defined. In so far as these side-effects are negative, making certain groups worse off, an acceptable position may be to ensure that urban transport decisions are Pareto-optimal and that compensation is actually paid. This would not be sufficient if the concern were with the positive side-effects of transport decisions: with those groups made relatively better off. Perhaps the most interesting case is to consider how far transport improvements and policies redistribute income towards the owners of land. The general effect of radial transport improvements is to extend the urban area and increase the amount of land at any given level of accessibility from the centre. Thus such improvements, by reducing the relative scarcity of land, will reduce aggregate rent in the city. However, in cities where the amount of space households and other land-users want is highly income elastic, the effect of transport improvements may be to increase the demand for land, thus increasing the share of rent in national income, as Alonso and Muth have shown [5, 6]. There is also an explicit discussion of the income distribution aspects of such a model in Mirrlees [7]. It will be assumed in what follows, however, that such positive distributional effects of transport policies are not the concern of the city decision-makers, by relying on Musgrave's dictum that distribution ought ordinarily to be the province of central government. 'Unless this is done, distributional adjustments at the state [or city] level may come to be nullified by interstate movements, and serious barriers to an optimal location of economic activity' [8]. Therefore the only distributional judgement made will be that change will be Pareto-optimal.

The principle that changes should be really Pareto-optimal, not just potentially so, implies that every sufferer from an effect of an urban transport decision should receive at least a *compensating variation*, to use Hicks' terminology. He should be on at least as high an indifference surface as beforehand [9]. However, as Mishan has pointed out, this does not lead to a determinate outcome unless the prior question of *rights* has been settled [10]. To adapt his example, it may well make a difference to the efficient outcome (because of income effects) as well as to income distribution, whether the legal position is that those living by a new motorway have a right to be compensated for the noise inflicted on them or whether the vehicles have the right to make the noise and those afflicted only the right, directly or through government, to bribe them to reduce the noise. Mishan appeals to equity in arguing that it is better that those affected should have the right to compensation rather than that the law 'place the burden of reaching agreement on the person or group whose interests have been damaged'. Unfortunately even if one were to accept Mishan's opinion that the sufferers should be compensated, this does not make the solution determinate. In a famous example taken from an actual legal decision, Coase cited the case of a Wigmore Street pastrycook. He had two mechanical mortars in an outhouse at the back of his house, one of which had operated for 60 years, the other for 26 [11]. A doctor bought the house next door. Years later he built a consulting-room out into his garden and against the outhouse wall in which were the mortars. The noise and vibration from the mortars was such that he could not use his stethoscope. He sued that the pastrycook should move or stop using them. Despite the time they had been in operation, he won his case. The significance of this case often seems to have been misunderstood. In another paper Mishan gives a very similar example to that given by Coase and treats it as a question of conflict of interest, which it undoubtedly is [12]. He then argues that 'the fact that a conflict of interest exists does not, however, always preclude judgement about culpability. If a burglar breaks into my house in order to steal my wife's jewellery, and I try to prevent him, there is a clear conflict of interest. For that matter, given the burglar's intention and his appraisal of the efforts and risks, an effective bribe to desist may be an overall Pareto-optimal solution. Yet it would be hard to conceive of any organised society having difficulty in deciding the rights of such a conflict.' Of burglary, yes, but it would not be so easy in respect of many environmental conflicts. Besides, the real issue here is not so much one of culpability as of expectations. When the pastrycook bought his shop the price he paid reflected both the existing state of externalities *vis-à-vis* the property and his expectations of how these externalities might change in future. The Court gave judgement for the doctor expressly on the grounds that he had a reasonable expectation of being able to extend his house into his garden without experiencing undue vibration and noise. In the same way the English law on compulsory acquisition of property for transport improvements and other purposes seems to begin with the assertion that the purchase of any property is a gamble. Depending on unforeseeable circumstances its value relative to that of other property may rise or fall. While the State must pay a fair market price for any property acquired, it is not its duty to compensate as if its proprietor had initially bought a certainty that his property would not be needed for development. The position seems to be even clearer where the issue is not acquisition of property but environmental damage to property that is not acquired, but is affected, say, by a motorway. The starting point from which the law is slowly moving is that people who acquire property must have a certain expectation of the probability of being adversely affected by externalities. To treat them as if they had a certainty of not being so affected is in effect to make them specially privileged by comparison with people whose amenities are damaged by private action, but not to an extent which the courts would regard as actionable. To take a more difficult case still, a house on a main street in a city may have experienced great vicissitudes of noise in its lifetime from when it was fronted by cobbles on which moved ironshod horses and iron-rimmed wheels. On what basis, and in relation to what absolute standard, can one say other than arbitrarily that those in such a house have a right to compensation from increased noise? Thus, contrary to what Mishan seems to be suggesting, the principles which should govern liability to compensation are far from self-evident and must be decided by more than straightforward economic principles. In what follows it will be assumed that it is important to establish what the compensating variation is; but the direction of compensation must be regarded as among the policy assumptions of the analysis.

It will be argued that it is generally most important to achieve efficient investment decisions in urban transport; yet it is pricing policy which has received the most attention, particularly in the theoretical literature, and which is probably best understood. The analysis of congestion charges is of particular theoretical interest. The adoption of an efficient road pricing mechanism reflecting differences in congestion, or other measures like parking charges and physical controls which can partially simulate their effect, would undoubtedly improve several aspects of the urban environment. Besides reducing congestion the resulting fall in vehicle mileage would reduce the visual intrusion of moving vehicles and so improve the appearance of the city. This would be even more likely if land or road space used for parking was charged on an opportunity cost basis to reduce the number of parked vehicles. While it is unlikely that a supplement to a congestion tax would be an efficient method of achieving any recognised environmental purpose, one could say that such a supplement could be chosen as a feasible method of moving towards an optimum or possibly as part of a package of measures, in total more efficient. There would also be a reduction in air pollution, since there would be fewer vehicles and the increase in vehicle speeds over the relevant range, together with the reduction in acceleration and deceleration of vehicles, would reduce the emission of pollutants per mile travelled. A significant reduction in vehicle mileage is also likely to lead to some reduction in noise, dirt and vibration, but it is more difficult to be sure that it will always lead to a reduction in the disutility experienced. Imposition of congestion charges will tend to spread the peak. While less noise and vibration will be experienced both in total and in the peak, more will be experienced off-peak. It is difficult to judge people's preferences between these two situations. A different question arises with the effects on accident experience, pedestrian journeys and neighbourhood severance where the actual effects largely depend on individual circumstances. Faster traffic generally means fewer but more severe accidents. It is difficult to know whether pedestrians will be able to move more easily and whether neighbourhood separation will be reduced. The imposition of congestion charges will also affect land use. If one sets up the problem in terms of an Alonso or Muth-type model which is monocentric (Alonso), where employment tends to be concentrated at the centre [6], or essentially monocentric, though allowing for suburban sub-centres (Muth), the effect of introducing congestion taxes will be to raise rents at the centre (and incidentally towards the centres of sub-centres) [13]. Because transport costs will rise in congested areas, there will be a tendency for those activities that value the greater accessibility of central sites to cluster more in the centre and thus to bid up rents. What the models do not reflect, however, is the interaction between residential and job decentralisation. One would expect that greater transport costs towards the centre would stimulate further movement of homes and jobs – those with a relatively lower valuation on central accessibility – away from the centre. The eventual outcome might thus be an extension of the area of the city and, *ceteris paribus*, a reduction in population and other densities. If one then makes certain simplifying assumptions, which do not seem too unrealistic, the exposure of the population to environmental effects of roads will diminish. These assumptions are:

(1) Population is distributed uniformly or randomly, except in so far as there is a greater tendency to concentration towards the city centre.

(2) Trunk highway route mileage can be regarded as forming the sides of squares (or other shapes) within the urban area. With given population, the number of these squares (or shapes) remains the same, but their sides lengthen. (One can suppose homes and other activities in the middle of these squares connected to their edges by minor roads on which the light traffic is less environmentally damaging.)

(3) The pattern and volume of trips is a constant function of population and income. On these assumptions the average distance of people and activities from main roads will rise as population density declines. Thus on average they are less likely to experience noise, dirt, visual intrusion, loss of privacy, loss of light and probably pollution.

However, while the introduction of congestion pricing is likely, in the long run, to affect population densities, the efficiency of introducing it will itself be strongly influenced by the pre-existing characteristics of the city – including its population density. Whether it is worth going to the expense of installing the infrastructure, as well as the administrative machinery needed to implement efficient congestion charges, depends on the demand elasticity and elasticity of the Marginal Private Cost schedule shown in Fig. 6.1. The elasticity of the

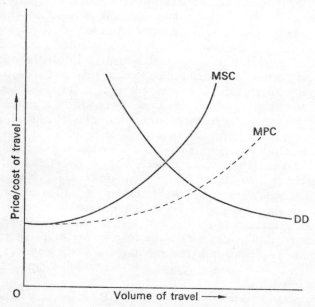

FIG. 6.1   Relationship between travel volumes and marginal costs

Marginal Social Cost schedule (M.S.C.), which differs from the Marginal Private Cost schedule (M.P.C.), in that it reflects congestion is such that $MSC = MPC \times [1 + \text{elasticity of } MPC \text{ curve}]$ [14].

As mentioned earlier, if demand is highly inelastic, road pricing would have merits as a tax, but not as an efficiency charge [15]. The substitute for car use which first influences the demand elasticity is the availability of good public transport which is itself free from congestion. In the absence of this, demand is still unlikely to be inelastic because the response to congestion at the centre will be (a) a greater clustering of activities with a high valuation of central accessibility and (b) a greater urban decentralisation than would otherwise be the case. Both Alonso [5] and Muth [6] assume that transport costs are linear with distance in all directions. If there is congestion towards the centre this will lessen its attractiveness as it will no longer be the point of minimum transport costs as the models assume. There will thus be more decentralisation, except for those activities which have other reasons for placing a high value on close contact. Imposing congestion charges, which further increase transport costs at the centre, will therefore have different secondary effects. Thus one would only be likely to find a highly inelastic demand where rent was high at the extensive urban margin either because the city is on a physically constrained site or its expansion is constrained by the vicinity of other cities so that rent at the extensive margin is not determined by agricultural rent but by rent at the extensive margin of the other cities. While it will vary with circumstances, it is often said the M.S.C. and M.P.C. schedules begin to diverge as speeds come down towards 20 mph. Whether the return from the introduction of efficiency charges will be high will be affected by how far below this the actual speeds are in private equilibrium as well as by the elasticity of the cost curves.

In a typical 'North American' city the demand elasticity for private car transport as a whole tends to be low because of the non-existence or atrophy of public transport. The greater decentralisation of both homes and jobs will also have made whatever public transport still exists less efficient than private transport. That the elasticity of substitution between public and private transport is usually very low is borne out by many studies [16]. It is also probable that the elasticity of substitution between roads in the system is comparatively high so that there is much less of a case for road pricing. While most complain of congestion it seems probable that it is far more localised in space and time in a 'North American' city. There will be less congestion of a kind which cannot be illustrated on diagrams such as Fig. 6.1 because these relate to a 'length' of road. It is characteristic of large British cities where there has been relative under-provision of express roads that the duration of peak congestion is longer and also that central peak congestion is more extensive. In the characteristic North American city the peak will be shorter and congestion will be localised. Efficient charges for congestion may not be so effective in diminishing existing congestion because they may represent a relatively small proportion of total journey costs. As a generalisation, the greater the provision of primary roads relative to population and real income per head, the less benefit will be derived from efficiency pricing. On the other hand there will be environmental benefits to set against the costs of generous road provision. While the mere existence of a larger primary road system will itself generate more traffic, on average it is probable that there will be less vehicle mileage per route mile. As has been argued earlier, this will realise certain environmental benefits. It is also likely that a larger primary road system will be associated with lower population densities [17]. Thus it will realise those environmental benefits associated with lower densities. What the net effects of these different configurations of traffic and environmental benefits will be, will be highly specific to place; and there has been little attempt to quantify, or evaluate, them systematically in terms of their physical characteristics. Indeed it is a fair point against advocates of congestion pricing that in general they do not conduct their analyses by assuming that the introduction of these charges should be made Pareto-optimal by compensating the losers. As the losers will generally be all private road-users, these should be compensated, presumably by lump-sum grants or in some other way which does not offset the effect of the congestion charges.

While the imposition of congestion charges, or the failure to impose them, will have environmental side-effects, there is every reason to suppose that an efficient system of environmental charges and regulations would not mainly be based on the introduction of congestion pricing. One might argue, however, that a city which had an efficient system of congestion pricing might be presumed to be in long-run transport equilibrium which, as we have seen, would have important implications for the size of the city, population densities and other matters affecting the quality of the urban environment. As Walters [18] has shown in equilibrium the congestion price or tax should tend to equal the return at the margin from expanding the urban transport system. If it were higher it would pay to expand the transport system to reduce congestion. If it were lower, there would have been overinvestment.

Howevei, there are reasons why it is difficult to imagine a city persisting in long-run transport equilibrium, apart from any question of the feasibility of introducing road pricing.

(1) While investments in the minor road system, as well as in buses and railway rolling stock, can often be regarded as the making of marginal adjustments, investment in new primary roads is notoriously indivisible. The recent practice of initiating so-called comprehensive land-use transportation studies has practically accentuated this. While expressways are still built piecemeal and sequentially, the studies try to evaluate alternative strategies of expressways (and sometimes public transport) usually by reference to some single target year in which it is assumed that each alternative network will be suddenly complete.

(2) Major transport investments are long-lived and in a rapidly growing city with more rapidly growing car ownership a large proportion of the benefits from an investment, even when discounted, may be predicted for the distant future. This throws great strain on

the accuracy of the forecasts. Because the costs of adapting or removing expressways and surface railways are very great, their longevity throws a large environmental shadow over the distant future. Formally this means that substantial negative benefits ought to be predicted for the distant future, representing the probability that the future may wish to obliterate or modify the structure, presumably for environmental reasons, at a positive cost. This may complicate the process of evaluation itself [19].

(3) It is rare that a transport strategy is built as it was evaluated.

(4) The methods of economic evaluation used are commonly far from perfect in relation to the costs and benefits they purport to measure. They generally ignore many environmental aspects.

The conclusion to be drawn is that it is most important to try to improve the quality of the transport investment decision. If these are often seriously wrong, in relation to their transport and environmental effects, then the role of charging policies and regulations will always be sub-optimal – they will simply attempt to make the best of a long-run disequilibrium situation. Moreover, a city which has, for example, markedly overinvested in roads or in mass transit will probably never be able to afford to reverse these investment decisions. In a very meaningful sense, it will have to live with its mistakes.

It is only during the last ten years or so that economists have done much research on the urban transport investment decision. The economic evaluation was, and still is in many cases, performed by engineers. Neuberger has found several common categories of mistakes [20].

(1) For example, it is sometimes enough in a simple situation to assume that the volume and distribution of traffic is the same before and after the improvement. The only change is that some traffic now uses the improved route. It is quite another matter to make a projection of traffic volume (and its distribution in space) for a target year, 10 to 20 years hence, which is determined principally by increases in population, income and car ownership and then to assign this, first to the existing network, and then to a proposed new network of facilities. This implicitly assumes that the demand forecasts are independent of changes in the network. This method – still in frequent use – may seriously overestimate the improvement in accessibility and in the relief of congestion. On the other hand if some allowance is made for additional traffic induced by the new network, evaluation on the basis of comparative total transport costs will, to that extent, understate the benefit, since the induced or generated traffic will be treated as if it incurs additional costs without generating any corresponding benefits. The 'do-nothing' alternative may also be badly

defined. It may be omitted altogether, in which case all one has is a set of incremental returns over the least preferred strategy and no reason to suppose that the return on all the resources involved is positive, or a supposed 'do-nothing' alternative might incorporate substantial new investments often on the rather doubtful grounds that they have already been decided on and are irreversible. The practical effect of these two errors is the same. There are many other errors which have also had to be cleared up – e.g. the treatment of taxation, network effects and changes in property values – which in some cases have seriously affected the value of the rates of return reached. It is now coming to be agreed generally that the correct maximand – setting aside questions of income distribution – is consumers' surplus measured for each link (or between every pair of traffic zones) separately and summed. (The consumers' surplus on any given link, however, if required to help decide on its construction, should be measured by summing the surplus changes on all links with and without the given link.) However, practice still frequently falls short of this.

(2) Closely allied to this is the desirability of always using capacity constraints in transport modelling to simulate for the investment decision, and the relationships between traffic volume and speed used in congestion pricing theory. To be useful such procedures must re-assign traffic between links according to the relation between speed, flow and capacity on each link until the result is realistic [21]. It will be more useful still if it makes reasonable predictions about the traffic that the congestion diverts off expressways; and in what proportions this traffic is assumed to use public transport, not to travel at all, etc. The greater realism of such procedure not only leads to better estimates of benefits from investment, but also generally does not hold out false promises that when expressways are built journey speeds will be high, particularly towards the centre of cities and in the peak.

(3) Most urban transportation studies in the past have tended to concentrate on the evaluation of highway networks and many are still only designed to evaluate such networks. Even after some cities began to ask their transportation studies to consider public transport alternatives, it took time to develop the necessary techniques. The difficulty was to develop sufficiently a sensitive demand forecasting procedure to predict what traffic would divert when another mode with distinct quality characteristics was introduced. Techniques have now been developed which make meaningful comparisons possible, especially in cities which already have some public transport [22, 23].

(4) The testing of alternatives has been costly so that normally

few alternative strategies have been tested. Each network tested has ordinarily been the existing primary network with very substantial additions, presented in total as a possible future transport system for the whole city. The costs of individual links will vary enormously. So will the traffic assigned to each and the traffic benefits predicted. Thus any average return on the whole network may give an exceedingly misleading impression of the return on a given link. Techniques have been developed for calculating returns on the major links separately. This makes it much easier to determine the relative importance of individual schemes and construct a more efficient overall strategy, as well as giving some indication of what might be the most efficient sequence in construction [24]. Further development is needed to model the actual effects of building links in sequence and to choose optimal strategies over time. However, even without this, what is now possible is a great improvement on what is commonly used.

(5) Not only is the choice of alternative strategies limited in number, but it is still common for the major alternatives to be conceived in the highways department. This is not always sensible. Frequently those who undertake the studies are presented when they arrive with a few extremely detailed plans for testing. More attention should be paid to developing techniques for the pre-selection of alternatives, and in particularly joint highway and public transport strategies. An excellent example of such pre-selection was the method by which the Commission on the Third London Airport [25] reduced a long list of possible sites down to four to which they gave detailed consideration. Logically 'pre'-evaluation should have the same maximand as full evaluation, but the estimation of costs and benefits should be simpler, allowing wider margins of error.

(6) Most transportation studies pay little attention to the effects of new primary roads and traffic growth on the secondary-road system. This normally understates total construction costs, since substantial improvement of the secondary network will often be needed to feed the primary network. The procedure also generally overstates traffic benefits, although some simplified procedures which allow for congestion on the secondary network are sometimes discussed. This is likely to be unimportant in a city with low population densities, a relatively straight orthogonal secondary-road system and a relatively high proportion of its land use already devoted to secondary roads. In an older city, on the other hand, the effective capacity constraint towards the centre may be on the secondary-road system. Improving the primary system may thus yield comparatively little benefit.

(7) Almost without exception a single year return is calculated for a target year, 10 to 20 years after the study year. While predicting a

time-path for costs and benefits is well beyond the present state of the art, and would greatly add to costs, there are biases in the present procedures which almost certainly normally lead to the overstating of benefits from investment. Gestation periods are normally long. Constraints on capacity in the system tend to have a depressing effect on the rate of growth of traffic benefits in the long run. While making one's basic evaluation still in terms of one year, it would not be difficult to calculate an N.P.V. allowing for the effect of the gestation period and allowing traffic predictions to run on in time to make a reasonable estimate of the time span over which congestion would be likely to diminish the growth of traffic benefits. Between the initial date of opening and the target year, and between the target year and the year in which substantial congestion is expected to begin (which could be before the target year, however), one would establish values by interpolation.

While there are many improvements to be made, particularly in the empirical estimation of demand and cost relationships, and in cheapening the operation of the studies, the state of the art is such that urban transportation studies can be far more meaningful than they are often allowed to be. In particular it should be possible to avoid many of the mistakes and procedures which in the past may have tended normally to exaggerate the return on highway construction in cities. It has also proved possible to make meaningful comparisons of disaggregated alternatives and between public transport and highway schemes, at least those public transport schemes involving substantial investment.

There have been substantial criticisms of land-use transport studies. Some have been of the techniques actually used, the biases in them and occasionally the unintelligibility of the results presented [26, 27, 28]. In essence, though perhaps not in detail, these have been the same kind of criticisms as those advanced in this paper. Boyce, Day and McDonald appear more sceptical [29]. Theirs is primarily a planning interest. They note that many of the more ambitious American studies of the late 1950s and 1960s set out to test how different land-use plans would affect transportation requirements (costs and benefits). They almost invariably found that no major differences in requirements was found. This was partly because the land-use plans tested normally had a large common component in as much for any existing city the possibilities of changing land use in the short-run were marginal. Cost and conservatism limited the alternatives considered. The exigencies of meeting deadlines and the difficulties of making computer models operational often meant there was not time to go back and try out new ideas. To this one may add that as long as one evaluates strategies as a whole, rather than disaggregated links, this will damp the differences between returns predicted for different plans. Moreover, a major difficulty here is deciding what are the costs and benefits associated with different land-use plans. While there is no particular difficulty in establishing an evaluation framework for such relatively localised developments as urban renewal, land-use zoning controls and other planning mechanisms which affect limited neighbourhoods, the benefits from different comprehensive land-use patterns for a metropolitan area are unlikely to be logically independent of transport benefits. It is only through refinement of models such as those of Alonso [5], Wingo [30, 31], Muth [6], and Solow and Vickrey [13] that one will be able to decide a meaningful logical evaluation framework without double-counting. Since, on the one hand, the evaluation methods for the transportation alternatives – themselves often flawed – did not come up with meaningful differences in the returns predicted, and on the other the ways in which planners tended to express their preferences for different land-use alternatives was not formalised, not economic and not consistent with the methods used in the transport evaluation, one cannot be surprised by Boyce's main finding. He argues that these studies should spend less time on costly computer models (which take ages to make operational and are then often of doubtful significance) in favour of using much simpler methods which enable the evaluator to learn from experience and to elaborate new alternatives during late stages of the analysis. What this assumes, however, is that it is important to choose between alternative *land-use* transportation plans rather than between transportation plans for a given city, which indeed, as Boyce has suggested, probably has little manoeuvre for alternative land-use developments except at the margin. If one is prepared to handle the comprehensive land-use planning issues separately until there has been sufficient refinement in techniques, then most of Boyce's objections lose their force.

A more pertinent objection is that the methods of urban transport planning we have described do not allow for the evaluation of environmental impacts. But before meeting that criticism directly there is one further point to be made on the evaluation process. During the last 10 years a number of urban transport studies have been made in the U.K. which partly meet, or can be modified to meet, most of the criticisms discussed earlier in this paper. In some cases not all the relevant findings are published; but the general impression, which must be tentative, is that returns on investment in large cities are low. (By comparison schemes in small cities appear to show higher highway but lower public transport returns. No systematic study has been done but it would seem that highway investment programmes for cities of between 100,000–200,000 commonly show first-year rates of return of between 25 per cent and 35 per cent; with public operations of 10 per cent to 20 per cent.) This is as true of the returns for individual schemes when disaggregated, with some exceptions, as it is for whole networks. It holds for expressways as well as for major mass transit investments; and for suburban as well as central city locations. While cost-benefit ratios of the order of 1:1·1 are not uncommon, it often seems that schemes for up-grading existing roads involving modest capital expenditure are responsible for a disproportionate amount of the benefits. There are a number of reasons why this effect may be more marked in the U.K. than in many other countries though undoubtedly other countries may approximate the same conditions:

(1) Land costs tend to be relatively high, particularly towards the extensive margin of cities [32]. This is because cities tend to be relatively close together and because urban green belts and zoning often raise the costs of urban land.

(2) Highway construction costs tend to rise progressively with population densities, independent of land costs.

(3) A high proportion of journeys tend to be short. The time savings experienced by those who divert to expressways and mass transit will thus be small and this will affect the volumes assigned.

(4) Congestion on the secondary road system often seriously affects the traffic benefits to be derived from new primary roads.

(5) In most cities there is already a fairly dense network of roads (and public transport) which also tends to reduce the time benefits to be derived from new links.

(6) There has already been very great investment in traffic control systems, and other forms of traffic engineering, to improve the performance of the existing street system.

(7) U.K. road-building in cities, excluding land costs, tends to be costly compared with the U.S.

While further investigation is required to establish the correct facts, and to explore similar hypotheses in other countries, the tentative conclusion must be that it will be difficult in the U.K. to make out a case for massive highway investment, or investment in mass transit for large cities, on the basis of traffic benefits alone. If correct, this must mean that the transport planner will increasingly have to rely on measures like:

(i) Improved bus systems which permit faster bus journey times on existing streets, usually at the expense of reducing the space available for private cars.

(ii) Improved traffic engineering measures which increase intersection through-put.

(iii) Piecemeal highway improvements such as the provision of under-passes and over-passes at busy intersections, selective street widening, etc.

(iv) Improving the performance of existing fixed track public transport systems.

(v) The introduction of road pricing and/or parking charges and physical controls to get more efficient use of the existing street system.

If one now turns to the environmental impacts of new urban expressways or surface railways, one needs to make a distinction between *relatively immediate* and *post decentralisation* effects. What often seems to be underestimated is the extent to which many of these environmental impacts, or at least elements in them, can be quantified and evaluated.

Environmental impacts on drivers and passengers vary according to the highways on which they drive. In principle it should be possible to estimate this from a more refined analysis of elasticity of substitution between modes (modal split) and between roads (assignment).

Noise measurement is well established and considerable research has been done on devising scales to reflect subjective preferences. As far as motorways or surface railways are concerned, the building of parapet accoustic walls or of earthworks is cheap, effective, but strangely neglected. Not only because of difficulties in establishing the direction of compensation mentioned earlier, but because of those of distinguishing between different causes of noise, it is probably more difficult, though by no means impossible [33, 34] to decide on the benefits of fitting double-glazing on noisy town streets.

Vibration effects can be severe, particularly when there are heavy trucks and when the buildings are old. While there are subjective costs from experiencing vibration, a minimum cost of damage or prevention can be established from experience and experiment.

Air pollution is one of the more difficult problems because of the complexity of the issues involved. Different pollutants have different effects. Since the effects of pollution are also a function of the concentration of pollution, the effect of any increase or reduction in automobile pollution will depend in part on the volume of pollutants from other sources. An expressway will also have localised pollution effects. The effects of pollution are also strongly affected by meteorological and even by micro-climatic conditions. While some of the costs of pollution – effects on paintwork, stonework, etc. – are in principle not difficult to cost, the medical effects are requiring, and getting extensive research, in their own right to establish causation and to attempt evaluation [35]. A rather arbitrary interim approach is not possible in many countries. There are often national or local regulations which require vehicles to fit equipment to reduce pollution. It does not seem unreasonable to assume that the State regards the implied cost per quantum of pollution reduced as a minimum implicit value to be placed on a marginal increase or decrease in a similar quantum of pollution achieved by other means [36]. Similar methods of implicit evaluation have been developed by Weisbrod [37] and Mera [38].

Dirt can be a considerable effect of new highway and surface railways as also of the build-up of vehicles on existing streets. It is not always dirt from, or stirred up by, vehicles that is relevant. The structures themselves can change the micro-climate in such a way as to affect the incidence of dirt. There is no difficulty in principle in measuring changes in dirt though it may be difficult in some cases to distinguish between these and other causes of increased dirt. This last difficulty, however, should be susceptible to controlled experiment. The additional paintwork and cleaning costs from dirt, including some evaluation of cleaners' and housewives' time, requires judgement but should not be beyond the possibility of getting some consensus.

Visual intrusion can have positive as well as negative aspects. If a motorway blots out an unsightly prison or railway yard, it may have positive benefits. On the other hand, the appearance of an elevated expressway or railway above a neighbourhood is one of the aspects most frequently complained of. In general, visual intrusion can be avoided by accepting the additional costs of putting a highway or railway at grade or in a cutting, though in many cases there may be cheaper solutions. As the additional expense may be greater and may well increase neighbourhood severance, it may be important to establish what costs it is worth incurring. Where the blight is direct it may be possible to use carefully-designed questionnaires to elicit values, because of the difficulty of disentangling the factors which cause changes in property values [39].

Loss of privacy from drivers and others being able to look at one in one's house and garden is another frequently disliked environmental effect. Walls and earthworks would prevent this, so that if these, being comparatively cheap, are justified to reduce noise, they would serve this end also. Otherwise they would also seem to require evaluation by questionnaire.

Loss of light is easier up to a point because part of the disbenefit can be valued in terms of the additional lighting costs of those affected; but there is probably a psychological element also which it would not be easy, or perhaps necessary, to disentangle where relevant from the last two items.

Neighbourhood severance can partly be quantified in terms of changed journey times and costs, and accident experience to pedestrians and traffic. Sometimes, however, a new journey, e.g. through a pedestrian subway, may be widely judged to be unpleasant so that there may be qualitative aspects. In some cases the lengthening of journeys may be considerable if the effect of the new structure is to remove a facility, so that those who journeyed to it have to go much further to serve the same purpose. In some cases the facilities removed from a neighbourhood – a hospital, school, factory – may be so great as to seriously alter the pattern of movement and activity affecting job opportunities and incomes. In principle the analysis of the costs of this is not different from that involved in determining the external economies resulting from building up industrial or other neighbourhood effects. Over and above that, there may again be particular subjective values attached to the neighbourhood severed or to the particular facilities removed.

Disturbance costs are all the costs, in some cases offset by benefits, which are experienced by people during the construction of new facilities: loss of business, excess noise, dirt, vibration during building and excess journey costs through diversions because of building.

Accidents are evaluated by well-established procedures of which perhaps the only major controversial aspect is the valuation given to human life [40]. A certain amount is known about differences in accident experience on different roads and in different circumstances. Again it would be possible to produce data, most of it of a cost-benefit kind, even if the decision on the value to be given to a life were avoided, which would be relevant to decision-making.

Relocation is defined here to cover compensation to those who relocate as a consequence of transport investments, whether property owners or tenants. While the theoretical position under many regimes is formally that of the compensating variation, practically it is often less than this. A correct procedure for estimating the compensating variation might be:

$$CV_r = f_t(H_1 + D + \Delta T + S) + f_p (IT + H_2)\pi$$

where f_t and f_p are technological and pecuniary externalities respectively. H_1 is the quasi-market value of the house, valued as if its value were not blighted by the prospect of the transport movement. H_2 is a pecuniary factor to reflect the change in the price of such houses or other property because the transport improvement reduces the stock of such property – this may be substantial if much property is being demolished in a short time – and the purpose is to convert from an *ex ante* to an *ex post* quasi-market valuation of the property. *D* is all real costs of disturbance or all costs associated with the move including the time costs of the tenant or owner in making the move. ΔT is the difference in transportation costs to the owner or tenant and his family, etc., from the move. This could be considerable if the effect of moving is to lead to longer journeys of several kinds. *S* is the subjective value placed on a particular property or neighbourhood – what the Roskill Commission called 'householders' surplus [41]. *IT* is (negative) income transfers and is different in that they do not represent a real cost. *IT* will normally only apply to businesses. For example, a small firm may lose profits temporarily or permanently because of a move, but its loss will be another's gain. As is evident from the Roskill Commission's work in determining plausible values in a similar situation – relocation because of a new airport – considerable quantification is possible which should greatly improve the basis for decision-making.

The item ΔT is difficult to value, since the house or property price reflects its *general* accessibility. If someone were to be fully compensated for his house but were then to buy a house at the same price farther from the centre but larger, it will be double-counting to compensate him also for the difference in transport costs already reflected in the house price. However, in so far as the journeys he and his family make are not reflected in the house price he would seem to have a case for some compensation. For example, he may live near his work, but when he relocates he may find it difficult – perhaps because of the transport improvement itself – to relocate near his work. There is no reason to suppose that disadvantages of this kind will be reflected in house prices; or any longer journeys his children may make to the same school, or the family in visiting relatives. Yet again differences in distance to shops may well be reflected in house prices. What one is after is a quantifiable element in his objective valuation of the amenities of his house.

If one collects together these categories of benefits (or disbenefits) each has elements which are susceptible to measurement and evaluation, whilst most also have elements which are less susceptible to measurement and evaluation. Yet even where one cannot go so far as giving money values, one can often quantify relevant facts in relation to different alternatives; so that the decision-maker may consider what weight to give to them in making up his mind – whoever he may be, an individual or a collective entity.

As well as Boyce, Day and McDonald's objections to the use of economic evaluation and the argument for its replacement by some other kind of evaluation, there have been other objections principally on environmental grounds. In many cases one feels they are contingent, not logical. Economists have become identified with the crude and incomplete rates of return mostly devised by engineers. Even where economics has had a greater influence, the broadening out to comprehend other (environmental) categories of costs and benefits has been slow. It cannot surprise one if authorities who persistently ignore important categories of costs and benefits, or make large changes which are not Pareto-optimal – whether or not they are potentially so – should stir up powerful political opposition from interests affected to the extent that, as in the U.S., it may be very difficult to build urban expressways or mass transit in most circumstances. Few of the *immediate* environmental effects of the construction of expressways or surface railways seem to be positive. On the other hand, they will have the indirect effect of stimulating decentralisation:

(1) The people relocated will tend to decentralise as will those sufficiently affected by the environmental consequences to prefer to move. These effects are equivalent to removing a sizeable chunk of urban land, usually a greater proportion towards the centre, and this can only be replaced further out

(2) The effect of better communications themselves will be to stimulate decentralisation as Alonso and Muth have argued; and, as has already been pointed out, this will be at lower population densities, though the extent of this will vary depending in part on the relative scarcity of land at the urban extensive margin.

In so far as one will expect negative environmental externalities to diminish with lower population densities, though probably at a decreasing rate, one would expect some environmental benefits from this decentralisation, while remembering that in some areas decentralisation will increase population densities. However, it is not impossible that, even if population densities do fall – and the existence of a green belt, for example, may prevent even this – that if negative environmental externalities decline at a decreasing rate, the net effect of decentralisation could be to increase environmental externalities per head because of the behaviour of those who must relocate. Falling population density is nevertheless not always associated with environmental improvement. Some environmental benefits are themselves a function of density – the pleasure of living overlooking crowded streets, etc. [42] What does seem probable even so is that a model which makes environmental impacts a function of population density will be the best way of linking changes in land use to transport improvements for environmental evaluation. One might eventually be able to compare the environmental impacts, for example, of allowing urban growth and decentralisation to continue (a) principally as a function of population and income growth; (b) stimulated in addition by the imposition of congestion charges; or, alternatively, (c) by transport improvements.

One could also add other theoretically feasible strategies for achieving a more efficient allocation of land – e.g. ending subsidies to home ownership, and constructing local fiscal regimes which allow for the efficient pricing of inter-governmental externalities [43].

If Mills' model (Chapter 7) represents the real world well and he is right that transport improvements effect little decentralisation, then the environmental benefits of highway construction will tend to be small except in so far as there is an actual reduction over the Do-Nothing projection in traffic on city streets through diversion to motorways. As has already been argued, in large British cities on average this would seem to be improbable. Under such circumstances the environmental effects may be expected to be negative. If one is also right that in British cities rates of return to traffic are much lower than would normally be used to justify an investment, then the case for investment is even weaker. If the relevant conclusions of Professor Mills' model do not hold, all depends on the actual effect on population densities.

REFERENCES

[1] D. Appleyard and R. Y. Okamato, *Environmental Criteria for Ideal Transportation Systems* (Centre for Planning and Development Research, Univ. of California, Berkeley, 1968).
[2] J. Rothenberg, 'The Economics of Congestion and Pollution: an Integrated View', *Amer. Econ. Rev.*, Vol. 60 (1970), pp. 114–21.
[3] A. Maas (ed.), *Design of Water Resource Systems* (1962), p. 62.
[4] H. Mohring, 'Land Values and the Measurement of Highway Benefits', *J. Pol. Econ.*, Vol. 69 (1961).
[5] W. Alonso, *Location and Land Use* (Harvard Univ. Press, 1964), pp. 111–13.
[6] R. F. Muth, *Cities and Housing* (Chicago Univ. Press, 1969).
[7] J. A. Mirrlees, 'The Optimum Town', *Swedish J. of Econ.* (March 1972).
[8] R. A. Musgrave, *The Theory of Public Finance* (McGraw-Hill, 1959), p. 181.
[9] J. R. Hicks, *Revision of Demand Theory* (Clarendon Press, 1956).
[10] E. J. Mishan, *Cost Benefit Analysis* (Allen & Unwin, 1971), Chapters 19 and 52.
[11] R. H. Coase, 'The Problem of Social Coast', *J. of Law and Econ.*, Vol. 3 (1960), pp. 1–44.
[12] E. J. Mishan, 'Pangloss on Pollution', in P. Bohm and K. V. Kneese, *The Economics of the Environment* (Macmillan, 1971), p. 71.
[13] R. W. Solow and W. S. Vickrey, 'Land-Use in a Long Narrow City', *J. Econ. Theory*, Vol. 3 (1971), pp. 430–47.
[14] A. A. Walters, 'The Theory and Measurement of Private and Social Cost of Highway Construction', *Econometrica*, Vol. 29 (1961), pp. 676–99.

[15] H. Hotelling, 'The General Welfare in Relation to Problems of Taxation and of Railway and Utility Rates, *Econometrica*, Vol. 6, (1938), pp. 242–69.

[16] L. N. Moses and H. F. Williamson, 'Value of Time, Choice of Mode and the Subsidy Issue in Urban Transportation', *J. Pol. Econ.* (June, 1963).

[17] Muth, *op. cit.*, (ref. 6), p. 307.

[18] A. A. Walters, *The Economics of Road User Charges*, I.B.R.D. Occasional Paper No. 5 (John Hopkins, 1968).

[19] M. D. Edel, *On Silent Springs and Multiple Roots: Cost Benefit Methods and Environmental Damage*, M.I.T. Econ. Dept., Working Paper No. 48 (1970).

[20] H. Neuberger, 'User Benefits in the Evaluation of Transport and Land-Use Plans', *J. Transpt. Econ. Policy*, Vol. 5, No. 2 (1971).

[21] R. Lane, T. J. Powell and P. P. Smith, *Analytical Transport Planning* (Duckworth), pp. 128–38.

[22] A. G. Wilson *et al.*, 'Calibration and Testing of the SELNEC Transport Model', *Regional Studies*, Vol. 3, pp. 337–50.

[23] Lane, Powell and Smith, *op. cit.*, pp. 116–28.

[24] House of Commons Expenditure Committee (Environment and Home Office Sub-Committee), *Urban Transport Planning*. Minutes of Evidence, Session 1971–72, especially 22 March 1972.

[25] Commission on the Third London Airport, *Minutes and Proceedings*. (H.M.S.O., London, 1971).

[26] Freeman-Fox, Wilbur Smith & Assc., *London Transportation Study*. (G.L.C., London), Phase III, Chapters 20 and 21.

[27] J. M. Thomson, *Motorways in London* (Duckworth, 1969).

[28] M. E. Beesley and A. A. Walters, 'Some Problems in the Evaluation of Urban Road Investments', *Applied Econ.*, Vol. 1, No. 40 (1970).

[29] Boyce, Day, MacDonald, *Metropolitan Plan Making* (Regional Science Institute, 1970).

[30] L. Wingo, *Transportation and Urban Land* (Res. for the Future, 1961).

[31] B. Harris, 'Quantitative Models of Urban Development: their Role in Metropolitan Decision-making', in H. S. Perloff and L. Wingo, *Issues in Urban Economics* (John Hopkins, 1968).

[32] M. Clawson and P. G. Hall, *Planning and Urban Growth: An Anglo-American Comparison* (to be published, 1973).

[33] A. D. J. Flowerdew, 'The Cost of Airport Noise', *The Statistician*, Vol. 21, No. 1 (1972).

[34] C. D. Foster and P. J. Mackie, 'Noise: Economic Aspects of Choice', *Urban Studies*, Vol. 7, No. 2 (1970).

[35] L. B. Lave and E. P. Seskin, 'Health and Air Pollution', in P. Bohm and A. V. Kneese, *The Economics of Environment* (Macmillan, 1971).

[36] G. Ridker, *Economics of Air Pollution* (Praeger, 1967), Chapter 4.

[37] B. Weisbrod, 'Income Redistribution Effects and Benefit-Cost Analysis', in S. B. Chase (ed.), *Problems in Public Expenditure Analysis* (Brookings Institution, 1968), pp. 177–222.

[38] K. Mera, 'Experimental Determination of Relative Marginal Utilities', *Q. J. Econ.* (August 1969).

[39] R. C. Wilson, 'Livability of the City', in F. S. Chapin and S. F. Weiss, *Urban Growth Dynamics* (Wiley & Sons, 1962).

[40] E. J. Mishan, 'Evaluation of Life and Limbs: A Theoretical Approach', *J. Pol. Econ.* (July/August 1971).

[41] Commission on the Third London Airport, *Minutes and Proceedings* (ref. 25), Appendix 3.

[42] J. Jacobs, *The Death and Life of Great American Cities*. Jonathan Cape, 1967.

[43] Muth, *op. cit.* (ref. 6), Chapter 13.

Discussion of Paper by Christopher D. Foster

Formal Discussant: Bolwig. There are five points in this paper which call for detailed comment.

1. The urban transport sector is only one of the sectors producing environmental side-effects. An isolated attempt to optimise within the transport sector will thus create a sub-optimal situation if the damage functions of pollutants are not fully separable between sectors, and as long as other sectors do not make appropriate adjustments for their own sectoral effects.

2. The aggregate income effect of environmental externalities may very well be significant. An efficient allocational solution will thus depend on the settlement of rights with respect to environmental rents.

3. The relative merits of charges versus different forms of direct regulations in urban transport are not explicitly evaluated in the author's paper. The social costs of implementing and administering a scheme of regulations may well be relatively small compared to a system of charges. In the case of water pollution the opposite may be the case, so that an important asymmetry in this respect should not be left out of consideration.

As an example of the direct regulation of traffic in city centres I would like to mention the case of Gothenberg [1] in Sweden where a relatively inexpensive method of regulating the central city traffic flows led to a substantial reduction of congestion and other external effects (e.g. by reducing the carbon monoxide content in the air). It also improved the capacity utilisation of an existing ring road.

Many traffic regulations are nearly self-controlling as soon as they have been introduced. The loss in welfare is a diminished choice of route alternatives or a less differentiated traffic service, but the welfare gain is less congestion and a better environment so that the forced standardisation of the 'traffic product' is obtained at a lower real social cost per unit of traffic service. Theoretically it is a sub-optimal solution, but the contention is that it may be less sub-optimal than a feasible scheme of charges.

4. The observation by A. A. Walters cited by the author that in equilibrium the congestion charge should equal the return on marginal investments to increase capacity (and the private marginal congestion abatement costs) is an application of the general principle for environmental effects stated by Beckerman: the charge (or bribe) for an environmental external effect should equal marginal long-run abatement costs through investments in installations for environmental improvements.

5. The problem of optimal traffic regulations, charges and investments in a given city has some similarity to the internal traffic optimising problem posed by buildings like hospitals, as mentioned by Buchanan [2].

Heggie noted that the author mentioned several factors which contributed to inadequate cost-benefit studies. He mentioned unconstrained traffic assignment models and forecasting techniques that did not allow for any interaction between demand and supply characteristics. Although he did not disagree with these comments he did not think that they constituted a complete answer to the inadequacy of cost-benefit techniques. One of the notable weaknesses of cost-benefit analysis was that it remained notably vague about procedures for selecting projects for detailed analysis. It clearly followed that no matter how sophisticated cost-benefit techniques might be they would not give the right answer when applied to the wrong problem. What was needed was a consistent method of generating a sensible list of projects ideas (planning alternatives); of screening them (using rough and ready procedures like the first-year rate of return) to arrive at a rough order of priority; to ensure that only promising projects were selected for detailed analysis. The problem of devising a consistent framework for carrying out this activity merited further attention from economists.

He also noted that the title 'Transport and the Urban Environment' meant that both harbours and canals should feature in the urban planning process. In the case of harbours we clearly wanted to avoid the adverse environmental effects associated with the shipment of traffics like oil and noxious products, while we wanted to take full advantage of the potential amenity value provided by a port – particularly by a fishing harbour.

In the case of canals he referred to the Passenger Transport Executives in the U.K., which are not only responsible for providing public transport services in the connurbations they cover, but are also taking over the residual responsibilities of the British Waterways Board in their areas. During the first few years of their existence, the P.T.E.s had clearly been preoccupied with their role as providers of transport services. However, they clearly also had a responsibility to preserve and enhance the amenity value of the canals they now administered and this raised a much wider issue. As transport facilities became redundant in urban areas – and this applied to railways as much as to canals – they often provided unique opportunities to add to the quality of life in an urban area. On the other hand, if they were simply abandoned, e.g. a derelict railway marshalling yard, they could represent a positive disamenity that detracted from the urban environment.

Albers observed that in the Gothenberg example, Bolwig should have distinguished between the cost of adapting an existing road system to a new functional use and – what seemed more important because it was less prone to accidental local conditions – the relative cost of building and maintaining two functionally different road systems. In the Gothenberg example, if the ring road was able to take the increased traffic there must have been unused capacity (unless the regulations themselves reduced overall traffic demand). In any case the real question was reducible to deciding on the size of the area from which through traffic should be excluded. We clearly had to choose the right combination of accessibility and environmental quality, as Buchanan [2] had pointed out.

Mills, referring to the low rates of return on urban road investment mentioned in the author's paper, hoped that people did not think that the long-term problem of transport had been solved. The post-war experience had shown that the real income elasticity of demand for transport was extraordinarily high. The 'product' itself was also extremely complicated: it included commuter trips, trips for recreational purposes, the shipment of goods – both as intermediate goods as well as final goods and services –

and so on. As economies become more industrialised and complex the demand for transport would also grow and become more complex. He therefore thought that more, rather than less, transport investment would be justified in future years.

Foster replied that he was referring to under-costed rather than under-priced road schemes. The motorway network in the U.K. was difficult to justify. It was therefore not only a question of not being able to charge the correct prices; it was a question of whether the roads should have been built in the first place.

Hoch said that it might not be as difficult to price transport services as the discussion indicated. For high-speed limited access facilities one could use toll booths or hoppers, where the motorist would pay for use. This would be analagous to tolls collected on bridges or on inter-state toll roads. By collecting tolls (i.e. by measuring the price elasticity of demand), we could then find whether road extensions were really economic.

He also argued that a fair case could be made for freeways in terms of accident reduction relative to arterial city streets. He had estimated that accident reduction costs equalled one-quarter to one-third of expressway construction costs for Chicago in 1960.

He finally referred to the author's comments on the impact of transport improvements on land values. One factor that was at best implicit here was that of the impact of induced immigration to the urban area by virtue of the transport improvement.

Foster replied that accident savings were complex and depended on how the new expressways relieved the city street system. He had argued in his paper that these reductions were less likely to be sustained in a British-style city, because the improvements generated more 'traffic' which, in turn, caused more accidents.

Tulkens, referring to Foster's discussion of expectation of rights, thought that one should draw a distinction between the type of uncertainty associated with whether a particular externality would be exerted and that associated with whether a law would be introduced to curb the externality. This clearly affected the attribution of environmental rights as well as observed market prices.

Kolm said that the paper argued that the return on investments in transportation was usually very low. However, in France, where the minimum acceptable rate of return was 12 per cent, the government had no difficulty in exhausting the funds budgeted for transport investment. Of course these calculations did not include such things as noise costs, and land values did not take account of amenity values, but the rates of return were nevertheless still fairly high.

Foster replied that it was not a question of whether or not the marginal rate of return on French urban roads was stated to be 12 per cent. What mattered was the validity of the methods used to calculate these returns.

Mills raised the question of compensation for external costs (attribution of environmental rights). The author's paper raised two questions. The first was that the proper compensation of the victims of external diseconomies did not necessarily interfere with efficiency criteria. The second was concerned with the definition of the 'victims'. Why did we not compensate all people affected by changes in government policy, e.g. people who lost money when government policy pushed down share prices? It was a fairly recent notion that everybody had to be compensated for everything that happened to them – directly or indirectly – as a result of public policy and it could be a dangerous notion to encourage.

REFERENCES

[1] F. Larsen, 'Trafikzonesystemet i Göteborg', *Byplan* 135, No. 5 (1971), pp. 157–9 (in Danish).
[2] C. Buchanan *et al.*, *Traffic in Towns* (H.M.S.O., London, 1963), pp. 33–52. Reprinted in D. Munby (ed.), *Transport* (Penguin, Harmondsworth), pp. 153–83.

7 Sensitivity Analysis of Congestion and Structure in an Efficient Urban Area*

Edwin S. Mills

7.1 INTRODUCTION

This paper is part of a continuing research project on the determinants of urban structure. By urban structure I mean a description of the kinds and amounts of goods and services produced in various parts of the urban area, the factor proportions with which they are produced and the ways that the transportation system links urban activities together.

In an earlier paper [2], the author formulated a linear programming model that makes it possible to compute an optimum urban structure under rather general conditions. This paper reports some initial computations with that model. The emphasis here is on the way optimum density of production and housing varies with distance from the city centre, on the optimum congestion of the transportation system and on the sensitivity of urban structure to changes in the transportation system.

Concern throughout is with the generic city, or metropolitan area. The terms city, urban area and metropolitan area are used interchangeably.

THE MODEL

The model analysed in this paper has been developed in detail elsewhere [2], where its relationship to earlier work is shown. That discussion will not be repeated here, but it will be convenient to set out the model briefly for ease of reference.

A land area at least as large as that to be occupied by the city is divided into a rectangular grid. It is assumed that fixed amounts of several goods produced in the city are to be exported from a predetermined point, which could be a railhead or harbour. Place the grid so that the export point is at the centre of the square designated

* The research reported in this paper was generously supported by a grant to Princeton University from Resources for the Future. The author is greatly indebted to John Yinger, who undertook the programming and computing reported here.

(0, 0). Then each square in the grid is identified by the ordered pair (i, j), $i, j = 0$, ± 1, ± 2, ... Transportation through the squares is assumed to be along rights-of-way running north-south and east-west through the centre of each square. In this model, resource allocation and transportation will be the same in all the squares that are a given travel distance from the city centre at (0, 0). It is easy to show that travel distance from the centre of (i, j) to the city centre is $u = |i| + |j|$ squares. There is of course one square whose centre is zero squares from the city centre and there are $4u$ squares that are just u squares travel from the centre, where $u = 1, 2, \ldots$. It is assumed that economic activity is distributed uniformly over the available land in each square. This is a good approximation to the optimum arrangement if the squares are small.

The two sets of variables in the model pertain to production and transportation. The production variables consist of a set $x_{rs}(u)$, $r = 1, \ldots \bar{r}$, $s = 1, \ldots, \bar{s}$, $u = 0, 1, \ldots, \bar{u}$. $x_{rs}(u)$ is the output per square of good r in s-storey buildings u squares from the centre. There are $\bar{r}$ goods produced in the city, $\bar{r} - 1$ export goods, and housing, which is good $\bar{r}$. Housing can be interpreted to include any locally produced and consumed goods. Item $\bar{s}$ must be at least as large as the number of storeys in the tallest building in the city. If aesthetic or other considerations dictate that the optimum city should have buildings no more than a certain height, then $\bar{s}$ should be set at that level. Otherwise, it should be set large enough so that the solution of the model yields $x_{\bar{r}\bar{s}} = 0$ for each r and u. The model can be used to compute the cost of artificial limits on building heights. If there is a physical barrier to extending the boundaries of the city, $\bar{u}$ should be chosen to reflect that limit. As now formulated, the model can accommodate only barriers that are the same number of squares of travel distance from the centre in all directions. If there are no barriers, $\bar{u}$ can simply be chosen large enough so that the solution yields $x_{rs}(\bar{u}) = 0$ for each r and s.

Production technology is of the usual linear programming kind. Item a_{qrs} is input of type q required per unit of output r in an s-storey building. Inputs are labour, land and capital. In the paper 'Markets and Efficient Resource Allocation in Urban Areas' [2], the model was formulated to permit labour input per unit of output to vary with building height. But no use is made of that possibility in this paper. $q = 1$ represents labour, $q = 2$ represents land, and $q = 3$ represents capital. The capital land substitution which building height represents is accounted for by choosing values so that a_{2rs} decreases in s and a_{3rs} increases in s for each r. These assumptions represent the fact that tall buildings require less land but more capital than short buildings per unit of output. An important advantage of the present model over these models [3] that employ neo-classical production functions, is that this model places no restrictions on the nature of the capital-land substitution. All manageable neo-classical production functions require the elasticity of substitution to be independent of factor proportions. It is assumed in this model that input-output coefficients do not depend on u.

The requirement that predetermined amounts of the goods be produced in the city can be expressed as

$$\sum_s \sum_u 4ux_{rs}(u) + \sum_s x_{rs}(0) \geq \bar{x}_r \quad r = 1, \ldots, \bar{r} \tag{1}$$

Unless otherwise indicated, sums are over integer values of the indicated index from one to the barred values. In inequality (1), $\bar{x}_r$ is the predetermined required output of good r. In this model it is assumed that each worker requires one unit of housing. Then the required output of housing services, $\bar{x}_{\bar{r}}$, equals the number of workers. Since the labour input per unit of output has been assumed not to vary with building height, total labour force is determined by output requirements. For convenience, output units can be chosen so that one worker is needed per unit output of each good. Then $\bar{x}_{\bar{r}} = \sum_{r=1}^{\bar{r}-1} \bar{x}_r$.

The second set of variables in the model is the amount of transportation of goods and workers in each square. Wherever in the city goods are produced, they must be shipped to the centre for export. (What follows can easily be reinterpreted to include raw materials imported into the city.) Likewise, workers must commute between their homes and work places. $T_r(u)$ is the number of units of commodity r that must be shipped through each square u squares from the centre if $r = 1, \ldots, \bar{r} - 1$, and the number of workers who commute through each square if $r = \bar{r}$.

The first step in specifying the transportation system is to relate the $T_r(u)$ to the $x_{rs}(u)$. Since all units of export goods must be shipped to the city centre, all units produced further than u squares from the centre must be shipped through one of the squares at u. Efficient use of the transportation system requires that the same number of units of a given good be shipped through each square at a particular u. Then,

$$T_r(u) = \frac{1}{4u}[\bar{x}_r - \sum_{u'=1}^{u-1} \sum_s 4u'x_{rs}(u') - \frac{1}{2}\sum_s 4ux_{rs}(u)$$

$$- \sum_s x_{rs}(0)] \quad \begin{cases} u = 1, \ldots, \bar{u} \\ r = 1, \ldots, \bar{r} - 1 \end{cases} \tag{2}$$

$$T_r(0) = \frac{1}{2}[\bar{x}_r - \sum_s x_{rs}(0)] + \frac{1}{4}\sum_s x_{rs}(0) \quad r = 1, \ldots, \bar{r} - 1 \tag{3}$$

The square bracket in equation 2 is the number of units of r produced more than u squares from the centre plus half the number of units produced in squares at u. The one-half represents the fact that the average unit must be shipped half way through the square in which it is produced. Equation 3 says that all units of r produced outside of $(0, 0)$ must be shipped halfway through $(0, 0)$, to the centre, whereas the average unit produced in $(0, 0)$ must be shipped a quarter of the way through the square.

If all output must be shipped to the city centre, it is inefficient for any workers to commute away from the city centre to work. If there were outward commuting, then total transportation could be reduced by an exchange between place of residence and place of work for workers who commute away from the centre. That all work-bound trips are towards the city centre implies that $T_{\bar{r}}(u)$ can be written

$$T(\bar{r}u) = \frac{1}{4u}[\sum_{u'=1}^{u-1} \sum_s 4u' (\sum_r a_{1rs}x_{rs}(u') - x_{rs}(u')) + \sum_r a_{1rs}x_{rs}(0)$$

$$- x_{\bar{r}s}(0)) + \frac{1}{2} \sum_s 4u (\sum_r a_{1rs}x_{rs}(u) - x_{\bar{r}s}(u))] \quad u = 1, \ldots, \bar{u} \quad (4)$$

$$T_{\bar{r}}(0) = \frac{1}{4} \sum_s \sum_r (\sum a_{1rs}x_{rs}(0) - x_{\bar{r}s}(0)) \quad (5)$$

Equations 4 and 5 say that the number of commuters passing through all the squares u squares from the centre equals the excess of employment over housing in squares closer to the city centre. Equations 4 and 5 are correct representations of commuting only if there is no outward commuting. This is ensured by

$$T_{\bar{r}}(u) \geq 0 \quad u = 0, 1, \ldots, \bar{u} \quad (6)$$

The technology of the transportation system is that the capacity of the system in a given square depends on the land and capital resources devoted to transportation in that square, but that varying amounts of traffic can use the system depending on the congestion level that is tolerated. The congestion level depends on the amounts of all kinds of traffic using the system. The total demand placed on the system in each square at u is represented by an index $T(u)$, where

$$T(u) = \sum_r t_r T_r(u) \quad u = 0, 1, \ldots, \bar{u} \quad (7)$$

t_r is the demand placed on the system by the shipment of one unit of good r through one square. It is convenient for numerical analysis to normalise the weights t_r by setting $\sum_r t_r = 1$. If commuters used a separate right-of-way from goods, Equation 7 would be an inappropriate representation of transportation demand.

Travel speed and, to a lesser extent, vehicle operating costs vary inversely with the traffic level. Therefore transportation cost per unit-mile of goods shipment or per commuter-mile varies directly with traffic volume. There is considerable uncertainty as to the precise form of the relationship and as to how it depends on the nature of the transportation facility. Write $c(u)$ for the total operating and time costs of the transportation in each square at u. For a fixed transportation facility, $c(u)$ is a function of $T(u)$. This function can be approximated to any desired degree of accuracy by a step function

$$c(u) = \sum_k c_k T^{(k)}(u) \qquad u = 0, 1, \ldots, \bar{u} \qquad (8)$$

$T^{(1)}(u)$ is the capacity of the system at congestion level one, e.g. no congestion. In general, $T^{(k)}(u)$ is the capacity of the system at the kth congestion level. c_k is the marginal cost of an extra unit of transportation at congestion level k. The sum is over $k = 1, \ldots, \bar{k}$, where $\bar{k}$ is the congestion level at which the system can absorb no more traffic. The system must use at least enough congestion levels to handle the traffic imposed upon it. This requires

$$\sum_k T^{(k)}(u) \geq T(u) \qquad u = 0, 1, \ldots, \bar{u} \qquad (9)$$

It is assumed that the capacity of the transportation system at congestion level one is proportionate to the land and capital devoted to transportation in each square. Then $b_2 T^{(1)}(u)$ and $b_3 T^{(1)}(u)$ are the land and capital employed for transportation per square at u. The only restriction imposed on the c_k's is $c_k \geq c_{k-1}$, $k = 2, \ldots, \bar{k}$. The fact that all the facility costs are imputed to the first congestion level means that restrictions are necessary to prevent the computer from trying to use higher congestion levels without using the first level. The appropriate restrictions are

$$T^{(k)}(u) \geq T^{(k+1)}(u) \qquad k = 1, \ldots, \bar{k} - 1 \qquad (10)$$
$$u = 0, 1, \ldots, \bar{u}$$

The final constraints ensure that production and transportation use no more land than is available in each square. They are

$$\sum_r \sum_s a_{2rs} x_{rs}(u) + b_2 T^{(1)}(u) \leq 1 \qquad u = 0, 1, \ldots, \bar{u} \qquad (11)$$

where, for convenience, distances have been measured in units that imply one unit of land area in each square.

An efficient allocation of resources in the city is one that minimises the cost of the required production and transportation. This can be expressed as

$$min\ Z = R[\sum_u \sum_r \sum_s 4ua_{3rs}x_{rs}(u) + \sum_r \sum_s a_{3rs}x_{rs}(0)$$

$$+ b_3 \sum_u 4uT^{(1)}(u) + b_3 T^{(1)}(0)] + R_A[\sum_u \sum_r \sum_s 4ua_{2rs}x_{rs}(u)$$

$$+ \sum_r \sum_s a_{2rs}x_{rs}(0) + b_2 \sum_u 4uT^{(1)}(u) + b_2 T^{(1)}(0)]$$

$$+ \sum_u \sum_k 4uc_k T^{(k)}(u) + \sum_k c_k T^{(k)}(0) \qquad (12)$$

In Equation 12 it has been assumed that capital can be acquired on a competitive market at rental R per unit and that land can be bid away from non-urban, e.g. agricultural, users at a rental rate R_A per unit. The first term in square brackets in Equation 12 represents the capital used in the city; the second square bracket is land used; and the remaining terms are transportation costs.

Minimisation of Equation 12 subject to Equation 1–11 is a conventional linear programming problem. The unknowns are the $x_{rs}(u)$ and the $T^{(k)}(u)$. Equations 2, 3, 4, 5, 7 and 8 define left-hand variables which are computationally inessential. By laborious substitution they can be used to eliminate the inessential variables from the inequality constraints. The programming problem is then to minimise Equation 12 with respect to $x_{rs}(u)$ and $T^{(k)}(u)$ subject to the constraints in Equations 1, 6, 9, 10 and 11 and non-negativity of all variables.

7.2 PARAMETER VALUES

The programming model in the previous section contains $(\bar{u}+1)$ $(\bar{r}\bar{s}+\bar{k})$ variables, not including slack variables. The criterion function is to be minimised subject to $\bar{r}+(\bar{u}+1)(\bar{k}+2)$ constraints, not including non-negativity conditions on the variables. These numbers would be much larger were it not for the assumptions that imply that all squares a given distance from the city centre are identical. Nevertheless, it is easy and tempting to choose dimensions for the model that make the calculations expensive and cumbersome.

For several reasons, it was decided to choose parameters that roughly typify U.S. cities of about one million inhabitants in the mid-1960s. First, such a city is big enough to be interesting, but small enough to avoid some of the complexity of large cities. Second, there are many cities roughly that size in the U.S. and elsewhere. Third, this was the city size chosen to analyse in *Studies in the Structure of the Urban Economy* [3], and it is interesting to compare the results of the two quite different models.

A typical U.S. metropolitan area of one million inhabitants has about 250 square miles of land area. It is computationally convenient to choose squares that are one square mile in area. That implies a $\bar{u}$ of about 11, but $\bar{u}$ was set equal to 12 on the hope that the computer would not completely use up the twelfth square. The tallest building in U.S. metropolitan areas of about a million people might be 15 or 20 storeys. It was decided to limit the city to 20-storey buildings but, to keep the dimensions of the problem small, only even numbers of storeys were permitted. This means that the computations were undertaken with $\bar{s} = 10$, although input-output coefficients are chosen to represent buildings twice that high. The results are reported in the next section for buildings with even numbers of storeys between 2 and 20. This is of course to be interpreted as an approximation rather than as a bias against odd numbers. Item $\bar{k}$ is the number of congestion levels and determines the accuracy of the step-function approximation to transportation costs. The term $\bar{k}$ is assigned a value of five, $\bar{r}$ represents the number of export goods and housing or labour types in the model. In the calculations there are two export goods and one kind of housing or labour, so $\bar{r} = 3$. Parameters are chosen below so that one of the export goods is produced near the city centre and one in suburban subcentres. Increasing the number of classes of labour and housing is a high priority in further calculations.

The dimensions just chosen imply that there are 455 variables and 94 constraints in the programming problem. The calculations were performed on Princeton University's I.B.M. computer, using the M for 360 program written by I.B.M. Each solution of the programming problem required about half a minute of computer time. The constraint matrix contained about 45,000 entries, of which about 7,000 were non-zero. A separate program was written to compile the entries in the constraint matrix from the parameters presented below.

The following paragraphs present brief justifications for the parameter values, which are summarised in Table 7.1.

A city of one million has a labour force of about 300,000. Labour input is measured in thousands, so $\bar{x}_3 = 300$. Good No. 1 is intended to be the output of the central business district. It is assumed that a third of the labour force works in the C.B.D. Measuring output of Good No. 1 by its labour input, $\bar{x}_1 = 100$. Good No. 2 is produced elsewhere in the city and must employ the rest of the labour force, so $\bar{x}_2 = 200$. These choices of units imply that the labour input-output coefficients in the two production sectors, a_{11s} and a_{12s} have values of one. No labour is employed in producing housing services, so $a_{13s} = 0$.

R_A is the rental rate per day (in thousands of dollars) per square mile of land in non-urban use. It is assumed that such land is valued at $3,000 per acre and that rents are capitalised at 10 per cent per year. These assumptions imply $R_A = 0.8$. R is the daily rental rate per $10 million of capital, measured in thousands of dollars. The capitalisation rate of 10 per cent implies $R = 4.0$.

TABLE 7.1

PARAMETER VALUES, MODEL A

s	a_{21s}	a_{22s}	a_{23s}	
1	0·50	0·50	0·70	$\bar{x}_1 = 100$
2	0·40	0·45	0·66	$\bar{x}_2 = 200$
3	0·35	0·40	0·62	$\bar{x}_3 = 300$
4	0·30	0·36	0·59	
5	0·25	0·32	0·56	$t_1 = 0.5$
6	0·20	0·29	0·54	$t_2 = 0.23$
7	0·16	0·26	0·52	$t_3 = 0.27$
8	0·12	0·23	0·50	
9	0·09	0·21	0·50	$c_1 = 2.0$
10	0·06	0·19	0·50	$c_2 = 3.0$
				$c_3 = 4.0$
				$c_4 = 6.0$
				$c_5 = 10.0$

$$a_{11s} = 1 \qquad s = 1, \ldots, 10$$
$$a_{12s} = 1 \qquad s = 1. \ldots, 10$$
$$a_{13s} = 0 \qquad s = 1, \ldots, 10$$

$R = 4.0$
$R_A = 0.8$

$$a_{31s} = 1.0 + 0.05s \qquad s = 1, \ldots, 10$$
$$a_{32s} = 0.45 + 0.06s \qquad s = 1, \ldots, 10$$
$$a_{33s} = 0.80 + 0.07s \qquad s = 1, \ldots, 10$$

$b_2 = 0.1$
$b_3 = 0.12$

$$\bar{u} = 12 \qquad \bar{r} = 3$$
$$\bar{k} = 5 \qquad \bar{s} = 10$$

The land input coefficients a_{21s}, a_{22s} and a_{23s} were chosen as follows. If the number of square feet of floor space required per unit of output were independent of building height, each a_{2rs} would be a_{2r}/s where a_{2r} depends on r but not on s. But the rectangular hyperbola overestimates the savings in land from tall buildings because extra provision must be made for elevators and building walls. On this basis it was guessed that each a_{2rs} probably decreases about linearly in s. A characteristic of an activity that justifies C.B.D. location is that capital is relatively easy to substitute for land. Therefore a_{21s} was made to fall more rapidly as s increases than was a_{22s}, since good one was intended to be the C.B.D. good. It was felt that there is probably more disadvantage to tall houses than to tall office buildings or factories, so a_{23s} was made to fall off more slowly with s than a_{21s} or a_{22s}. An additional consideration in choosing land input-output coefficients was that housing occupies about half the land in U.S. cities and production another quarter (the fourth quarter is used for transportation). The coefficients were adjusted to approximate this fact. Finally, the land coefficients were adjusted by minor amounts to produce some variability in building heights.

The capital coefficients a_{31s}, a_{32s} and a_{33s} were all made to increase linearly in s. Capital input per unit of output must increase with building height, at least beyond a few storeys, because of the need for elevators and supports. Capital input is presumed to rise less rapidly with height for the C.B.D. good, and more rapidly for housing than for either production activity. The capital coefficients were also adjusted to be consistent with known magnitudes in the U.S. economy. House values are about the same as annual family income in the U.S., about $10,000 in the mid 1960s. About 75 per cent of house value is capital, the rest being land. In addition, the capital-output ratio is near unity in U.S. industry. The capital coefficients in Table 7.1 are consistent with these magnitudes. (Capital is measured in units of 10 million dollars.)

The term b_2, the land input-output coefficient in transportation, was estimated by calculating roughly the transportation that the model would generate and choosing b_2 so that it would require about a quarter of the land area, b_3, the capital input-output coefficient, was estimated from data in *The Urban Transportation Problem* [1] for road based systems. These data imply urban road capital costs of about $500 per commuter mile in the mid-1960s. The value $b_3 = 0.12$ is based on that figure.

The terms t_1, t_2 and t_3 represent the relative demands placed on the transportation system by shipment of the two goods and by commuters. Since the two kinds of goods do not correspond to classifications of products in available data, there seems to be no easy way to estimate these numbers. Some experimentation with the model makes it clear that the t's are important, and perhaps sole, determinants of locations of the three activities in the urban area. The values in Table 7.1 were chosen so that Good No. 1 would be located near the city centre and Good No. 2 would be at least somewhat suburbanised.

The last parameters to discuss are the c's. The c's represent marginal operating and time costs of a unit of transportation at the five congestion levels. A one-mile round trip of relatively uncongested travel costs about $0.40 if travel speed is 20 m.p.h., operating costs are $0.10 per mile and travel time is valued at half a wage rate of $4.00 per hour. These figures are typical of the mid-1960s. Since t_3 is 0.27, a unit of transportation is about four one-mile round trips of commuters. This suggests a value of about $1.50 for c_1, which was rounded up to £2.00. Congestion cost rises moderately at first, but then more rapidly. The cost per one-mile round trip of a commuter at congestion level five is $(0.27)\frac{1}{5}\Sigma_k c_k = \$1.35$.

7.3 RESULTS

The solution of the programming problem, using the parameter values in Table 7.1, is summarised in Table 7.2. The first two columns show the height of the buildings in which Good No. 1 is produced

TABLE 7.2

CHARACTERISTICS OF MODEL A

uare	Good No. 1 Height	Good No. 1 Output	Good No. 2 Height	Good No. 2 Output	Good No. 3 Height	Good No. 3 Output	Trans- portation Conges- tion Level	Units	Land Shadow Price
0	—	—	—	—	—	—	5	48·0	239
1	20	3·56	—	—	—	—	3	23·6	36
2	20	10·72	—	—	—	—	3	10·4	19
3	—	—	—	—	10	1·26	2	5·9	12
4	—	—	—	—	10	1·42	2	4·1	10
5	—	—	—	—	10	1·52	2	2·9	8
6	—	—	—	—	6	1·45	2	2·1	7
	—	—	—	—	6	0·13	–	—	—
7	—	—	10	1·06	2	0·72	2	1·5	6
8	—	—	10	0·87	2	0·95	2	1·1	5
9	—	—	6	0·87	2	0·88	2	0·8	5
10	—	—	6	0·89	2	0·88	2	0·5	4
11	—	—	2	0·82	2	0·82	2	0·3	3
12	—	—	2	0·83	2	0·83	2	0·1	3

Criterion function: 4490.   Parameter values: Table 7.1.

and the output per square at each distance from the city centre. The next columns show the same information for Good No. 2 and for housing. The transportation columns show the highest congestion level used in each square and the number of units of transportation per square at each distance from the centre. The final column shows the shadow price per square mile of land at each distance from the centre. These numbers are values of the dual variables corresponding to the inequalities (11) in the primal problem. The shadow prices have a straightforward interpretation as components of the rent distance function.

The data in Table 7·2 correspond roughly to many characteristics of U.S. cities. Good No. 1 is produced in the C.B.D. and there is no housing in the C.B.D. (Square zero, to which all goods are shipped, is a somewhat artificial concept in this model. It is entirely devoted to transportation because the entire square is required to move the freight. It might be thought of as a railhead.) Good No. 1 is produced entirely in 20-storey buildings, whose height is limited by s rather than by economic considerations. Housing is produced in squares

3 to 12 and in buildings of from 2 to 10 storeys. Good No. 2 is produced towards the edge of the city, also in 2- to 10-storey buildings. The transportation columns show that congestion is great near the centre of the city and falls off rapidly with distance from the centre. There is almost no congestion beyond two miles from the centre. The results presented in this paper strongly indicate that a great deal of congestion is efficient near city centres. The land shadow prices follow the pattern that has been found consistently in theoretical and empirical research. Land rents are extremely high at the city centre, fall off rapidly close to the centre and nearly level off within about five miles of the centre.

The main purpose of this paper is to test the sensitivity of urban structure to changes in the transportation system. This is a complex matter because three sets of parameters affect transportation in the model: the c_k's, the t_s's and the b_q's. Many changes in a city's transportation system, such as the construction of a mass transit system, would have complex effects on all three sets of parameters. The most that can be attempted here is to obtain a feeling for the sensitivity of the solution to simple changes in parameter sets pertaining to transportation.

Tables 7.3, 7.4 and 7.5 show the effects on the solution of the model of changes in b_2 and b_3. These changes are easy to interpret. A reduc-

TABLE 7.3

CHARACTERISTICS OF MODEL B

Square	Good No. 1 Height	Good No. 1 Output	Good No. 2 Height	Good No. 2 Output	Housing Height	Housing Output	Trans- portation Conges- tion Level	Units	Land Shadow Price
0	—	—	—	—	—	—	4	48·0	101
1	20	6·32	—	—	—	—	3	23·3	28
2	20	9·34	—	—	10	0·06	2	10·2	13
3	—	—	—	—	10	1·37	2	5·9	11
4	—	—	—	—	10	1·49	2	4·1	10
5	—	—	—	—	6	1·43	2	2·9	8
6	—	—	—	—	6	1·48	2	2·1	7
7	—	—	10	1·15	2	0·82	2	1·5	6
8	—	—	10	0·84	2	0·98	2	1·1	5
9	—	—	6	0·88	2	0·88	2	0·8	5
	—	—	6	0·18	—	—	—	—	—
10	—	—	2	0·65	2	0·83	2	0·5	4
11	—	—	2	0·82	2	0·82	2	0·3	3
12	—	—	2	0·83	2	0·83	2	0·1	3

Criterion function: 4332.
Parameter values: Table 7.1 except $b_2 = 0·08$ (-20%).
$b_3 = 0·96$ (-20%).

TABLE 7.4

CHARACTERISTICS OF MODEL C

Square	Good No. 1 Height	Output	Good No. 2 Height	Output	Housing Height	Output	Trans- portation Conges- tion Level	Units	Land Shadow Price
0	—	—	—	—	—	—	4	48·0	98
1	20	6·32	—	—	—	—	3	23·3	28
2	20	9·34	—	—	16	0·06	2	10·2	13
3	—	—	—	—	10	1·37	2	5·9	12
4	—	—	—	—	10	1·49	2	4·1	10
5	—	—	—	—	6	1·43	2	2·9	8
6	—	—	—	—	6	1·48	2	2·1	7
7	—	—	10	1·15	2	0·82	2	1·5	6
8	—	—	10	0·84	2	0·98	2	1·1	5
9	—	—	6	0·88	2	0·88	2	0·8	5
	—	—	6	0·16	—	—	—	—	—
10	—	—	2	0·67	2	0·83	2	0·5	4
11	—	—	2	0·82	2	0·82	2	0·3	3
12	—	—	2	0·83	2	0·83	2	0·1	3

Criterion function: 4388.
Parameter values: Table 7.1 except $b_2 = 0.08$ (-20%).
$b_3 = 0.144$ ($+20\%$).

TABLE 7.5

CHARACTERISTICS OF MODEL D

Square	Good No. 1 Height	Output	Good No. 2 Height	Output	Housing Height	Output	Trans- portation Conges- tion Level	Units	Land Shadow Price
0	—	—	—	—	—	—	4	48·0	99
1	20	6·32	—	—	—	—	3	23·3	28
2	20	9·34	—	—	16	0·06	2	10·2	13
3	—	—	—	—	10	1·37	2	5·9	12
4	—	—	—	—	10	1·49	2	4·1	10
5	—	—	—	—	6	1·43	2	2·9	8
6	—	—	—	—	6	1·48	2	2·1	7
7	—	—	10	1·15	2	0·82	2	1·5	6
8	—	—	10	0·84	2	0·98	2	1·1	5
9	—	—	6	0·88	2	0·88	2	0·8	5
	—	—	6	0·16	—	—	—	—	—
10	—	—	2	0·67	2	0·83	2	0·5	4
11	—	—	2	0·82	2	0·82	2	0·3	3
12	—	—	2	0·83	2	0·83	2	0·1	3

Criterion function: 4366.
Parameter values: Table 7.1 except $b_2 = 0.08$ (-20%).
$b_3 = 0.12$ (0%).

tion in b_2 is a decrease in land input required per unit of transportation, and a reduction in b_3 is a decrease in the capital input. Such changes represent improvements in transportation technology such as the construction of an urban expressway or, possibly, construction of a public transit system. In Tables 7.3, 7.4 and 7.5, the land coefficient is 20 per cent less than in Table 7.2. In Table 7.3, the capital coefficient is also 20 per cent less, in 7.4 it is 20 per cent more and in 7.5 it is the same as in 7.2.

The reduction in b_2 frees some land from use in transportation and enables all three activities to concentrate somewhat closer to the city centre. In addition, in Tables 7.4 and 7.5 there is a small amount of housing in taller buildings than appear in Tables 7.2 and 7.3. But the important message in Tables 7.3, 7.4 and 7.5 is that modest changes in b_2 and b_3 have almost no effects on resource allocation in the urban area. Activity levels and transportation are almost unchanged from Table 7.2. This is a surprising and provocative result. It is important to know if it is a property of models of realistic complexity and parameter values. It is also interesting that the shadow price of land is affected much more, at least close to the city centre,

TABLE 7.6

CHARACTERISTICS OF MODEL E

Square	Good No. 1		Good No. 2		Housing		Trans-portation Conges-tion Level	Units	Land Shadow Price
	Height	Output	Height	Output	Height	Output			
0	—	—	—	—	—	—	5	45·0	589
1	20	4·55	—	—	—	—	3	22·1	40
2	20	10·23	—	—	—	—	2	9·8	21
3	—	—	—	—	10	1·28	2	5·6	12
4	—	—	—	—	10	1·44	2	3·9	10
	—	—	—	—	10	0·36	—	—	—
5	—	—	—	—	6	1·07	2	2·7	8
6	—	—	—	—	6	1·46	2	1·9	7
7	—	—	10	1·01	2	0·87	2	1·3	6
8	—	—	10	0·90	2	0·95	2	1·0	5
9	—	—	6	0·87	2	0·88	2	0·7	5
10	—	—	6	0·89	2	0·89	2	0·5	4
11	—	—	2	0·82	2	0·82	2	0·3	4
12	—	—	2	0·83	2	0·83	2	0·1	3

Criterion function: 4401.
Parameter values: Table 7.1 except

$a_{217} = 0·15$ $c_1 = 2·5$ $t_1 = 0·5$
$a_{218} = 0·10$ $c_2 = 3·0$ $t_2 = 0·2$
$a_{219} = 0·07$ $c_3 = 5·0$ $t_3 = 0·3$
$a_{210} = 0·05$ $c_4 = 10·0$
                       $c_5 = 20·0$

than is resource allocation. This is similar to results found by the author in his earlier model [3].

Since changes in the b_q's hardly affect resource allocation, changes in the criterion function almost exactly measure the changes in the cost of the fixed transportation pattern caused by changing b_2 and b_3. For example. Table 7.3 shows that 20 per cent reductions in b_2 and b_3 reduce transportation costs by about 150 [$\simeq$(4,490 – 4,332)]. This reduction is only about 3 per cent of the criterion function. Thus, one reason for the insensitivity of resource allocation may simply be that 20 per cent changes in the b_q's are too small to have much effect. This conjecture is supported by the fact that land and capital costs are a relatively small part of total transportation costs in the model.

Some further light is shed on these issues by the calculations shown in Tables 7.6 and 7.7. These tables differ from Tables 7.2–7.5 in several minor ways listed at the bottom of Table 7.6. But they differ from each other only in the values of the c_k's. In Table 7.7, the c_k's are smaller and increase less rapidly with k than in Table 7.6. The c_k's in Table 7.6 are about 20 or 25 per cent larger than those

TABLE 7.7

CHARACTERISTICS OF MODEL F

Square	Good No. 1		Good No. 2		Housing		Trans-portation Congestion Level	Units	Land Shadow Price
	Height	Output	Height	Output	Height	Output			
0	—	—	—	—	—	—	5	45·0	469
1	20	4·54	—	—	—	—	3	22·1	30
2	20	10·23	—	—	—	—	2	9·8	14
3	—	—	—	—	10	1·28	2	5·6	12
4	—	—	—	—	10	1·44	2	3·9	10
5	—	—	—	—	6	1·39	2	2·7	8
6	—	—	—	—	6	1·46	2	1·9	7
7	—	—	10	0·98	2	0·89	2	1·3	6
8	—	—	10	0·91	2	0·94	2	1·0	6
9	—	—	6	0·87	2	0·88	2	0·7	5
10	—	—	6	0·89	2	0·89	2	0·5	4
	—	—	6	0·14	—	—	—	—	—
11	—	—	2	0·69	2	0·84	2	0·3	4
12	—	—	2	0·83	2	0·83	2	0·1	3

Criterion function: 4066.
Parameter values: Table 7.6 except $c_1 = 2·0$.
$c_2 = 2·5$.
$c_3 = 4·0$.
$c_4 = 8·0$.
$c_5 = 16·0$.

in Table 7.7. Again we have the striking result that there are only negligible effects on resource allocation in the city. In this case the effect on the criterion function is not negligible, since it is 7·5 per cent smaller in Table 7.7 than in Table 7.6.

7.4 CONCLUSIONS

These calculations have the striking implication that urban structure is insensitive to changes in transportation costs and technology. If correct, this is an extremely important conclusion. Hordes of writers have claimed that the massive decentralisation of urban areas observed in many countries during the last few decades has resulted from transportation innovations in general and the automobile in particular. Of course, thoughtful writers have realised that transportation improvements have been only one of several causes of decentralisation. Others have been increases in real income and in the overall population of urban areas. But many scholars in several disciplines believe that the transportation system plays a key role.

There are at least three reasons why the results in this paper may understate the sensitivity of urban structure to changes in transportation parameters.

First, the model may be basically defective in the way it represents the determinants of urban structure. Urban model building is in its infancy and it would be surprising if future models did not reveal defects in existing models. My present view is that the most serious defect in the model is the assumption that all goods are shipped to the city centre to be exported. In fact, an important consequence of the shift of freight from rail to road during the last half century or so has been a growing tendency to export goods directly from suburban locations, without first shipping them to a city centre terminal. That possibility clearly has the effect of decentralising urban areas. I believe it requires major modifications in the model.

Second, the sensitivity of urban structure to changes in transportation parameters obviously depends on parameter values as well as on the basic structure of the model. Numerical values used in this paper were chosen rather casually, and they may be wrong. The fact that heights of buildings in which Good No. 1 is produced are determined by the artificial restriction of $\bar{s}$ in all the runs supports this view. A basic trade-off in the model is between tall buildings and transportation. Parameter values used in this paper produce a corner solution for that trade-off. This causes insensitivity for the reason that the demand of a consumer for a commodity he does not consume is insensitive to changes in its price. However, the constraint on building height was not binding for Good No. 2 and for housing and these building heights were also insensitive to changes in transportation parameters.

Third, the model is of an efficient city, not of an actual city. Of course the usual duality results of linear programming apply to this model. Those results imply that a system of competitive markets will sustain an efficient allocation of resources. The fact that the durability of structures requires long periods of time to adjust to new conditions is not relevant to the broad usefulness of the model. It would be an important explanation if the model showed great sensitivity to parameter changes, whereas real cities exhibited stable structures over time. But the situation is the opposite! The model structure is insensitive, whereas real cities have undergone rapid changes in structure. I believe the most important cause of deviations of actual from optimum urban structures is the difficulty of properly pricing congestion in the urban transportation system. The concept of optimum congestion tolls has been discussed extensively [4] and the analysis cannot be repeated here. There is a laborious but conceptually simple way of representing improper pricing in the model's transportation system, outlined briefly in the paper 'Markets and Efficient Resource Allocation in Urban Areas' [2]. But as a practical matter, the calculations reported here suggest that it is unlikely that the urban structures computed would be sensitive to modest distortions in transportation pricing. Such distortions can hardly be extremely large relative to the parameter changes that have been studied in this paper. But of course the urban structure may be more sensitive to improper transportation pricing with other parameter values than with those used here.

At this point I believe we should not preclude the possibility that urban structure is insensitive to parameters of the transportation system.

7.5 FUTURE DEVELOPMENT

There are of course many phenomena that are important in cities but are excluded from the model. Further research will be undertaken to incorporate several additional phenomena in the model. Among the possibilities are the possibility of exporting goods from places other than the city centre, scale economies in production, a more complex input-output structure for the urban economy, and demand or utility considerations. Some of these phenomena can be introduced at no cost other than increased computational burden, whereas others entail basic reformulation of the model. When the research was begun, it was believed that computer capacity would be a major limitation on the complexity of the model. But modern computers can do extraordinarily large linear programming problems, even without the use of decomposition procedures. The way is therefore open to introduce many additional phenomena in urban models, for both planning and economic analysis.

REFERENCES

[1] J. Meyer, Kain and M. Wohl, *The Urban Transportation Problem*. (Harvard University Press, Cambridge, 1965).
[2] S. Mills, 'Markets and Efficient Resource Allocation in Urban Areas', *Swedish J. of Econ.*, Vol. 74, No. 1 (March 1972), pp. 100–13.
[3] E. S. Mills, *Studies in the Structure of the Urban Economy* (Johns Hopkins Press for Resources for the Future, Baltimore, 1972).
[4] A. Walters, 'Theory and Measurement of Private and Social Cost of Highway Congestion', *Econometrica*, Vol. 29 (1961), pp. 676–99.

A Town Planner's View of Urban Structure as an Object of Physical Planning

G. Albers

In the industrial society the concept of urban planning, town planning or city planning goes back to the middle of the 19th century when it first became apparent that economic forces could not be relied upon to bring about a rational and socially acceptable urban structure. The main principles, as well as the legal framework for physical planning, were developed in the second half of the 19th century – obviously in opposition to the main stream of opinion which favoured the unrestricted play of market forces (*laissez faire*). Urban planning, although sometimes strongly biased towards aesthetic goals, contained from its very beginning an element of an alternative to the market process which, until then, had determined the use of a given piece of land.

Some consistency could be observed in the land-use patterns of the rapidly expanding cities of the 19th century. It was most apparent in the newer cities where developing land-use patterns were only indirectly influenced by the existing infrastructure, the presence of historic buildings or the traditional patterns of land ownership. It was therefore no accident that the United States was almost the only place in which theories of urban land use structure were postulated. Burgess [1] developed his theory of concentric zones encircling the central business district (light manufacturing and warehousing, zones of transition, tenement houses, single-family houses and a commuter zone). Hoyt [2], on the other hand, postulated a sectoral theory of urban development: he suggested that existing uses tended to spread from the centre like a fan. Both tendencies can be observed in practice; the concentric pattern of development seems to be most common, and is also most convincing, being in a way an extension of von Thünen's theory of the isolated state [3].

More relevant for planning than such explanatory theories were the attempts to deal with the shortcomings of the actual urban development process, as first experienced in Britain, then in France, and later in Germany and in other industrialised countries. The first acknowledged disadvantage was the lack of open space in the growing city – especially in the newest quarters. This resulted from economic pressures; no private proprietor was likely to forgo the potential revenue he could earn from a more intensive land use. The local authority thus had to step in and either buy land for use as open space or had to exclude certain areas from development (this often involved the payment of compensation).

A further complicating factor was the uneconomic use of infrastructure facilities (although the term itself was not yet employed). Overhead facilities like streets, sewerage networks, schools, etc., were treated as residual services to be provided by the municipality after private entrepreneurs had established the basic land-use pattern (just as shops in new development areas followed residential uses as soon as market considerations made it profitable). This made it difficult to plan infrastructure facilities on a rational basis. Schools, for example, were often overcrowded on one site and underutilised on another. Public transport was another pertinent example: a network designed to serve a haphazard distribution of residential establishments and work places cannot be expected to produce optimal results.

A third important implication followed from the haphazard siting of residences, factories, workshops and warehouses. It tended to impede industrial development and affected residential quality in a negative way.

All this led to the demand for a new approach to urban structure. It called for tools to influence this structure and for a set of rules and principles (or models) to guide any public intervention. The basic motivation for wishing to plan the urban land-use structure (judging from the literature produced around the turn of the century), can be listed as:

(a) To prevent the undesirable consequences of urban growth and haphazard public and private land-use patterns. In particular to prevent:
   - the devaluation of private investment through the proximity of incompatible land-use patterns (e.g. factories too close to residential areas; on these grounds the U.S. Supreme Court upheld zoning as constitutional in 1926);
   - public disinvestment through congestion of the city centre;
   - the unreasonable utilisation of the city's infrastructure.

(b) To create a framework within which the (conflicting) goals and preferences of the inhabitants could be satisfied.

Turning to possible solutions to the 'Urban Problem', we must first identify the elements of urban structure, then ascertain their space requirements and their desired relationships to one another and, finally, clarify how the individual urban elements can best be aggregated into a pattern or model which avoids most of the disadvantages of unregulated development.

If we define urban structure in our context as the pattern of human activities, we can broadly group these activities into those which are basically stationary and those which involve movement between these stationary locations. This corresponds to the distinction between 'adapted spaces' and 'flow systems' put forward by Lynch and Rodwin [4].

But for what kinds of activities are these spaces to be adapted? The famous Athens Charter of 1933 [5], the credo of the modern architects of that time, speaks of dwelling, work and recreation. In recent times, some attempts have been made to elaborate on this by adding other activities like education, the provision of goods and services, community activities, and so on. For most practical purposes, however, the five categories in the matrix shown in Table 7.8 seem to suffice. It does not seem necessary or desirable, as the Athens Charter indicated, to attribute to every such activity a separate spatial category. Some of these activities can easily be accommodated in similar categories, others call for spatial separation. Workplaces, for example, can have quite different properties – from a quiet studio to a noisy factory. Thus the main spatial categories do not fully coincide with the activity patterns, as the matrix clearly shows; open space is contrasted with three categories of built-up areas: residential areas, industrial areas and central locations. The term

TABLE 7D.1

CATEGORIES OF SPATIAL LAND-USE PATTERN AND
SOCIO-ECONOMIC ACTIVITIES
(Percentage of Total Area)

Activity Categories Space Categories	Dwell- ing	Work	Supply of Goods and Services	Education and Cultural Activity	Recre- ation	Move- ment*
Residential	75	10	10	10	10	10
Industrial	3	40	5	—	5	10
Central Locations	20	40	50	75	35	10
Open Spaces	2	5	5	5	50	10
Transportation Network	—	5	10	—	—	60
Public Utilities	—	—	20	—	—	—

* The percentage of education classified outside the central location, and the amount of movement classified outside the transportation network, depends on the scale of the spatial system. In this example, kindergartens and elementary schools have been treated as parts of the residential area; pedestrian walkways and access streets have not been treated as parts of the transportation network.

central location is meant to indicate an area in which those buildings, institutions and services are located which should be easily accessible to the general public (e.g. schools, shops, the town hall, the public library and the travel agency). The matrix shows – in a rough way – the extent to which these categories overlap: a town hall is both a work place and an institution which provides services to the citizen; the city's main sports grounds are open spaces as well as locations of central importance (at least temporarily). The figures in the matrix simply represent an 'informed guess' of the proportion of the total area occupied by each activity. However, they may help to illustrate the relationship between activity systems and land-use patterns.

Turning now to the space requirements of each kind of land use, we find the term already somewhat ambiguous. What is meant by 'requirement'? Technical data like road widths are important, but residential density ranges from a few people per acre in some American suburbs to several thousand per acre in Hong Kong. One must therefore distinguish between empirical averages, demand expectations (sometimes loosely called 'needs', e.g. 'the needs of motorised traffic in the eighties'), and social value judgements (e.g. how much space per person should be allocated for residential purposes, for open spaces, for schools, etc.). It is not the purpose of this paper to analyse these value judgements; it is sufficient to say that in the last decade several contributions from various European countries [6] support the general consensus that a large city should have between 160 and 260 square metres of developed land per inhabitant – including land for buildings, streets, railroads and public spaces, but excluding agricultural land and forest, waste land and major water areas. This amounts to a gross density of 38 to 60 persons per hectare (15 to 24 persons per acre).

More important in our context is the question of the relationship between different land uses; notably the relationship between residences and open spaces, between residences and work places, and between residences and central locations. Proximity of open spaces to residential areas was one of the earliest demands made for a 'healthy city structure'. Easy access for pedestrians from dwellings to some form of open space is still considered – and probably rightly so – one of the basic requirements of good urban planning.

The distance between residences and work places became a matter of concern to planners when it was seen that this was the root of many traffic problems. Two disparate approaches can be identified: the concentration of industrial sites in one, or a few, large industrial locations with a corresponding emphasis on public transport between them and the residential areas; and a systematic dispersion of industrial locations in an attempt to provide each residential area with its own work places within easy pedestrian access. The main advantage of this system was seen as the potential reduction in road traffic, especially during the rush hour. Its rigid application, however, is open to criticism on at least two grounds: it requires a static pattern of employment opportunities (unrealistic in a mobile society and in a growing economy) and it tends to group residential locations with work locations imposing the social hierarchy of the office and factory on that of the residential quarter.

The planners' concern with central locations is of relatively recent origin. It started in the 1950s and is probably connected to the advent of the 'affluent society' or the 'consumers' society'. We now know that the 'classic' factors in the theory of industrial location are increasingly supplemented, if not superseded, by the characteristics of the services and institutions provided by the urban centre. Since the city centre is also usually the focus of communications, information and publicity, it is also an important focal point for public opinion. We thus see attempts to develop a hierarchy of centres for different types of central functions and can again observe the tendency to provide certain services at a given centre combined with that of offering a choice of different centres to extend the range of choices offered.

The concept of a hierarchy of centres already hints at the concept of the separable elements of a city structure – elements on different scales which can be used as the basis of larger groupings. For a long time the concept of the neighbourhood unit dominated the scene: the idea was to group residences, shops, schools and other communal services together so that each institution could be operated economically whilst preserving convenient pedestrian access and excluding through traffic. Quite apart from the social romanticism which contributed to this concept, we find that the basic ideas are still valid, although they do not lend themselves to a simple rule-of-thumb procedure. Twenty years ago, neighbourhood units of 5,000 to 6,000 inhabitants seemed to offer the answer to the city's problems. Today we are more modest. We regard it as a limited answer, and the actual number of inhabitants, as a consequence of many considerations, may rise to 10,000 or more. The next level, of 30,000 to 60,000 inhabitants, is generally accepted as the basis for both secondary education and a diversified shopping centre, as well as for certain other important services. This seems to be the smallest size for a new town expected to develop a growth potential of its own.

A systematic discussion of the most important suggestions for a planned urban structure would surpass the scope of this paper [7]. This paper can simply indicate the main principles along which such models are organised. In a sense they can all be classified as derivatives and/or combinations of three basic organisational principles:

- the concept of a compact concentric city;
- that of a linear city based upon a transportation 'backbone';
- and, finally, the dispersed settlement structure.

There is more to these three schemes than the three geometric elements of the point, the line and the plane. The concentric settlement structure, with its differentiation of centres according to their degree of importance, is a typical corollary of the agrarian society characterised by the dependence of the town on its agricultural hinterland. The fear of overconcentration, together with the resulting social and economic disadvantages which this creates has done much to nourish the idea of decentralisation to which both linear development and dispersal offer theoretical solutions. The idea of a dispersed settlement structure owes much to the socio-cultural ideal of reconciling the natural tensions between town and country. This is based on the notion of technological progress implying the ubiquitous availability of energy and communication services [8]. The linear city, on the other hand, starts from the assumption that the important elements of infrastructure which offer decisive locational advantages for industry are normally developed in linear patterns and that to group them together would, in principle, multiply such advantages.

Most present schemes for large cities and city regions combine a series of linear developments along rapid transit lines with the development of a regional centre, which – partly for historical reasons – tends more towards a concentric and relatively compact settlement. Fig. 7D.1 shows some of the most important recent proposals although it does not claim to be comprehensive. It is not meant to represent a finite system; it simply indicates the way in which different elements contribute towards the various schemes. Clearly, both the central city with satellites and the compact city with a hierarchy of clustered centres are derivatives of the monocentric city (the 'point'). So is the compact city with a linear centre, which already hints at the concept of a linear city. Elements of both point and line are combined in the star-shaped city, a model frequently used, which leads to a potentially congested centre. This can be counteracted in various ways – one being the development of a central zone as in the comb-shaped pattern. This represents the transition from line to grid, in the same way that the star marks the transition from line to point. Between them lie closer derivatives of the linear city, like the scheme for Brasilia. If the grid pattern is interpreted as a dispersed settlement structure, Buchanan's proposal for a 'directional grid' constitutes another example of the transition from line to grid. Le Corbusier's plan for Chandigarh comes closest to a non-directional grid pattern and the idea of developing a regional system of settlement clusters, each of limited size and clearly separated from every neighbouring community, can be considered as marking the transition from a dispersed to a concentric structure.

The above description has been much abbreviated and has only given the barest outline of the most important concepts and techniques

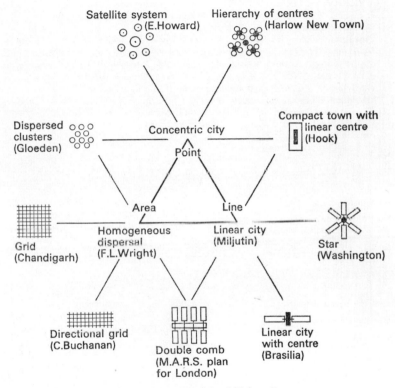

FIG. 7D.1   Some Models of Urban Structure

that are utilised. It may suffice, however, to give an economist some idea of the way in which the physical planner sees the evolution of an urban structure. It would be of great assistance to the physical planner if the economist could undertake a comparative evaluation of some of the above structural patterns. It is a field in which considerable research is still required and is an area in which the economist could render an invaluable service to the physical planner and, through him, to society at large.

REFERENCES

[1] E. W. Burgess, 'The Growth of the City', published in R. E. Park, E. W. Burgess and R. D. McKenzie, *The City* (Chicago Univ. Press, 1925).

[2] H. Hoyt, *The Structure and Growth of Residential Neighbourhoods in American Cities* (Federal Housing Administration, Government Printing Office, 1939).

[3] Von Thünen, *Der isolierte Staat in Beziehung auf Landwirtschaft und National-ökonomie, 1826–63* (Jena, 1930).

[4] K. Lynch and L. Rodwin, 'A Theory of Urban Form', *J. American Institute of Planners* (1958), pp. 201–14.

[5] J. L. Sert, *Can Our Cities Survive?* (Harvard University Press, 1942).

[6] London County Council, *The Planning of a New Town* (L.C.C., London, 1961); *Maatschappij voor Nijverheid en Handel, De stedelijke ontwikkeling in Nederland* (Haarlem, 1964); Internationaler Verband für Wohnungswesen, Städtebau und Raumordnung, *Der wachsende Raumbedarf in der Stadtregion* (The Hague, 1965); M. Leyh *et al.*, *Ermittlung des optimalen Einwohner-maximums für fixe Gemeindegebiete* (Unpublished, 1966).

[7] G. Albers, 'Toward a Theory of Urban Structure', *Proc. Town and Country Planning Summer School* (London, 1968).

[8] P. Kropotkin, *Fields, Factories, and Workshops* (B. Blom, New York, 1968; reprint of 1913 ed.); F. L. Wright, *When Democracy Builds* (University of Chicago Press, Chicago, 1945).

Discussion of Paper by Edwin S. Mills

Formal Discussant: Rothenberg. This is an extremely clever model of urban structure. It is useful as an exploratory device to see what characteristics and relationships have special influence on unfolding urban structure.

The paper essentially stipulates a number of activities, their technologies and interrelationships with one another, and then derives by linear programming that distribution of these activities over the urban space which minimises the total costs of carrying out the designated activities. A different 'optimal' city is generated for each of a number of parameter value assignments, these alternate assignments designed to reveal the sensitivity of optimal urban form to different relationships and influential variables.

The core of the model is the substitution between vertical and horizontal expansion. This is a very important kind of relationship for understanding the city and its development. The explicit relating of transportation demand to the relative location of production and 'housing' activities is extremely illuminating, as is the competition of transportation as a land use with other land-using activities. This last is shown dramatically in the optimal patterns under all parameter sets tried: the city centre is completely monopolised by transportation use – no other activity is located there; and it takes so much of land near the centre that the densities of other activities increase only progressively *farther from* the centre as a result of this competition.

Another very enlightening aspect of the model is the treatment of congestion as an explicit cost resulting from the relation between traffic and capacity, where both are variable, and the latter can be augmented but at a real cost.

The insensitivity of optimal urban form to transportation variables is potentially striking, and it is instructive when the multiple kinds of interactions transportation can have with other activities are explicitly accounted for. So on these scores the model is illuminating. But these evaluations must be qualified as a result of some very special characteristics of the model, characteristics which weaken the forcefulness of the demonstration.

'Housing' is sometimes discussed as if it really were literally *housing* and sometimes in the sense of the defined larger category of local goods. The very order of magnitude of the category depends on the distinction: in the latter, inclusive sense, it generally exceeds the total of all exported goods for the metropolitan area in the real world. It is certainly not a negligible sector. So the very special and counter-factual treatment of it in the model makes one uneasy about the representativeness of the whole:

(a) Production of 'housing' is deemed to require no labour or transport of goods.

(b) Overall output of 'housing' is assumed to be constant. It depends entirely on the assumed fixed proportion of population to workers, of workers to labour services supplied, and of labour services supplied to the total of export output. This represents an exceedingly crude base-multiplier formulation.

(c) The discussion of what parameter values are reasonable for the sector is couched in terms of the characteristics of literal *housing*. A compromise for the rather disparate sector intended may well diverge substantially from the literal housing component of it.

The exclusive use of single-worker households may be locationally misleading. The proportion of women in the labour force, and of multiple-worker households generally, are substantial and have been rising. The resulting multiplicity of work places for a single household should have some effect on its locational decisions. For example, whether it augments the attractive force of the dominant job cluster regardless of the location of the household's primary workplace (since this may magnify the probability of obtaining and holding second and third jobs) or increases the drawing power of the idiosyncratic minor job cluster where the household's second or third job actually is, matters for the character of optimal urban form. To exclude it may rob the model of applicability to modern metropolitan areas.

Transportation is an absolutely central aspect of the model, yet its treatment is limited in a very important way. The model requires that all squares at the same distance from the centre have equal transportation capacity and equal traffic using it. This assumption rules out all transport modes with scale economies. Arterial highways, expressways and all forms of mass transit are excluded. For each of these, only a few need be built to service traffic needs; this substitutes a few specialised concentrated transport corridors for symmetrical small-scale facilities and traffic throughout: the substitution of scale for number.

The absence of such recognisable transport modes damages the treatment of congestion, which is very important in the model. Congestion is a function of the concentration of traffic over space relative to the concentration of capacity over space. This relationship is surely influenced by the technological opportunities for scale economies by some modes – or, even more interestingly, by the differential economies of scale attainable by different modes. Omission of these modes may significantly misrepresent the effect of transportation on urban form.

This is seen also in the sensitivity analysis. The author interprets the successive versions of increasing transportation efficiency as investment in expressways or mass transit, and thus the resulting slightness of consequences as an insensitivity to the presence or absence – in differing degrees – of these modes. But the parameter changes he employs cannot be interpreted in this way, because the model still operates under the symmetry assumption that excludes all such modes. So the insensitivity of the model to such parameter changes may not really be an insensitivity to the kinds of recognisable real world changes in transport technology and capacity that other writers have considered.

The assumption that transport services require no labour input emphasises still further the very special nature of the transportation activity in this model. The treatment strongly suggests a single, highly individualised and localised transport mode: something close to the single-passenger private automobile mode for commuting, and the individual firm-owned truck for goods transport. But modal shifts which result from large lumpy investments in new modes involve a significant trade off in inputs, of which labour substitutions are important (e.g. the substitution of paid labour in mass transit for the 'free' labour in private auto use).

The significance of the relative insensitivity of spatial allocation to transport changes has to be carefully examined.

(a) Sensitivity of this sort reflects directly the cost of horizontal expansion versus the cost of vertical expansion. It is the *combination* of transportation parameters with vertical expansion cost parameters that matters. Given the lumpiness of congestion costs via its step function, observed optimal allocations may represent corner solutions. Therefore, modest variations in only transport technology may fail to dislodge such solutions. Yet appropriate variations in the two factors together might show considerable impact on allocation.

(b) In most land-use models since that of Alonso, households especially are treated as valuing both accessibility *and* land. Just as changes in relative prices or household incomes influence the amount of accessibility they wish to buy, so too do they influence the amount of land they wish to buy. Indeed the observed preponderance of rich households in some of the most distant portions of the metropolitan area is *not* predicted by these models – contrary to what many believe – unless the additional assumption is made that the income elasticity of demand for land exceeds that for accessibility. The attraction of lower land prices farther out is especially compelling when a household is willing to consider buying very substantial sized lots on those terms (a combination of large income *and* price elasticities for land). Thus quantity of land as a demand *variable* is probably rather influential in determining location decisions.

This variable is, however, totally omitted from the present model. Households demand – and obtain – a fixed quantity of 'housing' – which, of course, includes land. Changes in transport costs change the slope of the land price gradient from the city centre. But these changes in relative prices, in affecting only the gains from changing accessibility, do not change households' welfare greatly. If, in addition, the quantity of land were a variable argument of the utility function, transport changes would have a larger impact on utility and so locational decisions would be more sensitive.

(c) In this model congestion costs are formalised and explicit. They directly influence location, $1 of congestion costs being equivalent in this process to any other $1 of costs. In the real world, however, congestion costs are much less visible than here. Each participant in congestion is forced to pay only that part of the system congestion cost he generates which falls on himself; the much larger part falling on the other participants he escapes paying. Thus real world location patterns show much less influence of congestion than in the present model. In so far as it is spatial distributions that call for larger total transportation requirements – i.e. more diffuse form – which generate congestion, congestion will deter these more in the author's model than in the real world. This deterrent effect of greater dispersion through congestion is an offset to the impetus given to dispersion by lower transport costs. Thus, the transportation improvements tried here would be likely to have more offsetting mixed effects in the model – i.e. a smaller *net* effect – than in the real world.

(d) In the real world, at least some transportation improvements are likely to be of the 'arterial' kind – i.e. involve (1) economies of scale, (2) economies of long-distance versus short-distance hauls. Surely, major highway projects and mass transit investments are of this kind. These represent *lumpy* changes in transportation capacity, and they are not symmetric over space but intrinsically concentrated. True representation of such lumpy, spatially concentrated changes should induce important allocative changes – and these too will not be symmetric but asymmetrically clustered: e.g. along concentrated transport corridors. The model does not represent these kinds of change in transportation.

In sum, the manifest insensitivity of the model's spatial allocation to the hypothetical changes in transportation cannot be confidently generalised to real world systems. It does not seem to be a direct confrontation to other studies in the field that accord greater importance to transportation as a determinant of location, because it seems to rest on very special features of the present model which are seriously unrepresentative of real world urban systems. Thus the model and its consequences are illuminating; but one must understand very closely the refraction properties of the lenses through which one gains illumination before venturing to describe the underlying reality being illuminated.

Kolm noted that congestion taxes had been advocated in several papers at the conference, and this raised the following important issue. If we introduced a congestion tax, users would face two effects. On the one hand, they would have to pay; but on the other they would experience less congestion. Would they then, on the whole, be more or less happy with their condition? It had been suggested that they would always be less happy. Then the Pareto-improvement that the tax was supposed to provide could only be achieved by a lump sum redistribution of its proceeds to the users. But this was a serious drawback, since this compensating redistribution would have to be based on the service (road) used, and this would in fact amount to suppressing the tax.

In practice, it was possible that everyone was better-off with the tax, whatever was done with the proceeds. This was easy to show. Let u^i be the utility function of user i; x_i his consumption of the service (the number of trips undertaken by his family or firm during a given period), y_i^0 his initial income, and t the tax rate. His utility function would clearly be a function of x_i, of total traffic $x = \Sigma x_i$ because it was the cause of the congestion, and of his remaining income after tax $y_i = y_i^0 - tx_i$:

$$u^i = u^i (x_i, x, y_i^0 - tx_i).$$

We make the simplifying assumption that x_i/x is small, so that user i does not consider, when he chooses x_i, the effect of x_i on total congestion. This 'mass-effect' can be removed without changing the conclusion (although the optimum tax rate is then different for each user). User i

thus chooses an x_i which maximises u^i, given y_i and t. The choice $x_i(t)$ must therefore satisfy:

$$u^i_{x_i} - t u^i_{y_i} = 0. \tag{1}$$

The sensitivity of u^i to t is

$$\frac{du^i}{dt} = u^i_{x_i} \frac{dx_i}{dt} + u^i_x \frac{dx}{dt} + u^i_{y_i} \cdot \left(-x_i - t \frac{dx_i}{dt} \right)$$

$$= u^i_x \cdot \frac{dx}{dt} - u^i_{y_i} x_i.$$

Individual i's marginal willingness to pay for t is thus

$$v^i_t \equiv \frac{1}{u^i_{y_i}} \frac{du^i}{dt} = v \cdot \frac{dx}{dt} - x_i, \text{ when } v^i_x = u^i_x / u^i_{y_i}.$$

Now, $x_i \geq 0$ but $v^i_x < 0$ (congestion is noxious) and certainly $\dfrac{dx}{dt} < 0$ if the tax is efficient. v^i_t can thus be positive and can be positive for all i's. In this case, with $e = -\dfrac{1}{x} \dfrac{dx}{dt}$ the elasticity of demand and $v = -\sum_i v^i$ the social marginal value of a decrease in congestion, $e\, v > 1$. In addition, it would even be possible that some, but not all, users would consume more of the service in spite of the fact that they had to pay more for it, because its quality had been improved by the decrease in congestion. Of course, users who choose not to consume the service any more would necessarily be made worse off by the tax increase (except for possible indirect effects).

Lave argued that Rothenberg was not correct in suggesting that it was unfortunate that congestion costs were treated explicitly in the Mills model (since they are not explicit in the world). It was simply a matter of interpretation since Mills' congestion step function could either be interpreted as the average or marginal cost, depending on which item was of concern at the moment.

Uzawa did not dispute the usefulness of Mills' approach but felt that the major conclusions might be misleading. The premises of the model specified some of the elements which were crucial in the determination of urban structure. For example, the model had only one export point. If this assumption was relaxed the urban structure would change substantially. The assumptions thus seemed to determine the pattern of urban structure and affected the conclusions drawn from the model.

Foster felt that the unreality of assuming – at least for the centrally located export good – that its exit was at the centre of the urban area was less than at first appeared. In many cities it was office development which occupied most central area space and this produced no tangible export good, except in the form of management and services.

He then went on to elaborate on three of the points made by Rothenberg:
1. The model traded off building height against decentralisation which itself damped the decentralising effect of an increase in transport facilities.

But building height did not react instantaneously to a change in transport facilities, since there were substantial costs of adaptation. This tended to increase the effect of changing transport facilities upon decentralisation.

2. If efficient congestion charges were not levied, this would lead to lower rents in the centre, since this would lower individual travel costs and reduce the advantages of accessibility to central city locations. Because of the interconnection between transport charges and rents, one would not be surprised to find big shifts in location instead of the big changes in rent shown in the author's model.

3. In practice the alternative to congestion charges was not average cost pricing but a gasoline tax. This normally meant that tax costs per mile fell with highway improvements, irrespective of the costs of the improvement. But the price and income effects were likely to encourage people to buy more space for housing by being prepared to travel further than were implied by the author's assumptions.

Lave replied that Foster's comment (i.e. that demand is sensitive to the congestion toll) really does not contradict the author's result which implies that city structure is insensitive to transportation costs. An individual can react in five ways to the establishment of a congestion toll or to any increase in transportation costs:

(1) He can pay it and not change his behaviour.
(2) He can travel off peak.
(3) He can take public transportation.
(4) He can establish a car pool.
(5) He can change the location of his residence.

Only the last would result in a change in urban structure.

Evans suggested that it may in fact be true that both the urban system was insensitive to small changes in transport technology and that the decentralisation and suburbanisation which had occurred had been due to changes in transport technology. Over the last hundred years or so urban transport speeds had increased from about 10 m.p.h. or less by horse to 70 m.p.h. by car or train. This change was not small but very, very large. It might therefore have caused noticeable decentralisation over a period of time, even though the effects of a small increase in travel speeds might not have been noticeable.

Hoch, referring to Lave's list of possible reactions to a toll, suggested that 'change location' could mean (a) a change of location within the city, or (b) a move away from a particular city. He also suggested that the author's model could be made more realistic by specifying differing transport costs at point u (as a function of the distance from the centre) for both commuting workers and export shipments. This might lead to a more realistic case in between the two extremes of (a) central location only, and (b) the exploding metropolis with suburban export centres.

8 Cost-Benefit Analysis and Urban Traffic Congestion: The Example of Paris*

H. Lévy-Lambert

8.1 INTRODUCTION

This study was prepared in 1970 by the Forecasting Division of the French Ministry of Economy and Finance for an inter-departmental working party in charge of examining measures to improve, as of 1975, the financial returns of the Paris Public Transport Board (*Régie autonome des transports parisiens*), as well as traffic conditions in the Paris area [1, 2].

Because of the 1975 horizon, only short-run traffic management measures, such as organisation, regulation and pricing were considered. Investment schemes were precluded, since they generally take more than five years to implement from when they are first mooted [3]. Hence the problem examined here is that of the better use of existing facilities.

The main part of the study consists of a system analysis of Paris transport. This analysis rests on a study of user behaviour and provides the background for a comparison of possible alternative traffic patterns.

The chief management measure examined in this study is pricing for the use of private motor cars by means of parking charges. This represents the simplest form of indirect control in present conditions.

The first part of this paper reviews the basic principles of cost-benefit analysis as applied to road traffic pricing. The second part sets out the results of the study, but the only comparison given in detail is that between the reference solution, assuming the continuation of past trends with a peak bus speed of 9 k.p.h., and an alternative solution in which parking charges result in an increased peak bus speed of 14 k.p.h.

8.2 BASIC PRINCIPLES

Road congestion produces external effects which need to be internalised in order to achieve the economic optimum. This can be done by using prices based on marginal social costs.

* Translated from the French by Elizabeth Henderson.

The general case

In the general case, the problem may be formulated as follows [4, 5]. Overall vehicle-usage cost is defined as the sum of cash expenses and the money value of indirect benefits like changes in travelling time, accidents, convenience, and so on.

For any given road system, overall cost is a function $C(T)$ of traffic, T:

$$C(T) = P_t \, t \, (T) + k \qquad (1)$$

where t is the all-important travelling time, P_t is the value of time and k represents cash expenses (petrol, etc.), which is assumed to be independent of traffic.

This function is constant up to a certain traffic level, T_{min}, below

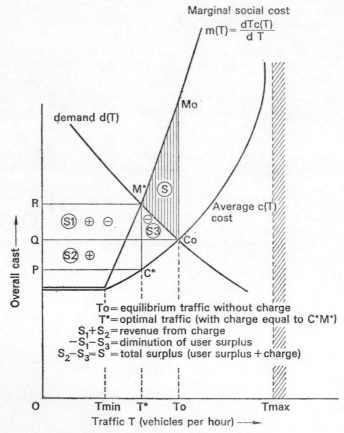

Fig. 8.1   Demand and Supply for Road Journeys

which vehicles do not interfere with each other; it then grows continuously up to the traffic level, T_{max}, which corresponds to complete congestion (Fig. 8.1).

The demand function $d(T)$ indicates the volume of traffic, T, generated at each level of vehicle-usage cost. The equilibrium volume, T_o, without pricing or regulation, is thus given by the intersection point C_o between the cost and demand curves, $C(T)$ and $d(T)$.

If T_o is higher than T_{min}, the equilibrium point is non-optimal, because drivers do not allow for the marginal social cost of congestion. Since the total cost of this traffic is the product $Tc(T)$ of the volume of traffic and the average cost, the marginal social cost $m(T)$ is

$$m(T) = \frac{dTc(T)}{dT} = c(T) + \frac{Tdc(T)}{dT} \tag{2}$$

Each driver pays the average cost $c(T)$. The road price or charge, $p(T)$, which depends on traffic conditions should thus equal the difference between $m(T)$ and $c(T)$:

$$p(T) = m(T) - c(T) = \frac{Tdc(T)}{dT} \tag{3}$$

or, by using Equation 1:

$$p(T) = TP_t\frac{dt}{dT} \tag{4}$$

Given the same demand curve as before, optimum traffic T^* is represented by the intersection point M^* between the curves $m(T)$ and $d(T)$, and the corresponding charge by the distance $C^* M^*$ between the overall cost curve $c(T)$ and the marginal social cost curve $m(T)$.

The reduction of traffic, from T_o to T^*, creates an additional surplus, S, which is shown by the hatched area $M^*M_oC_o$ between the demand curve and the marginal social cost curve:

$$S = \int_{T^*}^{T_o}[m(T) - d(T)]dT \tag{5}$$

The surplus S can also be shown to be equal to $(S_2 - S_3)$ representing the difference between the revenue received (the rectangle PRM^*C^* $= S_1 + S_2$) and the reduction in the user surplus (the trapeze $QRM^*C_o = S_1 + S_3$).

Competition between Public and Private Transport

We now suppose that travellers have the choice between two competitive means of road transport, namely, private cars (vp) and public transport (tc). To simplify the assumptions, total demand is taken to be inelastic, so that, with D constant, only the distribution of demand between vp and tc can vary. This distribution is assumed to depend solely on the difference between the overall cost of each mode, $(C_{vp} - C_{tc})$:

$$T_{vp} + T_{tc} = D = \text{constant} \qquad (6)$$

$$\frac{T_{vp}}{D} = f(C_{vp} - C_{tc}) \qquad (7)$$

Equation 7 is shown in Fig. 8.2 by an allocation curve separating the demand for private car travel on the left-hand side, from the demand for public transport on the right.

Travelling time is assumed to be a function of the total volume of traffic, expressed in passenger car equivalents, so that, assuming k to be in the region of 0·1 (assuming that a peak load of about 45

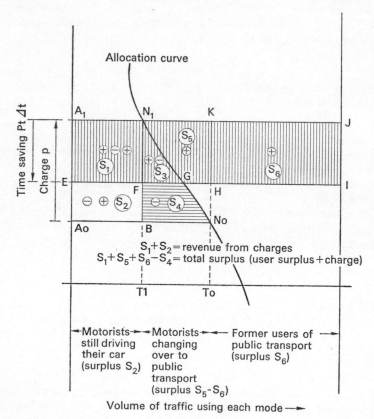

FIG. 8.2 Choice of Travel Mode: Private Cars versus Public Transport

passengers per bus creates roughly as much congestion as five private cars) we can write:

$$t = t\,(T_{vp} + kT_{tc}) \tag{8}$$

Let N_o represent the equilibrium position without any parking charges. The introduction of a parking charge p has a twofold effect as follows:

(a) It increases the cost difference $C_{vp} - C_{tc}$, by p, and shifts the equilibrium point from N_o to N_1.

(b) It reduces travel times by Δt, which reduces the overall cost of both modes of transport by $P_t \Delta t$. However, since it does not alter the cost difference, it does not shift the equilibrium point N_1. This assumption is not strictly correct, since driving speeds will change and other cost components (e.g. petrol) may also vary in different ways.

The first effect, (a), produces two changes in the surplus attributable to different beneficiaries. It reduces the motorists' surplus by $A_o N_o N_1 A_1$, or roughly $p\left(\dfrac{T_o + T_1}{2}\right)$, while it increases the surplus accruing to local authorities, who are assumed to levy the charge, by an amount to $A_0 B N_1 A_1$, or pT_1. The total surplus has thus been reduced by the triangle BN_oN_1, or roughly $p\left(\dfrac{T_v - T_1}{2}\right)$. The second effect, (b), raises the user surplus by an amount equal to $EIJA_1$, or $P_t \Delta t D$.

The overall changes in surplus are summarised in Table 8.1. It is apparent that the optimum, i.e. the highest total surplus, is obtained when the parking charge equals the marginal value of the time lost by all road users (as shown in Equation 4 above). The figures make no allowance for the cost of collecting the charge, nor do they allow for possible changes in the surplus accruing to transport enterprises when their marginal revenue exceeds their marginal costs. These changes have, however, been taken into account in the Paris case study discussed below.

8.3 *APPLICATION TO THE PARIS AREA*

As can be seen from Fig. 8.3, the Paris transport system consists of a number of loops. For instance, the demand for each mode of transport depends, among other things, on travelling speeds, and this in turn depends on aggregate demand. We therefore have to proceed by iteration.

TABLE 8.1

CHANGES IN SURPLUS

Group concerned	Volume of Traffic	Surplus	
		Graphical Representation (Fig. 2)	Unit Value
1. Former users of public transport	$D - T_o$	$HIJK = S_6$	$P_t \Delta t$
2. Motorists changing over to public transport	$T_o - T_1$	$FHKN_1 - BN_oN_1$	$P_t \Delta t - (1/2)p^*$
3. Motorists still driving their own car	T_1	$- A_oBFE = S_2$	$P_t \Delta t - p$
4. Local authorities (parking charges)	T_1	$A_oBN_1A_1 = S_1 + S_2$	p
Total	D	$EIJA_1 - BN_oN_1 = S_1 + S_5 + S_6 - S_4$	

* The term $- (1/2)p$ can be interpreted as a loss of convenience and is based on the assumption of a linear demand curve.

In practice, we first assume a set of values for the factors which determine transport demand (listed in the top row of Fig. 8.3). These include vehicle speeds, charges and the degree of convenience offered by each mode of transport (private car and public transport).

Next, the demand for each mode is determined by means of the allocation curves, and from this we can calculate the corresponding traffic speed with the help of the speed/flow relationships. If this traffic speed turns out to be different from that originally assumed, we have to start again with a different set of initial values. Two alternative solutions are discussed below:

(a) A reference solution, corresponding to a continuation of past trends, with no parking charges and a peak bus speed of 9 k.p.h.

(b) A solution with parking charges everywhere in Paris (2 frs per hour, or 15 frs per day, in the centre, and 1 fr per hour, or 8 frs per day, in the suburbs), and a peak bus speed of 14 k.p.h. A third solution examined the effects of a peak bus speed of 18 k.p.h.

The calculations assume an annual rise of 3·5 per cent in the general price level and of 6·5 per cent in wages.

Travel Analysis

A distinction is made between trips between home and work; and other trips, e.g. for shopping or recreational purposes.

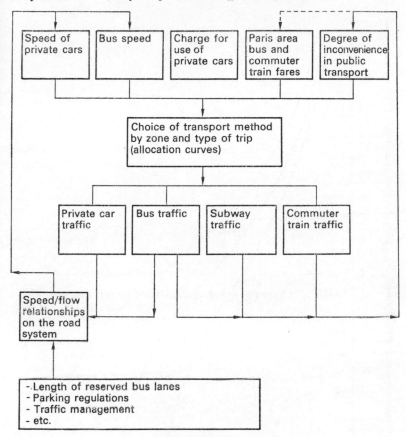

FIG. 8.3   The Paris Transport System

The Paris Town Planning Institute (*L'Institut d'Aménagement et d'Urbanisme de la Région Parisienne* – I.A.U.R.P.) had already done some work on user choices [6, 7] from which it was possible to determine allocation curves for both types. Those for trips between home and work are shown in Fig. 8.4 for the years 1962 and 1965 together with forecasts for 1975; differences in overall costs are expressed in hundredths of an hour and in 1975 francs. The shape of the curves depends on the level of vehicle ownership (maximum value) and in the availability of free parking facilities (minimum value). From these curves the value of time in 1967 was estimated, at 6 frs per hour for home-work trips and at 3.5 frs per hour for other trips, the corresponding figures for 1975 being 8·4 and 4·9 frs per hour respectively.

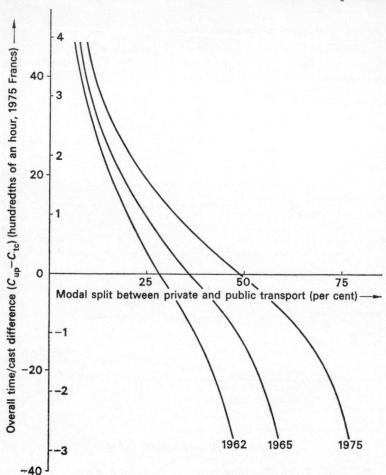

FIG. 8.4   Allocation Curves for Home-Work Travel

Next, the Paris Area was divided into ten zones as follows: Paris centre and suburbs; the inner commuter belt north, south, east and west; and the outer commuter belt north, south, east and west (see Fig. 8.5).

For each zone, apart from Paris centre and suburbs, three points were chosen as representative of traffic in the zone, and for each of these points the 1975 overall cost of travelling by public transport (C_{tc}) and by private car (C_{vp}) was calculated. With the help of the allocation curves, the percentage of car usage was then determined separately for trips to the centre of Paris and to the suburbs.

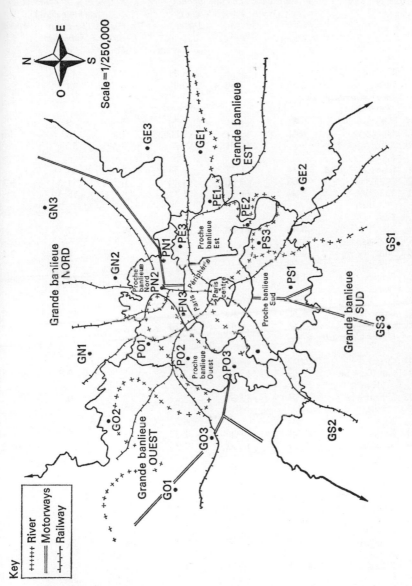

Fig. 8.5 Division of the Paris Area into Ten Zones

TABLE 8.2

THE USE OF PRIVATE CARS AND PUBLIC TRANSPORT IN HOME-WORK TRAVEL: 14 k.p.h. ALTERNATIVE
(Parking charge 2 fr. per hour in central Paris and 1 fr. per hour in suburbs)

Origin of Trips		Overall Cost (in 1967 Francs, per Trip to Paris Centre)			Proportion of Motor Car use (per cent)		
		Public Transp. a	Private Transp. b	Difference $C_{vp} - C_{tc}$ $c = b - a$	To Paris Centre d^*	To Paris Suburbs $e\dagger$	Avera $f\ddagger$
I –	**Paris**						
	Centre	3·15	6·86	3·71	6·7	12·7	
	Suburbs	3·55	7·53	3·98	6·6	11·7	
II –	*Inner commuter Belt*						
	West						
PO1	Argenteuil	6·81	11·51	4·70	5	9	
PO2	Nanterre	6·41	10·01	3·60	7·5	16	8·6
PO3	Saint-Cloud	7·77	11·01	3·24	8·5	22·5	
	South						
PS1	Chevilly-Larue	7·94	11·28	3·34	8	19	
PS2	Meudon	6·66	10·86	4·20	6·5	11·5	8·1
PS3	Maisons-Alfort	6·94	11·31	4·37	6	10·5	
	East						
PE1	Neuilly-Plaisance	8·90	11·45	2·55	11·2	31	
PE2	Joinville le Pont	6·48	11·24	4·70	6	8·5	7·1
PE3	Bobigny	7·06	10·88	3·82	7·5	14	
	North						
PN1	La Courneuve	7·06	9·96	2·90	9·5	25	
PN2	Saint-Denis	6·52	9·94	3·42	7·5	18	7
PN3	Clichy	5·48	8·62	3·14	8	21	
III –	*Outer Commuter Belt*						
	West						
GO1	Orgeval	10·97	14·74	3·77	7·5	15	
GO2	Conflans St. Honor.	8·19	13·35	5·16	6	7·5	9·3
GO3	L'Etang la Ville	10·04	13·29	3·25	8	20	
	South						
GS1	Evry	11·74	14·25	2·52	11·5	25	
GS2	St. Rémy les Chevr.	11·19	14·52	3·33	8	19	10·2
GS3	St. Geneviève des B.	9·02	13·73	4·71	5	9	
	East						
GE1	Chelles	7·79	10·47	2·68	10·5	28·5	
GE2	Boissy St. Léger	8·04	12·55	4·51	5·5	9·5	9·8
GE3	Villeparisis	10·22	12·93	2·71	10	28·5	
	North						
GN1	Taverny	10·42	12·33	1·91	16	27	
GN2	Sarcelles	8·37	11·40	3·03	8·5	22·5	9·7
GN3	Marly la Ville	10·99	13·99	3	8·5	23·5	

* For car owners (from Figure 8.2).
† On the basis of an overall cost difference equal to the figure in column c less 1·70 francs.
‡ Allowing for car ownership rates.

Table 8.2 shows the calculations for home-work trips on the assumption that peak bus speeds were 14 k.p.h. and that parking charges were imposed on the scale set out above.

Table 8.3 gives details of trips between Paris and the commuter belt in 1969, classified by trip purpose and mode of transport (excluding bicycles and walking). Table 8.4 gives the same information *extrapolated* to 1975, assuming no parking charges (assumption (a) above). Table 8.5 gives the same information calculated for 1975, assuming that parking charges are in existence. The calculations are based on Table 8.1 and on additional allocation curves showing the

TABLE 8.3

TRIPS IN THE PARIS AREA, 1969
(Thousand trips per day)

	Paris – Paris			Commuter belt – Paris			Total		
	Private Car	Public Transport	Total	Private Car	Public Transport	Total	Private Car	Public Transport	Total
Paris residents									
Home-work	238	987	1225	143	269	412	381	1256	1637
Other trips	323	753	1076	176	134	310	499	887	1386
Total	561	1740	2301	319	403	722	880	2143	3023
Commuter belt residents									
Home-work	98	45	143	459	1321	1780	557	1366	1923
Other trips	152	98	250	435	580	1015	587	678	1265
Total	250	143	393	894	1901	2795	1144	2044	3188
Combined									
Home-work	336	1031	1367	602	1590	2192	938	2621	3559
Other trips	475	852	1327	611	714	1325	1086	1566	2652
Total	811	1883	2694	1213	3082*	3517	2024	4965*	6211
Of which by:									
suburban bus		58			535			593	
urban bus		307			281			588	
railway		9			1118			1127	
subway		1509			1148			2655	
No. of cars at peak hour†	80			122			202		

* Including 778 commuter belt – Paris trips using both means of transport.

† On the basis of 1·12 passengers per car and a peak-hour coefficient of 13·2 per cent for home-work trips, and corresponding figures of 1·40 and 11·1 per cent for other trips.

proportion of bus and subway trips taken by public transport users. Table 8.6 shows the percentage changes between this solution and the reference solution.

From this last table it appears that, for a fixed number of total trips, the number of private cars on the road in Paris at the peak hour is 28 per cent less in the parking charge solution than in the reference solution. The number of buses is negligible compared to the number of private cars. There are 427 buses in the reference solution and 729 in the parking charge alternative. This means, if one bus

TABLE 8.4

TRIPS IN THE PARIS AREA, 1975: ASSUMPTION (a)
THE REFERENCE SOLUTION
(Thousand trips per day)

	Paris – Paris			Commuter belt – Paris			Total		
	Private Car	*Public Transport*	*Total*	*Private Car*	*Public Transport*	*Total*	*Private Car*	*Public Transport*	*Total*
Paris residents									
Home-work	229	1018	1247	147	300	447	376	1318	1694
Other trips	344	651	995	200	116	316	544	767	1311
Total	573	1669	2242	347	416	763	920	2085	3005
Commuter belt residents									
Home-work	107	53	160	504	1565	2069	611	1618	2229
Other trips	261	112	373	748	518	1266	1009	630	1639
Total	368	165	533	1252	2083	3335	1620	2248	3868
Combined									
Home-work	336	1071	1407	651	1865	2516	987	2936	3923
Other trips	605	763	1368	948	634	1582	1553	1397	2950
Total	941	1834	2775	1599	3387*	4098	2540	5213*	6873
Of which by:									
suburban bus		48			535			583	
urban bus		260			298			558	
railway		9			1228			1237	
subway		1509			1326			2835	
No. of cars at peak hour†	90			155			245		

* Including 888 commuter belt – Paris trips using both means of transport.

† On the basis of 1·12 passengers per car and a peak hour coefficient of 13·2 per cent for home-work trips, and corresponding figures of 1·40 and 11·1 per cent for other trips.

occupies the space of five private cars, that it only represents 3 to 5 per cent of car traffic. The reduction in car traffic is largely concentrated in home-work trips, which have fallen by 55 per cent; other trips have only fallen by 4 per cent.

It finally remains to check whether the number of cars on the road is compatible with the original speed assumption. This is done by means of Fig. 8.6, which shows the relationship between average driving speeds and the number of cars on the road in Paris during rush-hour traffic. The slope of this curve, which has gradually

TABLE 8.5

TRIPS IN THE PARIS AREA, 1975: ASSUMPTION (b)
USING PARKING CHARGES
(Thousand trips per day)

	Paris – Paris			Commuter belt – Paris			Total		
	Private Car	Public Transport	Total	Private Car	Public Transport	Total	Private Car	Public Transport	Total
Paris residents									
Home-work	75	1172	1247	147	300	447	222	1472	1694
Other trips	337	658	995	200	116	316	537	774	1311
Total	412	1830	2242	347	416	763	759	2246	3005
Commuter belt residents									
Home-work	38	122	160	180	1889	2069	218	2011	2229
Other trips	230	143	373	720	546	1266	950	689	1639
Total	268	265	533	900	2435	3335	1168	2700	3868
Combined									
Home-work	113	1294	1407	327	2189	2516	440	3483	3923
Other trips	567	801	1368	920	662	1582	1487	1463	2950
Total	680	2095	2775	1247	3989*	4098	1927	6084*	6873
Of which by:									
suburban bus		49			606			655	
urban bus		611			521			1132	
railway		9			1392			1401	
subway		1426			1470			2896	
No. of cars at peak hour†	60			116			176		

* Including 1138 commuter belt – Paris trips using both means of transport.

† On the basis of 1·12 passengers per car and a peak hour coefficient of 13·2 per cent for home-work trips, and corresponding figures of 1·40 and 11·1 per cent for other trips.

shifted to the right as a result of road investment and improved traffic management, was determined by spot observations on a number of roads. It was then adjusted in the light of the global data for 1965 and 1969, and extrapolated for 1975.

Balance of Gains and Losses

The changes in surplus attributable to the changeover from the reference solution (9 k.p.h. road speeds) to the alternative with 14 k.p.h. road speeds is set out in Table 8.7. It was based on the principles discussed earlier and lists the gains and losses in terms of cash, time and convenience.

New users of public transport are divided into two categories, 2(a) and 2(b), depending on whether or not they previously travelled by private car. As regards motorists still driving their own cars, there

TABLE 8.6

TRIPS IN THE PARIS AREA, 1975: ASSUMPTION (b)
USING PARKING CHARGES
(Changes against reference solution, per cent)

| | Paris – Paris | | | Commuter belt – Paris | | | Total | | |
	Private Car	Public Transport	Total	Private Car	Public Transport	Total	Private Car	Public Transport	Total
Paris residents									
Home-work	– 67	+15	0	0	0	0	– 41	+12	0
Other trips	– 2	+ 1	0	0	0	0	– 1	+ 1	0
Total	– 28	+10	0	0	0	0	– 17	+ 8	0
Commuter belt residents									
Home-work	– 64	+130	0	– 64	+21	0	– 64	+24	0
Other trips	– 12	+ 28	0	– 4	+ 5	0	– 6	+ 9	0
Total	– 27	+ 67	0	– 28	+17	0	– 28	+20	0
Combined									
Home-work	– 66	+21	0	– 50	+17	0	– 55	+19	0
Other trips	– 6	+ 5	0	– 3	+ 4	0	– 4	+ 5	0
Total	– 28	+14	0	– 22	+18	0	– 24	+17	0
Of which by:									
suburban bus		+ 2			+13			+ 12	
urban bus		+135			+74			+103	
railway		0			+13			+ 13	
subway		– 6			+11			+ 2	
No. of cars at peak hour†	– 33			– 25			– 28		

† From Table 8.5.

are three categories: those who go to Paris and pay the parking charge, 3(a); those who go to Paris but do not pay the parking charge, 3(b); and those who travel to the commuter belt, 3(c).

The revenue of local authorities (row 4) equals the additional expenses of motorists still driving their own cars, less any collection costs.

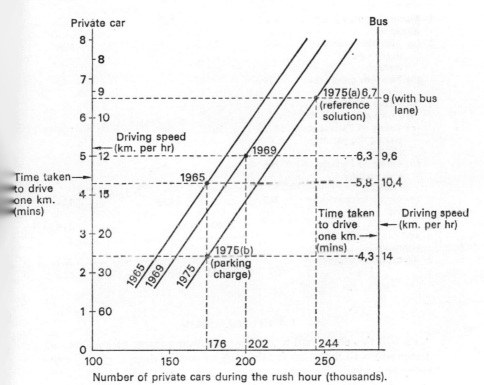

FIG. 8.6 Speed-Flow Relationships in Paris

Finally, allowance is made for the higher profits of transport enterprises, whose receipts go up because of the increased number of passengers while their unit costs diminish because of the higher bus speed.

The overall results are most encouraging. The total gain is 816 million francs per year, the bulk of which comes from time savings of 570,000 hours per day.

TABLE 8.7

BALANCE OF GAINS AND LOSSES AS A RESULT OF
INCREASED ROAD SPEEDS FROM 9 k.p.h. TO 14 k.p.h.
IN 1975

Group concerned	No. of Trips per Day ('000)	Gains (+) and Losses (−) (million francs per year)			
		Cash	Time	Con-venience	Total
1. Former users of public transport	558		+162		+162
2. (a) Motorists changing over to public transport	613	+ 25	+ 66	− 277	− 186
(b) New bus users other than 2 (a)	379		+ 42		+ 42
3. Motorists still driving their own cars					
(a) Going to Paris and paying the parking charge	1472	− 567	+393		− 174
(b) Going to Paris to free parking facilities	108		+ 54		+ 54
(c) Going to commuter belt	347		+133		+133
4. Local authorities (net revenue from parking charges)		+478			+478
5. Transport enterprises		+307			+307
Total		+243	+850	− 277	+816

8.4 *CONCLUSION*

Although this study had to employ a certain number of guesses and assumptions to make up for the lack of precise data, it clearly confirms how much the community stands to gain from restricting the usage of private cars in urban areas. It indicates approximately how high parking charges need to be in relation to the target speed of traffic, and it provides a basis for assessing the effects of such measures on the various groups concerned. On balance, the favourable effects far outweigh the unfavourable ones, even for motorists, for whom much of the extra expenditure and loss of convenience is offset by time savings.

However, the effectiveness of parking charges is limited by the fact that they do not reach motorists with free parking facilities. These are fairly numerous in the Paris area where regulations encourage firms to provide them. Parking charges likewise do not affect firms to provide them. Parking charges likewise do not affect through traffic, which may very well increase as a result of the enhanced road speeds.

Paris is now having its first taste of parking charges. It took the Paris Council years to make up its mind about parking charges (it was not until 1971 that it finally voted to introduce them) and they are only being applied to the city centre at the modest rate of 1 franc per hour. No significant effects can be expected until the system is applied more generally.

REFERENCES

[1] M. Barbier, 'La rationalisation du choix des investissements de transport pour le VI° Plan en région parisienne', *Bulletin R.C.B. No. 4* (April 1971).
[2] M. Giroux and B. Mourre, 'Le stationnement payant', *Statistiques et Études Financières*, Série orange, No. 5 (1972), pp. 3–14.
[3] H. Guillaume, *L'étude économique du Réseau Express Régional*, extrait de calcul économique, t. II, travaux et recherches de la Faculté de Droit et de Sciences Économiques de Paris (Presses Universitaires de France, 1971).
[4] H. Lévy-Lambert, 'Le péage sur les autoroutes et la théorie économique', *Transports* No. 104 (Septembre 1965), pp. 325–46.
[5] A. A. Walters, 'The Theory and Measurement of Private and Social Cost of Highway Congestion', *Econometrica* (1961), pp. 676–99.
[6] Institut d'Aménagement et d'Urbanisme de la Région Parisienne, 'Les transports urbains et leurs usagers dans la région parisienne – Choix du moyen de transport par les usagers', *Cahiers de l'I.A.U.R.P.*, Vol. 4–5 (1966), No. 2.
[7] Institut d'Aménagement et d'Urbanisme de la Région Parisienne, 'Analyse du choix du mode de transport par les usagers en région parisienne', *Cahiers de l'I.A.U.R.P.*, Vol. 17–18 (1969), No. 2.
[8] H. Lévy-Lambert and H. Guillaume, *La Rationalisation des choix budgétaires* (Presses Universitaires de France, 1971), Chapter V.

Discussion of Paper by
H. Lévy-Lambert

Formal Discussant: Rothenberg. This is a short but interesting and provocative paper. It bears comparison with the quite opposite results from the model by Mills (Chapter 7) at this conference, the study of mass transit subsidisation in Chicago by Moses [1], and the study of the effects of free mass transit in American cities by Domencich and Kraft [2]. Close comparison with these and other studies is, however, difficult; because the paper is somewhat too short on details about the actual derivation of its relevant measures.

Many of the author's calculations are based on avowedly sketchy data, 'guesses and assumptions to make up for the lack of precise information'. So we cannot lean too heavily on the exact magnitude of the policy results. Because of the central position played by the allocation curves in the analysis, and because details of their derivation in the paper are sparse, we also need to know a good deal more about them before we can fully appreciate the results. In particular, their derivation depends on assumptions about the value of time and is very sensitive to such assumptions. Yet the question of the value of time – of different kinds of time – is an unsettled and controversial subject.

Modal splits are treated here as dependent on differences in trip times between modes. But surely other characteristics of the respective modes are important too: operating costs, privacy, convenience, safety, and the quality and variety of the different modes available. This means that the prediction of modal split is really based on an equation of the following form:

$$m = f[P_\tau \delta\tau, \ \delta OC, \ \delta(Z), \ A]$$

where m is the per cent of total trips taken by autos;

$\delta\tau$ is the differential in trip speed between the two modes;
P_τ is the value of time;
δOC is the differential in operating costs per passenger trip between the two modes;
$\delta(Z)$ is the set of differential characteristics of the two modes other than speed and operating costs (safety, convenience, etc.);
A is the range of types and qualities of modes included in the public transit category.

In the general case, if the trade-off between time and operating costs is to be estimated by regression analysis (so as truly to derive a relationship between cost differentials and modal split), it must be performed by a multiple regression in which all the other variables are present *with adequate variability in the empirical observations.* If adequate representation of the other variables is missing, the coefficients of the time and operating costs variables, which enter the derivation of the allocation curves, will be biased. Application of the resulting predictor relationship to a situation in which variations in the auxiliary variables do not duplicate those in the estimation situation will simply result in poor predictions. The author does not indicate exactly how the allocation functions are derived; but his failure to mention the auxiliary attributes of the two modes, and especially the very important question of the sheer availability of mass transit forms with significant variety of quality level, raise doubts about the predictive power of the functions used.

There are grounds for believing that the procedure used overstates the trip-time saving that results from imposition of the parking charge:

(a) Bus speeds are calculated as a function of the amount of auto traffic at rush hour (due to the street interference of heavy auto traffic with bus progress). But any large scale shift of motorists to buses will tend – all other things equal – to *decrease* bus speeds by increasing loading and unloading times for buses.

(b) The impact of the charges on subway speeds is misrepresented, or not treated. While decreased auto traffic will increase bus speeds (decrease trip times) because of the inter-modal externalities between the modes on the streets, the externalities do not extend to subways. Subway speeds are not a function of the size of auto traffic. Thus, in so far as the induced modal shift is from autos to subways there will be no decreased speed on the subways. If the increased speed of public transit is meant to reflect all of the components of the public mode, then it is incorrect. If it is meant to reflect the overall impact on speed for the public transit mode as a whole, then it must really be a weighted average of different impacts on the different components of public transit. In the latter case, the overall speed increase – used to calculate the new overall modal split – must be less than what is established for buses alone.

It is not clear which of these two treatments is intended. What is clear is that the allocation curves should distinguish among the different forms of public transit, as they do not now. As presently treated, the response of modal split to some change in inter-modal cost differences is not invariant to which parts of public transport are largely affected.

The paper raises a larger issue than the specific magnitudes and mechanics of the effects of parking charges.

Parking charges, as envisioned in this study, do not distinguish between rush-hour and non-rush-hour use. Any differential impact on these two types of use results from any differences in the value of time involved in the two. But the significance of any given shift away from autos is much greater for rush-hour trips than for non-rush-hour trips. Since the former is much more concentrated in time than the latter, the former shift in mode has impact in a more concentrated period of time – its effect on congestion levels and thus trip times is likely to be much greater. This is true even if the congestion cost function is linear. So rush-hour congestion impacts should be a major focus of policy.

This suggests that we should examine parking charges more closely with respect to rush-hour impacts, and compare their efficiency towards this end with that of other policy tools, before too quickly accepting them. An emphasis on rush-hour impacts in this context is especially warranted because differential effects from parking charges result heavily from inherently controversial assumptions about differences in value of time for rush- and non-rush-hour travel. (It is not the trip time saving from faster speeds that induces the split, since this applies equivalently to both modes; it is the charge on one but not the other mode, with changes in relative costs between them, and the transformation of these changed money costs differentials into equivalent trip-time differentials. Assumptions about value of time enter at this step.) If the assumed value of time differential is really an exaggeration – as, for example, by systematically undervaluing housewife and other non-market time – then we would expect parking charges to have a smaller impact on rush-hour shifts than the model predicts.

Of course, parking charges can be used in a way that would give more direct discrimination towards rush-hour impact. The charges can discriminate by time of day: higher charges for rush-hour trip parking than for other trips. One method would be to charge a higher hourly fee for multiple hour parking than for short-period non-rush-hour parking (since the bulk of rush-hour traffic are work trips, where the auto is parked during the whole of the work day).

Having opened up the issue of the efficiency of parking charges in meeting the problem of rush-hour congestion, we recognise that other policy devices are available for doing this too. Moreover, there are policy considerations other than impact on rush-hour congestion. The real policy choice rests on a comparison among different types of instruments, which, like parking charges, can accomplish a variety of tasks. As a contribution to that choice it would be appropriate to point out some of the advantages and disadvantages of parking charges. Some advantages are: (1) relative to some other techniques, enforcement does not require observing cars in motion; (2) charges can be varied by location, time of day, duration of inactivity; (3) directly discourage the use of very valuable centrally located land for the dead storage of cars and release some for more active uses to which its location especially fits it. Some disadvantages are: (1) it cannot reach cars which are simply passing through a congested area but not stopping; (2) it cannot distinguish car use by route, but only by destination.

In sum, the impacts shown by the author are quite impressive. They make one wish to examine more closely the technical bases from which the impacts were calculated; and make one wish as well to examine more closely the appropriateness of parking charges relative to other policy approaches as an instrument for taming some of the unruly problems of urban transportation.

Müller said that when parking charges were used to regulate the allocation of traffic between modes, one had to consider what effect these charges would have on income distribution. Instead of a parking charge, or in addition to it, one could readily subsidise public transport to achieve the same modal split and offset some of the adverse distributional effects associated with parking charges alone. He felt, however, that public transport services should be subsidised to improve quality rather than to reduce fares.

Heggie said that recent empirical data based on the Oxford University Travel and Parking Survey [3] provided a useful insight into the likely effect of parking charges. The survey covered about 10 per cent of total employment in Oxford and roughly a quarter of all those employed in the Central Area. The sample numbered 7,250 persons of whom 6,150 (85 per cent) replied to the questionnaires. In spite of being confined to University and College employees, the sample covered a wide cross-section of income groups and professions. The largest group, some 38 per cent, consisted of domestic, janitorial and maintenance staff. Academic staff only comprised 25 per cent; the administrative, library and museum staff comprised a further 20 per cent of the total; leaving a residual of technicians (13 per cent) and 'others' (4 per cent) to complete the number.

The Survey asked car drivers whether they would pay, park further out or abandon their car in favour of another mode if charges were made for all private and public (on-and-off-street) daytime parking within the University area. Two levels of charges were specified separately: £30 p.a. for regular use or £0·12 per day for casual use; and £50 per annum or £0·20 per day for casual use.

He pointed out that surveys like this can be unreliable for a variety of reasons. He did not, however, propose to rehearse the numerous potential sources of bias implicit in the data: they were all carefully discussed in the Report itself. He simply wished to present two of the summary tables to give some idea of how the sample said they would respond to the two different levels of charges. Table 8D.1 shows how the 2,000 respondents who usually drive to work by car (there were 3,321 car owners in all) answered the two questions.

TABLE 8D.1

RESPONSE TO PARKING CHARGES – CAR DRIVERS
(Percentages in brackets)

£50	£30	Pay	Park Further Out	Abandon Car	Other Answer	No Answer	Total
Pay		291	—	—	—	6	297
		(14·5)				(0·3)	(14·8)
Park further out		139	343	—	—	2	484
		(6·9)	(17·1)			(0·1)	(24·1)
Abandon car		121	29	415	—	4	569
		(6·0)	(1·5)	(20·7)		(0·2)	(28·4)
Other answer		23	3	2	290	1	319
		(1·2)	(0·2)	(0·1)	(14·5)	(0·1)	(15·9)
No answer		96	54	61	8	118	337
		(4·8)	(2·7)	(3·0)	(0·4)	(5·9)	(16·8)
Total		670	429	478	298	131	2,006
		(33·4)	(21·4)	(23·8)	(14·9)	(6·5)	(100·0)

(Source: *University Travel and Parking Survey* [3], Table 16.)

The six blank cells did have some answers in them but they were moved into the diagonal by the validation programme. However, not all the answers were necessarily irrational. The sum of each column shows the number answering the £30 question in each of five ways. The sum of the rows does the same for the £50 question.

The data, which included information on income, occupational group, place of residence and place of work, was then used to derive *arc* elasticities. The travellers were classified by income group and the elasticities were then calculated on the basis of three different assumptions. The assumptions related to the way the 'other' and 'no answer' cells were dealt with in the analysis and effectively constituted minimum, central and maximum assumptions. Assumption 1, for example, assumed that only those who specifically stated they would pay would in fact do so. The results are shown in Table 8D.2.

TABLE 8D.2

ELASTICITY OF DEMAND FOR PARKING FOR DIFFERENT INCOMES

	Assumption 1			Assumption 2			Assumption 3		
				(Prices d. per day)					
Price range	0–30	30–50	0–50	0–30	30–50	0–50	0–30	30–50	0–50
Average price	15	40	25	15	40	25	15	40	25
Income				Elasticities					
Under £900	0·75	2·18	0·92	0·68	1·23	0·81	0·44	1·24	0·66
£900–£1,350	0·66	1·91	0·86	0·54	1·50	0·76	0·32	1·50	0·62
£1,350–£2,400	0·51	1·83	0·78	0·43	1·54	0·70	0·34	1·54	0·64
£2,400–£4,200	0·30	1·14	0·54	0·22	0·91	0·43	0·19	0·92	0·40
Over £4,200	0·17	0·88	0·37	0·12	0·58	0·26	0·11	0·57	0·25
Unknown	0·55	2·17	0·84	0·46	1·80	0·75	0·32	1·79	0·67
Total	0·50	1·54	0·74	0·40	1·22	0·63	0·30	1·29	0·56

(Source: *University Travel and Parking Survey* [3], Table 19.)

He pointed out how closely the answers resembled our intuitive notions of the effect of income differences, giving us some idea of the potential distributional effects of parking charges.

He was not sure to what extent the results could be extended to the situation in Paris. It did suggest, however, that provided parking charges could be extended to all on-and-off-street commuter parking places in medium size U.K. Provincial Cities, a fairly modest charge (e.g. £0·12 per day) could reduce commuter car traffic by up to a half in the built up Central Area. It was true that the quarter parking further out would create further problems (an aspect with which the author's paper did not deal) but the potential reduction of a half in Central Area car traffic would have significant benefits. The £0·20 charge clearly had an even more dramatic effect. In conclusion he thought that the author's paper, and the Oxford Travel and Parking Survey, did illustrate very clearly how Central Area traffic could be regulated in a fairly practicable way without having to wait – who knew how long? – for a fully-fledged system.

Münnich was rather suspicious of this type of investigation. He felt that people usually knew the purpose of the investigation and deliberately gave misleading answers. Only experience with a real charging system could demonstrate how people would actually behave.

Foster said that British experience suggested that efficient parking charges would be substantially higher than on the author's principles, because the travel-cost elasticity of through traffic was high and because there was a tendency for people to park further out in order to pay a lower charge. The author mentioned the first of these possibilities, but did not take account of it in his calculations. A more refined calculation would include a few other factors besides those mentioned by Rothenberg. Since the effect of congestion on buses was more sensitive to changes in volume than it was for cars, any decongestion was likely to improve their relative performance more. If specific measures were introduced to speed up buses, the shift would be even greater. On the other hand, the benefits of a shift to subways in the peak might be exaggerated, since they would be further congested, and while this might not affect journey times, it would affect the comfort of travel and therefore the relative attractiveness of the mode.

Lave observed that the evidence from U.S. studies suggested that the value of commuting time was about the hourly wage. Travel time differences were therefore crucial in modal choice decisions. There had also been studies showing that modal choice decisions were relatively insensitive to price. As an example, making the Boston Metropolitan Transit Authority free [4] would only decrease auto traffic by 10 to 15 per cent.

REFERENCES

[1] L. N. Moses and H. Williamson, 'Value of Time, Choice of Mode, and the Subsidy Issue in Urban Transportation', *J. Pol. Econ.*, 71 (1963), pp. 247–64.
[2] T. A. Domencich and G. Kraft, *Free Transit* (Lexington Pub. Co., U.S., 1972).
[3] University of Oxford, *University Travel and Parking Survey* (Oxford University Press, 1972).
[4] Charles River Ass., *Boston Metropolitan Transit Study* (Charles River Ass., Cambridge, Mass., 1970).

Part III

Evaluation and Consolidation Panel

9   Urbanisation and Environment: Retrospective and Prospective Views

Ian G. Heggie, Henry Tulkens, Rainer Thoss, Karl-Göran Mäler and Edwin S. Mills

A Retrospective Summary: Ian G. Heggie

The main theme of this conference was 'Urbanisation and Environment' and it followed close on the heels of the U.N. conference on the Environment held in Stockholm last week. However, it would be misleading to pretend that the collected papers presented at this conference represented an organised attempt by economists to become involved in the present controversy surrounding the relationship between man and the environment. Nor should they be interpreted as a definitive statement of the role the economist feels he can, and should, play in managing the environment. Rather, it must be interpreted as a series of separate statements linked by the common themes of Urbanisation and Environment.

The papers presented at the conference can be divided into four main groups:

(1) The macro economic approach to understanding urban and regional structure.
(2) The macro economic approach to managing water resources.
(3) The role of transport in the urban environment.
(4) The management of the environment by means of charges and regulations.

Although each topic represents a separate field of study, all are linked by their emphasis on the environment. This immediately raises one of the recurrent themes of the conference: what is the role of the economist in planning man's environment? In simpler terms, what can economists, as a profession, contribute towards the achievement of an optimum urban and regional environment: the term 'optimum' being interpreted in terms of human satisfaction. The answer is partly given in the papers we have considered. So many of the issues discussed at this conference have either required, or have pointed to, the need for a multi-disciplinary approach. The discussions on urban structure, on transportation, and on water resources relied, to an important extent, on material contributed by physical planners, psychologists, sociologists, natural scientists and engineers. It was likewise apparent that much prospective work in these areas – I have in mind the references to the Streeter-Phelps models – can only be effectively prosecuted in a multi-disciplinary context. As economists, we should therefore ponder what role we can best play in initiating such research.

The discussion following each of the 15 papers presented at this conference generated several recurring topics from which the panel selected eleven for inclusion in this summary. The mode of presentation will be for me to briefly summarise each topic after which Tulkens, Thoss, Mäler and Mills will sequentially introduce a few brief comments on the further research they think is required in each area. The first three discussants will introduce three topics each; Mills will introduce the remainder. After introduction the topic will be thrown open for general discussion.

1. *Preferences.* The first recurrent topic was that of preferences. It is clearly desirable to have a working knowledge of people's preferences to provide the basis for optimum decisions. However, we are not only interested in the displayed preferences of people and firms explaining why and how they presently behave; we must know enough about the fundamental determinants of behaviour to frame a set of incentives capable of achieving stated policy goals. It is not enough to simply explain why people migrate; if the optimum solution – including externalities – requires that they should not migrate then how do we persuade them not to?

2. *Distribution.* The second recurrent issue was that of distribution. This is clearly important in all studies of the environment and has to consider the regional distribution of environmental variables as well as the distribution of costs and benefits between individuals and its distribution over time. The central question is, who is doing what, to whom and by how much? It is also important to distinguish between the distributional effects of policies affecting existing, as opposed to potential, firms and individuals. In other words 'sunk costs' should feature in all our distributional calculations.

3. *Objective Functions.* At first glance this seemed a fairly simple issue and was initially discussed in terms of efficiency versus distribution. This clear distinction disappeared, however, once further complications were introduced. It was suggested that 'policy statements' should be clearly distinguished from 'policy intentions': in some countries policy statements were issued, and not implemented, to achieve maximum political impact; in others they were explicitly not stated to avoid the divisive effects that such statements frequently

induced. Another suggestion referred to the objective of preserving a unique environment. Although this was light-heartedly characterised as simply another way of providing 'outdoor relief' the objective does gain credibility when related to the preservation of unique cultures in developing countries (e.g. the Masai) or to the preservation of the historic centres of so many European cities.

4. *Environmental Effects.* A recurrent theme under this heading was 'what is the environment' and 'how can it be measured?' It was pointed out that the concept of environment cannot stop short at the statement of residuals. Environment is a question of quality as well as of sewerage, and one must avoid allowing a clinical definition to result in cultural suffocation. At a more technical level there was the question of measurement: D.O.* concentrations cannot readily be translated into degrees of satisfaction. The question of reversible versus irreversible effects was also raised; as was that of the durability of residuals and the possible catastrophic breakdown of systems. The malleability of input-output coefficients was also raised and this tied in with the questions of the sequence in which decisions were taken, the durability of capital assets and their adaptability over time.

5. *Micro versus Macro Models.* There was some genuine conflict on this subject. The micro modellers argued that macro models remain abstract, and while such models have their utility and aesthetic appeal, it is only infrequently that they can be used to solve genuine decision problems. The plea was made that the economic modeller should try to capture in his model as much of the real world as possible. Input-output models came in for considerable criticism because they are usually estimated by sector and thus dismiss the problem of space which is so important in most residual studies. In return it was argued that different types of models serve different purposes and part of the skill of the research worker was related to choosing the best model to suit the problem being analysed. International trade models and models simulating the effect of the new auto anti-pollution legislation were cited as examples supporting the usefulness of the macro approach.

6. *Growth Models and the Environment.* In spite of its importance, this topic generated very little discussion. The problem with most macro economic growth models is that they do not accurately replicate the growth process over extended periods of time because they do not systematically allow for the effect of technological innovation in their coefficients. Very few incorporate a finite set of

* D.O. = Dissolved oxygen content and is a measure of a certain type of water pollution.

natural resources and they likewise do not allow for the cumulative effect of residuals on the environment. Because this topic has only received limited attention at the conference, I hope that participants will feel free to contribute further ideas in the discussion this morning.

7. *Pollution Controls.* This resulted in a very wide ranging discussion related to the choice between charges and/or subsidies versus regulations and bribes versus charges. It was difficult to disentangle the questions of efficiency from those of effects. The degree of generalisation possible was also limited. Effluent charges in a river basin appeared to be efficient and easy to administer; charges for auto emissions, though possibly efficient, appeared extremely difficult to administer. Even parking charges – in Paris at least – seemed likely to have a problematic effect. There is likewise no guarantee that congestion charges in urban areas will necessarily lead to everyone being better off. It was suggested that if pollution costs were included in prices then such charges would become regressive. It was also doubted whether congestion charges would have much effect on city size. It might lead to a reallocation of resources between cities of different size, but may result in little decentralisation whilst at the same time fortuitously increasing the rental income of Central Area landlords. The dual problems of efficiency versus effects thus loomed large in the discussions.

8. *Compensation.* This topic produced a great deal of discussion. The central issue was, who is entitled to compensation and what implied rights do, and should, the public enjoy? Everyone is affected by some aspects of public policy, but why do we intuitively feel that people are entitled to be compensated for some effects and not for others? A great deal seems to hinge on 'reasonable expectations' and hence on the degree and type of uncertainty associated with the loss (or gain) of amenity. A further point, which did not clearly emerge from the discussion, was the relationship between the rights to compensation and Hicks' equivalent and compensating surplus. Amenity values generally constitute a large part of a person's real income. When he suffers an amenity nuisance, or when he gains added amenity, the effects are therefore often non-marginal and the difference between the compensating and equivalent surpluses can no longer be ignored.

9. *Economists and Public Policy.* This topic was less well discussed. There were several references to what economists thought policy makers should do, but none to the specific role of the economist in the decision-making process and to the mode of communication most appropriate to our status and profession. Attempts to change

the world will never succeed as long as they are directed at the wrong people, in the wrong place and in the wrong way. If we wish to influence policies and if we wish to improve the urban and engineering planning process, it is essential that we direct our ideas, in a fluent and coherent form, to the most responsive parts of the relevant decision process.

10. *Empirical Studies*. Apart from those examples embodied in the written papers, nearly all the references to empirical studies have come from the U.S. True, we have been treated to some anecdotal references to the anti-social behaviour of Parisian parkers, but this has not measured up to the great weight of empirical data turned out by our American colleagues. There are clearly many areas in which further empirical studies are required. There is clearly scope for a detailed study of personal preferences; why do firms choose one location instead of another (they never seem to behave as economists want them to); what incentives would persuade them to move; how are people in different situations likely to respond to parking charges; how would this response be affected by complementary improvements in public transit services; and so on. In other words, can we not tabulate, on an empirical basis, how people react to different types of environmental variables?

11. *Urban Structure*. The central issue discussed in this area was what are the causes and consequences of changes in urban structure. These two aspects were not always clearly distinguished. At times transport facilities were said to 'cause' urban migration; at others it was the urban migration that led to the 'need' for new transport facilities. Both are consistent, but it means that many of the phenomena observed in urban environments can only be interpreted against the backdrop of the way in which the particular urban centre has developed and the natural legacy of capital (sunk costs) and the established patterns of behaviour that it has inherited.

That concludes my brief summary of the main issues that have been discussed at this conference. I will now hand over to the four panelists and ask for their ideas on what prospective research they now think is desirable in each area.

Preferences, Distribution and Objectives: Henry Tulkens

I have been assigned the risky task of raising the three following types of problems: (i) the choice of objectives in environmental analysis; (ii) the determination of society's preferences in that domain; and

(iii) the treatment of the distributional issues involved.

As regards the *choice of objectives*, it appears from the set of papers presented at the conference that a certain division of labour is taking place among economists. If we draw a production possibility curve (see Fig. 9.1), we can summarise the final objectives of all economic analysis in the environmental field as those of *determining*

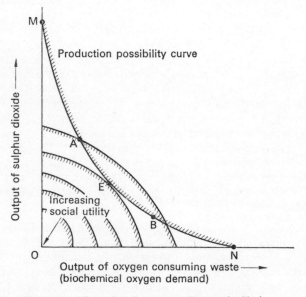

FIG. 9.1   Effect of Pollutants on Economic Choices

a point such as *E*, and of *finding procedures* to help society to get there. At least four of the papers, which I would call 'efficiency-oriented', choose as objective how to reach some point, say *A* or *B*, lying on the boundary *MN* of the production set. In three other papers, on the other hand, the objective is exactly point *E*, i.e. they are 'welfare (or optimality)-oriented'. Given the complexity of the problem involved, such a division of labour is surely a good thing, provided communications continue between the two types of studies.

As far as efficiency studies are concerned, I find it comforting to notice that existing general techniques of economic analysis, such as mathematical programming or input-output analysis, prove to be applicable to this new field; no genuinely new techniques seem to have been devised or are needed. Moreover, these techniques appear to be precise enough, to allow for a genuinely multi-disciplinary approach to be adopted. Clearly, for example, the Kneese [1],

Russell and Spofford [2], Thoss and Wiik [3] programming models appear as bridges between engineering knowledge and economic calculus. This suggests that both the stochastic and dynamic components of pollution phenomena might now usefully be incorporated into the optimisation process.

When it comes to the welfare-oriented studies, we clearly confront one of the most basic problems of economics, namely the *determination of society's preferences*. The papers by Kolm [4] and Uzawa [5] have shown the static and dynamic implications of the well-known Pareto-optimality principle. But, even within that rather simple framework, some essential elements of social preferences with respect to the environment remain obscure: for instance 'merit wants', which have barely been alluded to in Hoch's paper (Chapter 3) and by Kolm in the discussion, or the inter-generational choices involved in the dynamic analysis of resource conservation and the use of social overhead capital.

The analysis of decision procedures also requires further research. From the presentation and discussion of Haefele's model, one can only conclude that our conceptual tools for analysing preferences and understanding social decisions are too dependent on our concepts of observed market behaviour. The many non-marketable goods and services involved in any environmental analysis call for more conceptual progress and scientific imagination before we can be sure that our conclusions are not founded on our own preferences rather than on those of society.

Finally, on the distributional issues, I would like to observe that it is not always clear that environmental policies should always be distributionally neutral, instead of being used as a tool of redistributive policy. In practice, it seems that most governments take the latter attitude (as they have often done in the past with respect to other kinds of public goods). This should perhaps influence the orientation of our thinking in this field. I realise how difficult it is to do good distributional economics without introducing arbitrary value judgements; but I wonder whether the issues raised by environmental problems will ever be treated in a relevant manner without tackling that question more substantially.

Discussion of Paper by Henry Tulkens

Kolm agreed that it was time someone commented further on the time aspect of environmental problems. We knew that they differed very widely in the following respects: some environmental disruptions ceased when their causes stopped (noise); while others had long-lasting or even permanent effects (destruction of a unique site or of a species). But we had to be careful to consider all effects: noise could have durable consequences through physiological or psychological disruption. Of course, long-lasting effects raised especially difficult problems for their economic evaluation, since future generations were not here to tell us what importance they attached to a given aspect of their environment.

But, beyond economics, this raised very important and difficult philosophical problems. The tastes of future generations were largely determined by the values we gave them through culture, education, etc. If our only criterion was happiness (or *bonheur*, which was better), then we had to take this into account while shaping the tastes of future citizens. For instance, if we could teach them that Notre-Dame of Paris was not what we usually think of it but simply a funny heap of old stones, we could replace it with a nice parking lot and everybody would be happier. We make things difficult for future generations by giving them tastes which are costly to satisfy. Of course, some of these tastes may be genetically, rather than culturally, determined but, although the distinction is difficult to make, culture does have some effect. Do we therefore have the right to make future citizens unhappy by inculcating them with hard-to-satisfy tastes simply because they correspond to our own tastes?

Foster replied that we could all think of ways of measuring people's preferences under different conditions. The real problem consisted of a widely held belief that *the culture* was a tradition carried on by a minority who chose to interpret certain cultural artifacts as 'merit wants' of the people. Planning was, furthermore, a profession largely engaged in by people who had a strong sense of overriding notion that the culture must be carried on. There were thus areas, like the preservation of the countryside, where one could not say very much except that there were people who had sufficient power – and a feeling of justified 'merit wants' – to preserve these things.

On the question of manipulating preferences through education, *Foster* thought that there was little historical evidence to suggest that sustained changes in preferences could be achieved through education.

Kneese suggested a slightly different approach to the question of intergeneration preferences. He argued that one of the problems of utility maximisation models was that one could not accurately predict preferences and utilities over very long periods of time. It might therefore be better if we tried to develop other types of objective functions in these models. For example, we could perhaps keep the options of future generations open by not engaging in activities which produced irreversible effects.

Foster agreed with Kneese and commented that the problem of preferences, viewed in the context of traditional utility maximisation models, was insoluble. We could readily predict what the cost of rebuilding Notre Dame, or of demolishing an urban motorway, would be but we could not predict, even in probabilistic terms, what the preferences of future generations were likely to be and hence what the net social costs of keeping or of demolishing Notre Dame would be.

Mäler disagreed with this analysis. He felt that we already took account of the preferences of future generations by expressing them in our own preference functions. Utility maximisation models should, therefore, continue to maximise the utility of present generations since these models already implicitly subsumed the utility of future generations.

Uzawa did not think that the conference should be quite so complacent about the present generation of utility maximisation models. During the past 20 years a great deal of the natural and social environment in Japan, and in Tokyo in particular, had been systematically destroyed in the name of economic growth, efficiency and progress. He felt very strongly that our utility maximisation models had to be adapted, as he had tried to do in his paper, to explicitly allow for the consumption of natural resources and environment. It was only by doing this that one could realistically draw conclusions about the implications of alternative public policies.

Lave requested permission to speak on behalf of the Philistines. He felt that the conference was in danger of losing its objectivity. It was true that some people complained that too many historic buildings were torn down, but there were others – who had not yet been represented at the conference – who felt that too few were torn down. It was not merely a question of *conserving* resources, it was a question of conserving and investing them wisely. We should not, therefore, allow our misgivings about the preferences of future generations to result in the wasteful creation (or preservation) of public goods that were only desired by a few.

Hoch sympathised with this point of view. He felt that 'merit wants' often involved the expression of vested interests, e.g. that people wanted something for nothing. For example, national parks generally involved a subsidy to high income groups. They were the principal users of such facilities, yet they paid very little for their use. He felt that this was true of many appeals to virtue (i.e. that they were upper-income subsidies).

Rothenberg felt that one could interpret the well-being of future generations as the satisfaction that the present generation derived from various provisions for the future. He agreed with Lave that he preferred to live in 1970 than in 1700, but why? How many of us, he asked, were responsible for the benefits we were able to enjoy in 1970? We were all born with absolutely nothing – having earned nothing and deserving absolutely nothing – yet we were given absolutely everything based upon thousands of years of human effort on our behalf. He felt that we therefore owed to the future a great deal more than we had been given ourselves.

This suggested that we should (a) recognise that we were only here at the sufferance of those who went before us and that those who come after us would be similarly beholden to us and (b) he would not presume that his judgements today should commit future generations to the range of possibilities open to the present generation. So many of our preferences were superficial, casual and capable of being altered by the flimsiest changes of fashion. We should, therefore, allow for the possibility that others might be wiser and better informed than we were and should, therefore, preserve the options of any future generations.

Micro and Macro Models, Environmental Effects, and Growth versus the Environment: Rainer Thoss

I have been asked to say a few words about micro and macro models, environmental effects, and growth versus the environment. I would like to begin with what has been referred to as the antipathy between the micro and the macro model builders. I do not personally believe that such antipathy exists. During the course of this conference it has become apparent to the macro builders that micro-economics is a very powerful device for solving theoretical welfare problems, but I think it has also become apparent that for certain practical problems aggregated models are often the most suitable. The term aggregated does not of course imply that the models necessarily rely on national aggregates: it is rather that they utilise grouped data of one kind or another.

In spite of some apparent conflict, one of the main outcomes of this conference has been to enable the micro and macro modellers to gain a better appreciation of what each was attempting to do. As a macro modeller, I have certainly become more aware of the need to structure macro models along the same lines as the micro ones. This means of course that much of the prospective work in this field will have to follow the lead given by Tinbergen, Theil and Frisch whose models have been classified as flexible target policy models. This is probably essential if the macro models are to be applicable to general micro welfare analysis.

The most important link between the micro and the macro analysis seems to be the introduction of ambient standards. The role of the imputed price of these standards (for calculating optimal charges) has been clearly demonstrated at this conference. The imputed price of an environmental standard is thus one of the common features that links the micro and the macro models. The macro model, whose solution defines the best primal solution, should thus go hand in hand with a micro analysis of the optimal charges required to achieve this overall optimum. This represents an integration of both micro and macro approaches.

On the question of 'environmental effects' the discussion at this conference has shown how difficult it is to estimate empirical damage functions. The discussion of ambient standards was again relevant in this context since I believe that, until we can effectively estimate these damage functions, a crude ambient standard provides the best substitute to counter environmental degradation. Indeed, the resources required to estimate empirical damage functions need not be expended if an effective ambient standard can be devised.

Let me finally turn to the apparent conflict between growth and environmental quality. I think everyone agreed that there was no real conflict in the short run. It was likewise the composition of output, and not its volume, that was important when questions of environmental quality were being examined. Future research should thus seek to develop more disaggregated growth models (intermediate models half way between the present macro and micro models) unlike those used by Meadows and Associates which cannot show the opportunity cost of different environmental policies but can only diagnose an overall conflict of goals. Of course to compute the price of changing the composition of output (i.e. the price of environmental quality improvement) we need a model that explicitly allows for the resources required to bring this improvement about (clearly our measure of national output should also include some measure of the positive value of these quality improvements).

In the long run there is a further conflict of goals. Any diversion of current resources to improve environmental quality reduces the overall level of investment and hence of physical consumption in the future. This was one of the main conclusions of Uzawa's paper which suggested that further research was required on production functions to quantify what goods and services we have to forgo in the future for the sake of environmental quality improvements now.

Discussion of Paper by Rainer Thoss

Førsund argued that the usefulness of macro models for planning and for formulating economic policy needed no elaboration. The question was whether it was any use studying environmental pollution at the aggregated level of a macro model. He thought that it was and advanced the following four reasons:

(a) It meant that the process of gathering all the relevant data on pollution was structured within a balanced, meaningful framework for the understanding of possible economic developments.
(b) The scale of the problem was emphasised facilitating comparisons with other economic magnitudes.
(c) The direct and indirect repercussions of each policy measure would be analysed, showing how the composition of goods and services was likely to be affected.
(d) In a dynamic setting (as in the M.S.G.-model) the trade-off between traditional growth and environmental quality (as a function of discharge of residuals) could be exposed.

Finally, as economists, he argued that it was also relevant to consider the resources required to obtain useful results in the various types of pollution research. Utilising an operational macro model, the returns from a modest input of human capital clearly justified the investment.

Kneese observed that economic concepts had a tremendous capacity to integrate the work of different disciplines. For example, an idealised production function which could be applied to resource problems, or a model for optimising the allocation of resources, could be put into a quantitative framework which would then provide a coherent conceptual framework within which many disciplines could work in a highly effective manner. The model discussed in the Russell paper [2] (e.g. the residuals model for the Delaware River) provided an opportunity for professions from various disciplines to work in a highly integrated fashion. The team included an ecologist, a systems engineer, a specialist in operations research, two economists and a political theorist. The need for this multi-disciplinary team had emerged from the modelling technique chosen and there seemed to be great scope for using economic models to integrate such disciplines.

Lave noted that one aspect of economic models that was rarely discussed, particularly in relation to distributional problems, was that undue accuracy often compromised against the acceptability of a policy. If we specified who gained and who lost (and by how much) too precisely then vested interests very often undid the purpose of the analysis. General conclusions, which did not specify things too precisely, often gained much wider public acceptance for unpopular policies.

Mrs. Lave argued that one of the difficulties about the growth versus environment debate was that, by and large, the people who were most likely to benefit from improvements in the environment were high-income groups, while the people most likely to benefit from growth were the lower-income groups. The debate about growth versus environment thus had important distributional effects. For example, the cost of the new U.S. auto legislation was going to fall most heavily on the poor – they would be paying higher prices for cars and they were generally least concerned about the environment.

Strøm commented that if a significant part of the pollution problem was connected with physical stocks of residuals in the environment, or if the damage done by pollution was dependent upon the discharge of residuals in the past, then it was necessary to study pollution within a dynamic model. He thought that these stock problems accorded with our actual experience. As far as the actual presence of physical stocks was concerned, it was sufficient to mention residuals like lead, mercury and cadmium, or pesticides like DDT. The other case, which amounted to more or less the same thing – depending on how the environment was defined – could be illustrated by the potential harmful effects of cigarette smoking. The disease was attributable to past rather than present behaviour. Even a heavy smoker would take a long time to recover after he had stopped smoking.

At a given point in time the potential externalities caused by the discharge of residuals belonging to an accumulating category cannot therefore be controlled by regulating the discharge of residuals now. The externalities occur at a later point in time. This complicates both the theoretical and the applied work in the field of environmental studies. If one neglects these stock problems, however, a significant part of the real world pollution problem is overlooked.

Kolm disagreed with Mrs. Lave. He felt that people always assumed that environmental management would have distributional effects that would be regressive. However, many of these effects could be progressive. High-income groups were able to buy themselves a satisfactory private environment. When we spoke of public parks we meant that they were available to poor and rich alike. A public park could thus be thought of as a positive form of income distribution.

Uzawa pointed out that there were similarities between the management of the environment and labour management. At the end of the 19th century one of the most serious socio-economic problems was the exploitation of labour. However, when labour legislation, which sought to regulate working conditions, was first introduced it was violently opposed on the grounds that it would halt all economic growth. In fact, this did not happen and people eventually realised that good working conditions were complementary to long-term economic growth. The same was true of the debate on growth versus the environment. They were not contradictory but complementary.

Mäler agreed with Uzawa. He also suggested that there seemed to be a connection between the quality of the natural environment and the working (factory) environment.

This had not been discussed during the conference. In Sweden people had observed that damage to the natural environment could often be predicted from a knowledge of the factory environment. If workers were harmed by the use of some chemicals, then the natural environment would probably also be harmed by the same chemical although the effect of the damage took longer to appear.

Environmental Policies and the Role of the Economist in Influencing Public Policy: Karl-Göran Mäler

I have been asked to initiate a discussion on environmental policy measures. The following measures have already been discussed during this conference:

1. Markets	Polluters and pollutees negotiate over the amount of pollutants and over any compensation.
2. Property rights	The government (or any other authority) issues rights to use the capacity of the environment to assimilate waste. The price of these rights are determined by supply and demand.
3. Effluent charges	A tax on the amount of waste discharged into the environment.
4. Bribes	A subsidy based on the reduction of waste discharges.

5. Effluent standards Limits on the amount of waste that can be
   discharged into the environment.
6. Regulations   Requirements that firms and other polluters
                        use certain waste treatment or production
                        processes.

I will offer a very brief discussion of each of these measures.

1. As environmental quality is a public good, a market solution
will incur extremely high transaction costs. The government must,
therefore, intervene to establish the desired markets. Moreover,
there are the familiar problems connected with public goods, e.g.
non-convexities, etc. It does not, therefore, seem to be efficient to
rely on a market solution.

2. Given the capacity of the environment to assimilate waste, one
can conceive of negotiable rights to use this capacity. It is not clear,
however, how the supply of these property rights can be determined
when there are trade-offs between different pollutants, e.g. between
biochemical oxygen demand (BOD) and thermal pollution. It is likewise not clear what price should be charged for these rights when
they are issued. If a non-equilibrium price is charged, one hopes
that the markets are sufficiently stable for the price to converge. In
such cases the scarcity rent of the assimilative capacity will be
socialised, and no compensation will be paid.

3. We know that charges are efficient from the point of view of
information requirements and that charges will result in a least cost
combination of waste discharges. Rents are socialised. There are
two main problems with charges: (i) how can one find a good approximation for the optimal charge? and (ii) how can one devise a trial-
and-error procedure to ensure that the actual charge converges on the
optimal charge?

4. Bribes can be made equivalent to effluent charges, but they are
generally more complicated. In some cases, as Kolm has pointed out,
bribes are necessary. For example, when non-convexities are involved,
a subsidy must be used. The same is true when there are very high
monitoring costs. If it is feasible to let the polluter prove that he has
reduced his pollution, on the other hand, bribes may be superior
to charges.

5. Effluent standards generally require more information than
effluent charges and are not as efficient. They generally also require
the same monitoring of waste flows. Rents are not socialised.

6. Regulations may be used when it is impossible to meter the
waste flow.

Let me now turn to the impact on technological development.
Many people regard the incentives to change the present technology

as the most important effect of different environmental policy measures. Since we know very little about the causes of technological development, except that economic incentives play some role, it is almost impossible to offer a satisfactory analysis of the effects of environmental policies on technological development. A very simple comparison between standards and charges is illustrated in Fig. 9.2. In this diagram *MC* represents the marginal cost of reducing waste discharges. The horizontal axis measures the amount of waste discharged. Assume now that it is possible to develop a new technology giving the marginal cost curve *MC'*. With a charge, *OH*, the firm

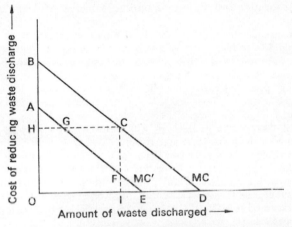

FIG. 9.2   Effect of Environmental Policy on Development
of new Technologies

will then save $(OHCDO - OHGEO) = CDEGC$ by adopting the new technology. With an emission standard *OI* on the other hand, the firm will save $ICD - IFE = CDEFC$ by adopting the new technology. This is less than the *CDEGC* saved by introducing the charge *OH*. Charges, therefore, seem to be more effective in encouraging technological improvements.

The conclusion of my discussion is, therefore, that charges seem to provide the best basis for any environmental policies. This leads to an important issue, not discussed in this conference so far. How do we convince our politicians and our authorities that economists can contribute to the improvement of environmental policy. There is no simple answer. However, I will offer a few comments, based on my own experience. If you meet a politician individually it is relatively easy to convince him that, for example, a charge should be levied on the discharge of wastes. But when he is back in his natural habitat, he is subject to much stronger pressures. The problem is that the economist can only argue on an intellectual level while other pressure groups have much stronger incentives.

Moreover, in Sweden at least, the civil servants in the government are mainly lawyers and I think that many lawyers are completely impervious to economic argument.

Discussion of Paper by Karl-Göran Mäler

Kolm said that Mäler's six categories did not exhaust the methods of dealing with pollution. There were also other ways of dealing with it. He suggested two further categories: (i) voluntary restraint in conjunction with civic education and (ii) internalisation by merger of the polluters and pollutees.

He then asked why markets fail in the matter of pollution control? He felt that Mäler had put too much emphasis on the matter of non-convexity. In examples of non-convexity the problem had been specified in terms of one polluter and one pollutee, each supplying or demanding pollution at a given price. But in a bilateral bargain, no such unit price was given to each bargainer. Then convexity, or its absence, becomes irrelevant. And when a larger number of agents were concerned with a pollution question, if there was a problem it was because of a collective concern ('public' good or bad) structure somewhere, often among the victims. Even if we assumed that there were two price-taking agents, it was still possible to define environmental rights in such a way that the difficulties caused by non-convexity did not arise. Finally, market failures, and the rationale for public intervention in environmental questions, arose for two reasons: firstly, because of a collective concern (especially among victims); and, secondly, because of the absence of any definition of rights. The latter reason was attributable to the fact that environmental goods were usually free and this incited the parties to fight politically for these rights before resorting to free exchange between themselves.

Mäler replied that internalisation, by nationalising (socialising) a firm was not really an environmental policy measure because even a state-owned firm could pollute. The government had, in one way or another, to impose controls on the amounts of waste the socialised firm discharged and it was these controls that took the form of regulations, standards, etc.

Kneese did not see why, in some cases, bribes should be superior to charges because the burden of proof was put on the polluters. It was possible to put the burden of proof on the polluter with charges as well.

Fφrsund observed that Mäler had not mentioned the problems associated with the high adjustment costs of a fixed technology. For example, charges tended to penalise established firms (with a fixed technology) in relation to new entrants.

Lave, returning to the role of the economist in the social decision process, suggested that there was some confusion about the proper role for the economist to play. We had no comparative advantage in attempting to change society's values or to impose our own values upon society. Our proper role was to determine the implications of programmes – implications which would not otherwise be evident – and to advise society on the best way to achieve its objectives. It was the function of the economist to spell out the implications of child labour laws, occupational health and safety laws, and the implications of a shorter work week. The conventional wisdom of the late 19th century was that these were costly luxuries: time had shown that they led to higher productivity and higher incomes.

Benefit-cost analysis had similarly shown that pollution abatement constituted a net benefit to society. Our task was to publicise this fact: not to wander off and dream of imposing our tastes for many more public goods on a reluctant society. We should recognise that markets are able to reflect inter-temporal choices. For example, assume that there was a bottle of wine that would remain undrinkable for 200 years. Would it have a zero price because no person presently alive could enjoy it? Of course not. The bottle would be valuable in 199 years time; in 150 years time; and so on up to the present. The market allocation of durable goods (and resources) was an efficient one, given our state of knowledge. Any conservationist views can be expressed as our uncertainty, our inability to realise the consequences of our preferences, or as too high a rate of discount. We could argue about each of these, but he felt that growth theory had more or less eliminated all three as important possibilities.

We were, therefore, left with the possibility that we were climbing the wrong mountain, that the curves we were dealing with were the wrong shape, or that markets were too inefficient. He doubted that we could think of any gross changes, along the above lines, that would make us better off. He felt that we should instead return to the task of benefit-cost analysis to sketch out the implications of environmental policies and decisions related to the provision of public goods. His own prejudice was that Society allocated too little effort to study. It should be part of our function to remedy this since the costs of study were so small in relation to the benefits of improved decisions.

Further Empirical Work and the Causes and Consequences of Changes in Urban Structure:
Edwin S. Mills

I have been asked to comment on two things: one is further empirical work and the other is the causes and consequences of changes in urban structure. Especially with the first I think it is a well-known theorem that any second-rate economist can ask more questions than the rest of the profession can answer. I will, therefore, confine myself to two issues which I find particularly interesting.

When I look at the empirical studies which have been presented here, I am struck by the fact that the work on the cost side of alternative means of abatement is fairly far advanced. There are still problems of course but the whole field is fairly well developed. The cost side is very much further advanced than the benefit side which is usually dealt with by assuming an absolute standard or goal and then finding the cheapest way of meeting it. Relatively little has been said about how you decide what environmental quality improvements are sufficiently beneficial to be worth it. This is clearly the more difficult side of the balance sheet, but it is the side where economists have a real role to play in this field and to which they should devote some attention. We have one excellent study of water quality improvement on the Delaware and the profession has clearly got its money's worth out of that study. It is quoted again and again and is virtually the only economic study in the environmental area that has had any measurable influence in the public arena in the U.S. In spite of its influence, and the rigour of its analysis, it is nevertheless one in which the procedure for estimating the benefits cannot be easily defended. It was extraordinarily crude and I think we should have some more such estimates. Except for some work by Lester Lave in measuring the benefits from improving air quality there is little else that I know of that can be called 'careful' by the standards that economists tend to use. Both for air and water pollution, and also for congestion which has received a fair amount of attention at this conference, a good deal more research on the benefit side would be justifiable. I also think that, in a sense, doing such work provides one of the keys which unlocks the door to the political process. I think the politicians and the business people always ask what they are going to get from cleaning up the environment, i.e. what are the benefits of doing so.

Very closely related, and this is a very special prejudice of my own, is how externalities really work. We have had a good deal of discussion of fees versus subsidies and standards. I found this very educational and I hope I've learned something. There has been a lot of theoretical work done in this area but I think everyone would agree that externalities which remain after markets have done their work are very much a matter of transactions costs which are not in the interest of private parties to incur. The public sector is, therefore called on to do something. But underlying all of this is some presumption that the transaction costs incurred in the public sector are small relative to those in the private sector. I think this is probably a reasonable presumption but we need some study of what kinds of transactions costs are involved with what kinds of public sector policies – fees subsidies, standards, etc. We have not really studied the kinds of transactions costs that private parties incur and the kinds of transactions costs that arise in various kinds of public policies in a very systematic way.

Let me now conclude briefly with some comments on urban structure. It is a good question to what extent environmental problems, however defined, are intimately related with the process of urbanisation. Clearly in some broad sense they are but it is not clear how specific this relationship is. Furthermore, it is not very clear to what extent environmental problems cause changes in urban structure or to what extent the opposite causation is responsible; changes in the structure of urban areas cause, or possibly even cure, some environmental problems. The twin observations that a lot of people have made and which I think are the basic ones about urbanisation in the last century or so in the industrialised world are the rapid growth of urbanisation, i.e. massive migration of people to urban areas, accompanied by a rapid and very large decentralisation of urban areas. These two get confused in a lot of popular discussion. To some extent environmental conditions may affect both of these trends in the future. To some extent the trends will certainly affect environmental problems.

Now for a few personal observations. In the United States now, and in many West European countries, about three-quarters to four-fifths of the people live in good sized metropolitan areas. This suggests that in the U.S. the process of very rapid urbanisation is about to come to a halt. It has come to a halt, or vastly slowed down, in some of the Northern European countries in much the way that I suspect it will do in the U.S. It is rather unlikely that the rural areas will literally be emptied out and if that is correct we cannot have a very much larger proportion of the population living in metropolitan areas. That has substantial implications for the likely future of environmental problems in urban areas. I also agree that growing environmental problems in urban areas are themselves an influence on the rate of growth of urban areas and this is what Hoch's paper was all about. I personally find that empirical work among the most interesting and provocative pieces of work I have seen in the field of urbanisation and environment in recent years.

To some extent environmental problems, especially congestion problems, have been the cause of decentralisation in urban areas. It is a very reasonable hypothesis and many people believe that down-town congestion and pollution have, in the U.S., led to suburbanisation of both housing and employment. Whether or not that is true, decentralisation has had an effect on environmental problems. To some extent it decentralises the discharge of residuals which is an improvement and it clearly reduces the amount of congestion that would otherwise have occurred. In fact, the conjecture has been made in the U.S. that the most serious urban congestion problems are likely to cure themselves in the next decade or two. Total employment in downtown areas in U.S. has been virtually stagnant since World War II and it is unlikely to increase whether we have congestion charges, effluent fees or subsidies. There is very little that the public sector can do to influence this. The great increase in congestion has come about mainly from the substitution of cars for other forms of locomotion like buses, walking or subways which require less land for rights-of-way per commuter. Given the difficulty and expense of increasing the right-of-way in built up areas this substitution has led to congestion. This process is now more or less complete. About 90 per cent of commuting in the U.S. is by car and that can hardly increase much in coming years. In fact it will probably decrease slightly as public transit improves. This suggests that congestion will not get any worse in most U.S. cities in the foreseeable future. Now this process is clearly not complete in many European cities. It obviously depends on public policy towards the use of the automobile, the alternatives available and especially the quality and cost of public transportation. In general it suggests, however, that the relationship between the congestion of the environment and urban structure may be a somewhat complex one whose future is difficult to predict on the basis of forecast trends since the Second World War.

Discussion of Paper by Edwin S. Mills

Kneese observed that by the end of this century the world would probably have 7 billion people and that by the middle of the next century his most probable estimate was that it would have 15 billion people. Nearly all of this increase was going to take place in Asia, Latin America and Africa. These countries already had some of the world's largest cities and their growth rates were unbelievable. São Paolo, for example, was growing at a net rate of 300,000 people per year and, although there might be some cause for complacency in the developed world, he thought that we could be much less optimistic about the developing countries. We must expect to see monster cities developing during the next 30 years and this was an area where urban economists interested in the environment should now turn their attention.

Rothenberg agreed that this was a very serious problem. One needed to pay more attention to the urbanising process as leading to environmental problems because of the very heavily mortgaged use of space, and the competition for space, over time.

REFERENCES

[1] J. G. Rothenberg and I. G. Heggie (eds), *The Management of Water Quality and the Environment* (Macmillan, 1974), Chapter 3.
[2] *Ibid.*, Chapter 7.
[3] *Ibid.*, Chapter 4.
[4] *Ibid.*, Chapter 5.
[5] *Ibid.*, Chapter 1.

Index